Global Militarization

Also of Interest

†Available in hardcover and paperback.

Westview Special Studies in Peace, Conflict, and Conflict Resolution

Global Militarization
edited by Peter Wallensteen, Johan Galtung, and Carlos Portales

Repression, armed conflicts, interstate wars, the international arms trade, military regimes, and increasing worldwide military expenditures are all indications of one particularly significant development in world politics: global militarization. In this volume, an international group of scholars describe, explain, and evaluate the roots of this development and suggest ways out of the increasing spiral of militarization.

The authors first explore the historical, sociological, organizational, and political origins of the many-faceted phenomenon of global militarization, placing particular emphasis on the role of the state. Then, in a series of case studies, they investigate the militarization of internal politics in Third World countries and analyze, in contrast, theoretically plausible and empirically attempted alternatives to an otherwise gloomy future. Professor Galtung provides a discussion outlining possible trends for the present decade.

Dr. Peter Wallensteen is associate professor of peace research at Uppsala University in Sweden. He served as a visiting professor in the Department of Political Science at the University of Michigan in 1984 and is the author of *Dilemmas of Economic Coercion: Sanctions in World Politics* (1983). **Dr. Johan Galtung** is professor of peace and conflict research at the Science Center in Berlin. He is the author of *Essays in Peace Research*, Volumes 1–5 (1975–1980) and was the founder of the *Journal of Peace Research*. **Dr. Carlos Portales** is a researcher at FLACSO in Santiago, Chile, and teaches part time in the M.A. program of the Institute of International Studies of the University of Chile.

Global Militarization

edited by Peter Wallensteen,
Johan Galtung, and Carlos Portales

Westview Press / Boulder and London

Westview Special Studies in Peace, Conflict, and Conflict Resolution

Copyright © 1985 by Westview Press, Inc.

Published in 1985 in the United States of America by Westview Press, Inc., 5500 Central Avenue, Boulder, Colorado 80301; Frederick A. Praeger, Publisher

Library of Congress Cataloging in Publication Data
Main entry under title:
Global militarization.
    (Westview special studies in peace, conflict, and conflict resolution)
    Includes index.
    1. Sociology, Military—Addresses, essays, lectures.
2. Militarism—Addresses, essays, lectures.
I. Wallensteen, Peter, 1945– . II. Galtung, Johan.
III. Portales, Carlos. IV. Series.
U21.5.G57 1985   355'.0213   84-13186
ISBN 0-86531-699-6

Printed and bound in the United States of America

10   9   8   7   6   5   4   3   2   1

Contents

PART 4
THE SEARCH FOR ALTERNATIVES

Tables

Preface

Militarization and Civilian Society

Ours is the age of militarization. Ours is also the age of questioning militarization. In the long history of human society, military attitudes, military behavior, and military structures have never been as widely represented as they are today. The war machines controlled by the United States and the Soviet Union have no historical comparison. The most devastating wars ever fought have occurred during this century, and several of them belong to the so-called postwar period, i.e., post 1945. The proliferation of arms trade, arms production, and military regimes makes the phenomenon of militarization a global one. It has many faces and shifting forms, but in toto, it limits the scope for civilian development. The parallel to a cancerous growth in a body is drawn by many.

At the same time, ours is an age of questioning militarization. The nineteenth century saw a growth of nonmilitary institutions that was also unprecedented in history: economic corporations, trade unions, political parties, cooperative movements, peace organizations, religious associations, to name only a few. Many of these civilian organizations explicitly questioned the role of the state, particularly its roots in military organization and dynastic control. Others, by their mere existence, showed that there were alternative forms of organization to the state and the armed forces.

Thus, we find ourselves in an era of rising militarization but also in an era when this trend is questioned more than before. The purpose of this book is to analyze the militarization trend and to suggest ways in which it can be changed. Thus, this volume seeks to understand what is going on and searches for alternatives. It will certainly not be the final work on this topic, but the authors hope it will contribute to the necessary process of questioning. The urgency of the topic cannot be denied. The qualitatively new turns of the arms race make military alternatives more likely in confrontations between superpowers, the influence of military institutions and attitudes shift resources away from badly needed civilian development, and the control of government by military regimes results in repression and continued violence.

Militarization is here understood to have two forms. First, militarization is a *social formation and structure*, that is, institutionalized and routinized relations within states and between states, in which military behavior comes to be preferred. This institutionalization can be seen in the form of a more or less permanent but informal structure, such as the balance of deterrence, or in a more formal sense, such as governments' remaining for a considerable period of time in the hands of military leaders. Modern societies tend to be run as integrated bureaucratic-corporate-intelligentsia alliances (BCIs); under militarization, such an alliance becomes an MBCI complex—subservient to the military system and values.

Second, militarization is also *behavior*: the preference for violent courses of action at the expense of nonviolent ways of influence. This choice is always a possibility in relations between two contending armed actors (such as between states), but it is equally possible in relations when only one actor has armed force at its disposal (such as within states). Militarization in this sense is a matter of options: the choice of certain forms of actions. Militarization in the first sense is one of institutions: a structured pattern of behavior with a certain permanence and stability. Of course, in real life these two forms intermingle. It could be that military regimes have a greater propensity for military action than civilian regimes have; it could also be that civilians utilizing military actions soon might find themselves losing control over events and becoming replaced by military institutions. However, no relationship is necessarily linear or clear-cut, and the intricacies of these links are illustrated in some of the chapters in this volume. Still, militarization can be seen, on an international level, as a reaction against an increasingly pluralistic world emerging in the aftermath of decolonization and, on an internal level, as a reaction against growing demands for democratization and participation.

The phenomenon of militarization cannot be understood without a concomitant analysis of conflict. Military institutions are there to wage conflict; and military behavior is one form of conflict behavior. Thus, militarization is linked to conflicts within and between societies. Parallel to the two forms of militarization are two concepts of conflict: incompatibility and conflict behavior. Incompatibility (sometimes called conflict formation, societal contradictions, structural cleavages, or the like) points to the basic conflict of interest between actors in a given society or relationship. At the same time, it requires the existence of conscious actors and conscious definitions of interest. Military institutions can, by definition, be part of such incompatibilities (as is the case in the incompatibility between military and civilian forms of society). Military conflict behavior refers to the actual use of military action by an actor pursuing a certain interest. In order to understand present developments, an analysis has to incorporate incompatibility as well as conflict behavior.

Obviously, the significance of states cannot be circumvented. The state apparatus (government, official administration, armed forces) is one of the most powerful institutions in any society. The origin of the state apparatus and many of its present forms date to military organization, as the dynasties shaping the present-day states often came into being because of internal or external wars. In wishing to increase the level of civilianization, the state has taken on many additional functions, which in some countries has reduced the significance of the military element, but in no instance eliminated it. However, the role of the state has to be seen in the light of incompatibilities and conflict behavior. The control of the state is one resource, an attractive and scarce one, that is useful for many actors and for many goals other than those originally thought of, thus inviting contention and struggle. The shaping of the state through these continued conflicts is a perspective of some of the chapters in this volume.

Outline of This Book

The question of militarization has been analyzed in many contexts and with many different approaches. In his analysis of these analyses, Johan Galtung suggests that military formations should be viewed in the context of the social formations in which they are embedded, which are often of a particularly complex nature. So far, no attempt has been able to come to grips with all elements, and a comprehensive approach is called for.

As the question of militarization is a global one, it is necessary to appreciate the links between developments that are external and internal to societies, and three of the chapters deal with this problem. Johan Galtung, when outlining the pertinent global conflict formations for the 1980s, not only illustrates his own quest for a comprehensive approach but also elaborates on such linkages. Charles Tilly particularly emphasizes European conceptions of the state and raises questions about the similarities and differences between the European historical experience and the contemporary Third World experience in state formation. Finally, Keiichi Matsushita attempts to link the internal urbanizing developments of industrial states to their new forms of involvement in international war.

Three other chapters point to the local and historical peculiarities of militarization, and all three heavily emphasize its institution-building aspect. First, Chulacheeb Chinwanno traces the roots of the strength of the military in Thai society to the developments prior to the Second World War. Different kinds of threats have been used at different times, resulting in a continuous enhancement of military influence in Thai society. Carlos Portales in analyzing the constitutional development in Chile points to the changing balance between civilian and military leadership in controlling the armed forces. The 1980 Chilean Constitution emphasizes the concept of national security in order to assure the subordination of civilian to military values. Björn Hettne points to the repeated military coups in Ghana, tracing the use of force to the continued cleavage in Ghanaian policy between pro- and anti-Nkrumaist forces. Together, these three chapters suggest different forms of militarization, which are perhaps indicative of the differences among the three continents of the Third World. In the Thai case, the king and traditional authority have played a particular role in militarization of the society; in the Chilean case, militarization has been linked to the uneven industrialization of the society; and in the Ghanaian case, militarization has a more elitist and personalist flavor. All three chapters illustrate the complexities in maintaining civilian control over an increasingly alert and self-conscious military establishment in societies that are marked by deep contradictions.

The last part presents three chapters that consciously search for alternatives in a world that has few alternatives, as, of course, is to be expected in an age in which militarization is the dominant trend. Dietrich Fischer, focusing on interstate relations, points to some of the conclusions that can be drawn from the Swiss experience of combining a low level of vulnerability with a nonprovocative defense. Paul Wehr, analyzing the developments prior to and after the introduction of martial law in Poland in 1981, attempts to explore the utility of nonviolent forms of struggle for internal change. Together, these two chapters suggest the significance of, as well as the need for, studies of low- or nonmilitary forms of conflict behavior. In the third chapter of Part 4, Peter Wallensteen makes some general remarks on the question of conflict resolution, suggesting ways as well as examples of how to settle incompatibilities so that the parties are allowed to remain parties.

The origin of this volume was a conference on militarization in the context of goals, processes, and indicators of development in general, which was held in Oslo in May 1981. The support of the Swedish Agency for Research Cooperation with Developing Countries (SAREC) made the conference as well as this volume possible. Also, the support of the Department of Peace and Conflict Research at Uppsala University in Uppsala, Sweden, is gratefully acknowledged. Not the least important has been the contribution by Mr. Robert Häggqvist of Stockholm.

Peter Wallensteen
Johan Galtung
Carlos Portales

Part 1

The State of the Art

1
Military Formations and Social Formations: A Structural Analysis

Johan Galtung

Introduction

With the total world budget for military systems rapidly approaching $300 billion, in other words about $75 per capita for each member of the human race,[1] there is no doubt that the military formation is a major part of contemporary society. At the same time, there are about half a hundred regimes that can be characterized as military, and an additional number that, although not military in the formal sense of having come into being through a military coup, are relying on military support to the extent that the civilian government sometimes can be referred to as a front. If a young boy in most developing countries asks the question, How do I make a career in this society? the honest answer would probably be "join the military, it can lead you anywhere." In fact, the present growth rate of the military system is much higher in the Third World than in the First and Second Worlds, a factor that will be discussed later in this chapter.

The ultimate purpose of the military system is destruction—destruction of human lives, the man-made environment, and the environment in general. Deterrence is based on the probability that the system is both motivated toward and capable of destruction, first of the other side's military system and ultimately, as mentioned, of anything.[2] The Indochina wars have provided the most frightening examples of what the human mind, combined with military organization, is able to concoct in terms of destructiveness. Given this purpose, the military system can be said to be a strange part of human society indeed, both in the sense of being "funny" and in the sense of being "alien." It drains resources and once in a while has to prove its destructive capability in order to remain credible. The idea of controlling its growth so as to arrive at a

1

constant size, the idea of trimming this size downward, and the ultimate idea of eliminating the military system completely are, as ideas, logical consequences of the nature and expansion of the military system. As ideas they are old and have been relatively highly regarded in this century; in practice, the present situation bears ample testimony to the fact that these ideas have not been very effective. There must be some reasons for that, and the present chapter is concerned with some of those reasons. What maintains military systems? and Why do they exist?

Four Ways of Thinking About Military Systems

To give some answers to those questions, let us start by making two distinctions. One may choose to analyze military systems, both their software (manpower) and hardware (arms) components sui generis— i.e., as if they were isolated systems, detached from the social environment. Military systems sometimes invite this type of analysis: They command a separate ministry with a separate budget; the software is kept in separate quarters, often far away from other people; and the hardware—both its production and its storage—is kept well hidden, often even from most members of the military system themselves. In some countries, the military system actually constitutes a separate society with its own production facilities and its own distribution machinery, producing and distributing not only the materials that are necessary for the military system as such but everything else that is needed for the reproduction of the system—food, clothes, housing, medical services, schooling, etc. It is, in fact, a society within society, and to focus on it sui generis would appear highly warranted.[3]

But this type of approach neglects at least two very important factors. First, the military system is ultimately intended to be used, and to be used in a conflict. But a conflict can be analyzed as a conflict formation, consisting of parties and a conflict issue. To analyze the military system without taking this factor into account would be a little bit like analyzing a hospital without any reference to patients or diseases, or analyzing a school system without any reference to pupils. One might learn something, but the analysis would tend to remain very abstract, detached from social reality. Distinctions, or taxonomies, may be made between military systems that mainly operate on land (armies), at sea (navies), and in the air (air forces), as was done in the old days, or they may be made between military forces that are intended for *megawar* (nuclear capabilities, weather modification, artificially triggered tsunamis or earthquakes, etc., not to mention large-scale bacteriological and chemical warfare); *macrowar* (such as most of the systems used in the two world wars) and *microwar* (guerrilla actions, "terrorism," etc.)—superconventional, conventional,

Table 1.1. Four approaches in analyzing military systems

	Intersystem Approach	Intrasystem Approach
Military system sui generis	actio-reactio analysis	*Eigendynamik* analysis
Structural context	conflict formation analysis	structural compatibility analysis

and subconventional systems would be more suitable classifications today. Such taxonomies are useful, but only insofar as they can be related to a structural analysis, using conflict formations as a basic analytical tool.

The second neglected aspect is how the military system relates to the social structure in which it is embedded, the society that produces and reproduces the system. The degree of interdependence—the society forming the military system and vice versa—will become more pronounced as the military system becomes stronger and more "developed." Since the concern about military systems today to a large extent is a concern about their growth, there is every reason to pay particular attention to this interdependency.

Implicit in what has been said above is a second major distinction in analyzing military systems: the intersystem approach versus the intrasystem approach. Usually "system" stands for society in the sense of a polity, meaning, for all practical purposes, a country—sometimes organized as a nation-state. Just as one gets different perspectives on, for instance, disarmament or demilitarization processes depending on whether one focuses on the military system sui generis or on the general structure, different types of light are shed on the problem depending on whether one looks at relations between systems or what happens inside them.

Taken together, these distinctions give rise to a fourfold table (Table 1.1). Let us try to spell out typical perspectives arising from this map of analytical orientations, following the arrows since this sequence is more or less the way analysis has proceeded, and, one might add, progressed, in recent years.[4]

The Actio-Reactio Model

The actio-reactio approach seems outdated today, not because it will not give very adequate insights into many situations, but because it leads to high levels of mystification when taken too seriously. L. F.

Richardson[5] did a service by putting the model in mathematical form because doing so made its crudeness more evident. A differential equation presenting the level of armament in one country as a function of the increment of the armament in another country is a very good baseline model, not so much because of what it shows as because of the many things it obviously does not show. Such a model portrays the military system as being essentially other directed, propelled by what happens in other military systems, not by its own dynamics, or by the structure or structures in which it is embedded. It does not help to equip the differential equations with some parameters or constants if these are not tied explicitly to other variables; if they are, the insufficiency of this perspective is brought out more clearly since these variables have to be fetched from one or more of the other three categories in Table 1.1 (or from other sources). Parameters become ways of escaping theoretical exploration by focusing on curve fitting instead.

The Eigendynamik *or Autistic Model*

In the *Eigendynamik* model, the growth of the military system is seen as being propelled by internal forces, and since the focus is usually on the hardware component and how it is produced, the model is essentially an economistic one. In order to produce military hardware, the same economic factors are needed as for the production of any hardware: raw materials, capital, labor, research, and organization (in the sense of administrators, i.e., a mixture of managers and bureaucrats with the ratio of the mixture varying from system to system). This model, in and by itself, does not reveal any built-in expansionism, except in the usual sense that when there is an imbalance in the supply of factors for the production of anything, the tendency may be to fill up on the lagging factor(s), not to cut down on those that are in excess.[6] Thus, if the raw materials are there, the labor is there, researchers have done their work so that the model of what to produce exists, and the whole administrative machinery is present, there will be a tendency to try to provide the missing capital rather than to send the raw materials back, dismiss the workers, let the research findings be shelved unused, and transfer the administrators to something else. In fact, this reaction is probably particularly likely if the people involved can prove convincingly that the lag is in one factor only, making it look very uneconomical not to fill up on that one.[7]

However, there are other strong factors in the internal dynamics that also cause expansion. First, there is the very simple circumstance that the military system is commanded by military people who, like most other people in a modern society, would like to have an expanding share of the total social product because their power and prestige are related to the military system's relative size inside the society. It is in that society that power and prestige are measured, not when the system is pitted against an enemy during a war—as wars, after all, are exceptional periods in human and social history. In order to justify their claims, military people use actio-reactio model reasoning or the *Eigendynamik* model type of reasoning, to at least keep their share of the social product constant.[8]

How successful they are depends on how successfully they are controlled by other sectors of society. If this control is relatively strong, expansion has to be achieved through other channels, and the most effective channel from the military point of view is to have the civilian sector want an expansion of the military sector because of what it can do to help the civilian sector. At this point, the reasoning shades over into the structural compatibility model: It becomes a question of what the military system does to the surrounding society.

It also belongs to the *Eigendynamik* model, however, because the reasoning remains so close to what has already been presented: It is essentially production oriented, and economistic. Human beings are involved in the production of military hardware as workers, researchers, capitalists, and bureaucrats, and an expansion of this aspect of the military system may also expand the power and prestige of these people. For that reason, such expansion might be as desirable to them as it is to the military people themselves. There is the question of how well coordinated these expansionist interests are, which may be a question of the same person appearing in multiple roles or having relatives and friends in other parts of the total system. The harmony of interest in expansion, as measured in power and prestige for military personnel, military researchers, and military bureaucrats and in terms of profit for the capitalist, is what is usually referred to as the military-industrial complex (MIC) or the military-bureaucratic complex (MBC) for the market and centrally planned economies, respectively. However, much too clear a line is usually drawn between the two types of economies. It might be much more fruitful to talk about the military-capitalist-bureaucrat-researcher complex (MCBRC), since that seems to be the type of alliance that is at work—"capitalist" meaning also the top administrators of centrally planned economic organizations ("state capitalists").

However, the military production system also has a great impact on the surrounding society, which is where the analysis shades over into the structural compatibility model. The system is capable of putting to use excess capital (which might produce inflation) or excess labor (meaning unemployed people, which would also include unemployed researchers, bureaucrats, and capitalists in times of real distress), thereby serving a Keynesian function in the economy.[9] Remarkable in this connection is the absorptive capacity of the military system. It is simultaneously capital intensive and labor intensive as it can absorb any amount of capital into its hardware components and any amount of any kind of labor into its software components. There has to be a reason, however, to accept the military as the recipient of all these economic factors, and it is at this point, of course, that the politics of tension management become important. The thesis that there should be some kind of proportionality between the rate of increase in military capacity and the tension level seems reasonable, but hardly unconditional. Thus, a sufficiently autocratic regime might simply increase its military capacity regardless of what the tension level is for the reasons mentioned in discussing the intrasystem approach models. However, if a tension image can be produced, it probably will be produced, for no other reason than because of the mores surrounding the military machinery: There is an assumption that the machinery should be relevant for conflict in an intersystem setting.

If there should happen to be two systems—two countries, blocs, alliances, etc.—tied to each other because of a credible conflict but with the same internal economic problems, then they might both make use of the *Eigendynamik* model as an approach to stabilize their economies. It should be pointed out that this utilization can hardly be successfully analyzed in terms of a quest for profit or power; it should be seen instead as parallel quests for equilibrium in the economic systems. If at the same time there is a tension between the two systems, it will seem as though the actio-reactio model is at work, each system being inspired in its military buildup by what it observes in the other system. In reality, however, the notion of two parallel autistic developments might be more useful in understanding what is happening.[10] At this point, one should not be confused by the use of "incidents" as a part of the tension-management process. A submarine in the coastal waters of one country and an infraction of the airspace of another might be used by either to justify its military buildup. But one should not disregard the obvious hypothesis that there could be a gentlemans' agreement, according to which one incident would be traded off for the other, which might serve the joint interest of the same type of people in both countries of increasing their share of the total economy.

A critical point to look for in justifying this kind of analysis would not be so much to what extent the civilian and the military sectors are intertwined but the extent to which the military sector is a mirror image of the civilian sector, even when kept totally segregated from it. If the military sector absorbs economic factors in roughly the same proportions as the civilian sector, then it is obviously a parallel society and has a considerable cushioning effect. It is the homology rather than the lack of clear borders between the two sectors that is important here, but the two factors together would of course contribute even further to the use of the military sector for the purposes of internal economic stabilization.

In all of this analysis the profit motive and the power motive stand out as important forces in their own right, particularly if the military sector can promise quicker returns in either or both than the civilian sector can. The speed factor connected with military production, the need for quick utilization of money and power, will probably be associated with higher returns, if for no other reason than because there are less elaborate control mechanisms when everything has to happen quickly. Quick action has to be rewarded.

But analyses in terms of profit motives of either kind are insufficient. The type of equilibration upward in order to produce an administratively neat structure and the use of the military as a parallel society, providing momentum to the civilian sector in low energy periods, can just as well be carried out by bureaucrats employed at a fixed salary.

The Conflict Formation Model

In the conflict formation model, which is rational and in a sense conventional, the military formation is related to conflict formation. The military system is seen as a response to conflict, in some cases also as triggering or engendering conflict. The question, then, becomes what conflict and how to analyze it, and here it is important to consider the notion of a conflict formation as being something consisting of an "issue" and parties, the latter with motivation and capabilities—capabilities that to a large extent coincide with the military system.

By and large three kinds of major conflict formations can be distinguished on the international level: conflicts between two center countries (the C-C formation), particularly the superpower conflict; conflicts between two periphery countries (the P-P formation), such as in the Middle East; and the center-periphery conflict (the C-P formation), which is by far the most ubiquitous and important type of conflict in the post–Second World War world.

If we now assume that the C-C formation might easily lead to a megawar and the P-P formation to a macrowar, the question remains, What about the C-P formation? The safest answer would probably be to say it could lead to all kinds of war—mega, macro, and micro. This possibility, however, depends on which form this conflict formation takes, and there are at least three possibilities:[11]

1. a national war of liberation: the center country against the periphery country;
2. a peoples' war of liberation: the people in the periphery against the whole center country joined by its bridgehead in the periphery;

3. a Marxian formation: the people in periphery and center against the elites in periphery and center.

One might now speculate that for the first of these configurations a macrowar would be the most likely result; for the second, a microwar as there would almost have to be a guerrilla war with "insurgency" and "counterinsurgency"; and for the third, a sort of parallel microwar in both theaters. The third is the least likely given the general disharmony of interests between the periphery in the center and the periphery in the periphery, as witnessed by the general tendency of the working classes in the center countries to fight against, not with, the people in the periphery in the typical C-P wars of the last generation.[12] Another factor that makes the Marxian formation unlikely is the social distance between the center and periphery, both in standard of living terms and in racial/ethnic/civilizational terms.

The problem that arises in using this kind of perspective is the relationship between the conflict formations and the military races. The race that has captured the public eye, the strategic arms race (particularly in the field of nuclear arms), seems to be geared to a C-C conflict, but the most frequent wars fit the first two C-P patterns.[13] This problem gives rise, and should give rise, to the smoke-screen hypothesis: that an arms race may not necessarily stand in any evident and direct relation to the underlying conflict formations. Thus, it may very well be that for both superpowers, the most important conflict formation—indeed, so important as to be a matter of life and death—is the C-P formation: the United States with the Third World and the Soviet Union with China. It may also be that, as conflict formations, these are less legitimate than the East-West conflict, which constitutes a reason for using the East-West conflict formation as a basis for legitimizing expansion of the military systems while at the same time directing real attention toward the C-P or North-South formations. Thus, there are good reasons to say that the East-West formation is somewhat without an issue. To the extent that the issue at one time was, Who shall rule over Eastern Europe? it has probably been solved through a complex bargaining technique, a type of horse-trading whereby the Soviet Union is given political and military ascendancy on the condition that the West is permitted to penetrate economically and culturally—through joint ventures and the free flow of information and, partially, of people. Needless to say, all of these aspects were to some extent sanctified by the Final Act of Helsinki 1975. The losers in this deal were the Eastern European peoples, who became part of a double periphery. They had no say in the conflict "resolution" process either, nor was that the intention. The point is that as an issue separating East and West, the conflict over control in Eastern Europe has to some extent evaporated except for details in the bargaining process and in the compromises attained.

The same is not true for the North-South conflicts. Both the First World–Third World conflict configuration and the complex web of the Soviet Union–China conflicts[14] are more than real enough in ways it is unnecessary to spell out in any detail here. It is the conclusion that matters: that the conflict issues seem increasingly to be located in the North-South context whereas the conflict capabilities are—presumably—located in the East-West formation. That fact is at the root of the mystification or smoke-screen hypothesis: Although only partly intended, the giant machinery makes people believe that the real problem is to control, even limit, the capabilities in the East-West formation, whereas the basic problem seems to be how to resolve North-South conflicts. Of course the two are related: There is the considerable danger that the so-called North-South conflicts may spill over into the East-West config-uration and trigger off the latent conflict formation from the Cold War—although the location of conflict is not as likely to be in the European theater as in other parts of the world.[15]

It is evident that the strategic arms limitation talks (SALT) have not led to the limitation of strategic arms, although they may have resulted in some limitation of the rate of increase in strategic arms. What, then, have they led to? One tempting hypothesis, and a part of the general smoke-screen theory, would be that the talks are actually about the limitation of strategic arms *targets*. Thus, is it really reasonable to believe that the superpowers are so stupid as to agree with each other that they are each other's target of the horrible destructive capability they have developed? Would it not be more reasonable to believe that they could both agree to a bargain that "in case of war, I shall use your satellite as a target on the condition that you use mine—on a quid pro quo basis—and we do not attack each other."[16] It has, of course, been argued that the P-P formation is exactly this: vicarious warfare between the two central powers, at least serving as a testing ground for their weaponry systems, be it warfare in Indochina, the Middle East, or elsewhere. But there is also a European dimension to the theory that should eventually make the satellites (allies in more polite language) of the superpowers in the North Atlantic Treaty Organization (NATO) and the Warsaw Treaty Organization (WTO) understand their common interest, seek contacts, and ultimately either withdraw from the alliances and join the nonaligned countries or even band together against the superpowers. That possibility may still belong to the future, but perhaps not the distant future.[17]

Table 1.2.   A typology of social structures

	Collectivist	Individualist
Vertical	Model 1: conservative ──→	Model 2: liberal
Horizontal	Model 3: communal ──→	Model 4: ?

The Structural Compatibility Model[18]

According to the structural compatibility model, which again is an intrasystem model, the basic point would be the general structural relation between the military formation and the social formation. In order to explore this point, we need a minimum typology of social structures, and one such taxonomy in four types, using the two dichotomies vertical/horizontal and collectivist/individualist, would be as in Table 1.2. Examples of types of societies for each model might be, for model 1, medieval, feudal societies; for model 2, "modern" liberal, corporate societies; and for model 3, the people's communes in China. Model 4 as yet has no example—it may be some type of future configuration that is both horizontal and diverse.[19]

The important point now is the idea that military systems can also be categorized in accordance with this type of general taxonomy of social systems. Thus, the model 1 system would obviously be a very tightly organized army, very much centered around the general, the caudillo or cacique—the leader who would embody the army, which would essentially belong to him and move with him wherever he went. There would not be much individual mobility between the various rank levels. Most people would be born to their level in the army, and the loyalty and general spirit of servitude would be rather complete. To leave the army would be worse than treason, it would be spiritual death.

And then there is the modern army, the model 2 army: rational and based on individual mobility, military competence, and promotion into the upper ranks. Similarly, there is the model 3 army: small units, very horizontal, very little difference between the ranks, strongly collectivist—in other words, the guerrilla unit. And then there is the fourth possibility: the combination of horizontality with a diverse, even individualist, orientation. One way of interpreting this possibility would be to say that the single unit of defense is horizontally organized, which means that it has to be relatively small, but that there is also diversity, meaning that there are several types of approaches, different ways of providing defense, in order to ensure security. Most important in this connection would be a combination of the guerrilla approach with nonmilitary defense.[20] Structurally, those two approaches have some similarities as they both have to be organized in a horizontal manner. Functionally they are rather diverse, and it might be discussed (and is indeed discussed) to what extent they are combinable.[21] The answer is probably related to the social context: If the context is sufficiently diverse, diversity in matters of defense will emerge.

Thus, the point of departure for this type of analysis is the idea that on the one hand there are four types of social formations and on the other hand, four types of military formations. The question is, How do the social and military formations relate to each other? Of course, a general answer is that one is a mirror of the other, and since the military system in general is embedded in the social system, the military will be a reflection of society in general. "Tell me what society you have, and I shall tell you what type of military system you have" would be the basic guiding rule. The military is a society within the society, of course deviating in details but to a large extent reflecting the basic properties of the macro structure. More particularly, in a modern, developed, vertical/individualist society, the military formation is of the same type, albeit with some model 1 characteristics also present. The officer in charge will still have a tendency to talk about "my boys," and there will still be paternalistic rather than managerial behavior patterns, but the general inclination will be toward objective, cool and universalistic, *sachlich,* interaction.

This particular case is important because the model 2 society is the predominant model of development in the world today. It is considered a crowning achievement by the developed societies—rich, capitalist (private or state), Western societies—and it is considered the model to be imitated by most Third World countries, whether they opt for the liberal Western European/North American variety or the more autocratic Eastern European/Soviet variety.

We now must consider the inertia hypothesis. The point is simply this: The military performs a function within the development dynamic of the society, and as long as no functional equivalent has been found that can perform that function more or less equally well, and/or as long as no other development model has been accepted, the military system becomes close to being indispensable to the society as a whole, from the point of view of the ruling elites. More particularly, in the developed countries in which development is seen as a problem of adjustment of details and above all as stabilization, as status quo main-tenance, the military has exactly that function. It is a reserve society that can be set in motion in times of crisis, guaranteeing the maintenance of the basic pattern. Thus, if governments do not perform satisfactorily, a military coup can be launched, and the top military leaders will form a reserve government to be substituted for the civilian one. And correspondingly, if, for instance, workers launch a general strike, the bottom part of the military formation, the soldiers, can be put in their place—sent to work in the mines, on the docks, etc.[22] In a truly grave crisis, both processes may take place at the same time, at least for some period—the military will, in fact, act as an occupying army. But for this situation to occur while at the same time key features of the system are maintained, the military formation has to be a model 2 formation, both for the military people to fill the gaps in the ordinary social structure created by their political moves and for the people who interact with the new statusholders to feel that they are nevertheless operating in a familiar context. A guerrilla army would not be able to keep the economies of certain capitalist countries running the way the elites of those countries would want them to run, nor would a classic medieval feudal army. What is needed is an army whose officers know how to respond when they are "called upon"; officers who know something about political timing—when to come to the rescue of the country, i.e., the class.[23]

In "developing" countries, the picture is different. Here the question is not one of status quo maintenance but of pushing what is usually an exceedingly complex social formation with strong model 1 features "into the twentieth century," meaning a model 2 structure with a corresponding social ethos. A modern model 2 army can constitute a training ground for living in a model 2 society, whether on the level of the private or on the level of the commanding officer. Individual detachment and mobility away from fellow soldiers, upward and sideward, are much less known in other social formations, but they can be close to the rule in a modern army. In the classical army a division moves with the general and vice versa; in a modern army a general can be detached from "my boys" and placed at the head of another division—meaning that neither the former nor the latter are really "his boys."[24]

Further, a modern army provides training in discipline—in this respect, of course, it does not necessarily differ from any other military formation. The general problem that so many developing countries think they are facing is similar to the one the Soviet leaders faced in the early years of the young Soviet republic: how to make the Russian muzhik—usually considered lazy, dirty, unshaven, uncouth, and often drunk—into an industrial worker capable of appearing on time; performing boring, routine operations without protesting but with exactitude, with a sense of detail and responsibility; leaving on time and reappearing the next morning. One answer was, put them in the army, discipline them there, and send them out again. That solution applies to both the lower ranks and the higher ones, except that the latter, the officers, could also be seen as potential managers.

A third function of the military is to instill into its people a certain ethos, generally speaking a Western ethos, that seems to be about the same in military structures and in capitalist corporations, private or state. In both there is the same idea of a center ("headquarters" is the term used in both cases) and periphery units that operate according to blueprints and standard operating procedures devised in the center. In both there is a keen sense of drama, of crisis: a way of nursing time so that crises can occur and recur, providing enough tension and motivation to keep people always on the move, never relaxing, never feeling that any final solution has been attained (thus, impending defeat and impending bankruptcy have relatively similar structures).[25] Further, in both capitalist corporations and military structures there is the same simplistic devotion to a low number of key variables, dimensions along which the game is played:[26] investment and input/output ratios in one case; launching of hardware/software and a comparison of losses and gains on either side in the second case—e.g., in terms of casualties versus territory and other items of value conquered. The simple tool of cost-benefit analysis along a couple of quantifiable dimensions provides the necessary information to know whether one is winning or losing. Still further, there is the man over man syndrome, competitive individualism, in both. Indeed, there is also the man over nature idea: The capitalist use of nature with highly insufficient regard for any ecological imbalances that are created is only exceeded by the military approach to nature, total and instant ecocide.

Thus, capitalist construction and military destruction are sufficiently isomorphic to let one of them serve as a training ground for the other. Consequently, it is small wonder that a typical career pattern in developing countries today is a relatively quick ascent through the military structure and then a horizontal move into a position of management in a private or state corporation. And correspondingly, one's position as a soldier may be an intervening step from an essentially tribal existence to that of a "modern" industrial worker. In this case, the inertia wheel is used, not as a braking force, but as major energizing factor, providing a sufficient amount of social energy for the transition from a model 1 to a model 2 social formation. People who deplore this function should ask themselves, What other social institution can provide a corresponding training ground, both in the structure and in the ethos of a model 2 society?[27]

In today's "socialist" countries, it is probably correct to say that the military system fulfills two functions at the same time: that of stabilizing the society through autocratic control and that of providing this typeof training ground. In capitalistic developed societies, the latter function is not so important as all of society is already changed in that direction—

schools to a large extent and even family relations, associations, etc. For that reason, future managers in those societies are given more technical training—for instance, the kind of training that is acquired in commercial colleges and schools of administration (such as in L'École Nationale d'Administration, France's civil-service academy, but even there, living and working in structures with a certain ethos is usually considered better training than learning in the traditional university manner). As a consequence, the military system becomes less necessary.

All of this discussion, incidentally, may also serve to shed a different light on the military coup. It may not be so much a phenomenon to be analyzed along the lines of a democratic versus a dictatorial political system as it is a question of having in society an institution that at least potentially can search all corners of society for talent that can then be sifted upward and toward the center through a system of mobilization and mobility. The military acts as a detection device to discover people who have sufficient talent to warrant promotion, even though only some of those discovered will remain in the military while others will move into other sectors of society. A shorter or longer period of service as a high-ranking officer may serve to advance a peasant's son, who otherwise would have no chance of making any headway in society—since formal education would be much too time consuming and much too uncertain.

Some Implications for the Theory of Disarmament

There are, then, four approaches to or four ways of thinking about military systems. What would be the four corresponding ways of thinking about disarmament? One can conceive of disarmament in a very simple manner: It is a question of reducing—unilaterally, bilaterally, and multilaterally—the destructive capacity of military systems, both software and hardware components.[28]

According to the actio-reactio paradigm, the theory is relatively simple: Inverse the armament spiral. If a positive arms increment on one side can lead to a positive increment on the other side, then a negative increment, a decrement, could/might lead to a decrement on the other side. Instead of a 5 percent increase per year there might be a 5 percent decrease. The optimist would feel that this approach could even work unilaterally: If one party announces its intention to set aside x percent of the money devoted to its military annually for, for instance, development, then there will be some kind of contagious effect leading other parties to do the same. At this point, it should be added that whether or not this idea holds empirically is one question, another question is whether such an action would be good for development. Many people might feel that development is not so much a question of more capital as it is a question of self-reliance and social structures that promote human and social development—hardly things to be bought for money; money may even stand in the way.[29]

As an approach to disarmament this theory appears naive, although not so much for the reasons usually given, viz., that people are not that idealistic, that some governments will cheat, or that some governments may even make use of the situation to improve the standing of their own military systems. Although all these reasons may be valid in an analytical approach, they are not the point I have in mind.[30] They disregard the question of whether governments in general and military decision makers in particular are really that free to act; whether they really can disarm following signals from others even when they want to. The three other paradigms will inform us that they are not free: There are strong forces in the productive systems attached to the military formation, there is the whole problem of conflict formation between the two parties and possibly smoke-screen games that may have been going on for some time, and there is the question of the structural contribution of the military to the society. To disarm even by a small percentage may seriously upset all these more or less fine-tuned and equilibrated mechanisms.

The second paradigm, the *Eigendynamik* idea, would then take that statement as a point of departure and say that we have to change society first. One idea might be to remove the profit factor, for instance, by putting arms manufacturers on a fixed salary. However, that idea has been tried and found very much wanting. By far the biggest arms dealers and manufacturers in the world today are national governments—and in general (with the exception of some corruption in the form of bribes), the managers of these arms corporations are on fixed salaries. But they are closely linked to people who are concerned with the trade balance, with the economic growth of the country, with how to secure permanent and full employment; instead of getting their reward in the form of profit, they might like to contribute to such goals, and those who have less lofty, more individualistic goals might be quite satisfied with power profit rather than money profit. One might then speculate that they could possibly also have their power position frozen, and in general be put in such a situation that there will be nothing personal to gain at all from an increase in the military's destructive capacity. Such systems can be imagined (see under the fourth paradigm below), but they might still not solve the problem because the collective interest in what could accrue to the country as a whole as a result of an increase in hardware and/or software might provide sufficient motivation.

An economy that is less prone to crisis and less in need of a military (or some other) sector that can be used as a Keynesian, countercyclical mechanism might be desirable, and such economies might be emerging.[31] It is, however, quite clear that this idea brings us much deeper into social analysis than the path that has so far been followed in this century, nationalization of the private arms industry and the arms trade.

The third paradigm, the conflict formations paradigm with the smoke-screen hypothesis, leads us to one insight that is simple to formulate but rather difficult to practice: If you want to disarm, you had better find out what the conflict is about. It may not be the conflict the parties say it is, it may be some other conflict—one indicator would be to what extent the military level is related to the level of tension in one or the other conflict formation.[32] When/if the conflict formation has been found, the next approach is to try to do something about the conflict—which could lead to conflict resolution or even to conflict solution.

This is not the place to enter into any detail about conflict negation theory. Suffice it to say only that conflict negation may not necessarily result in disarmament, and not necessarily only because there is another, hidden conflict under the apparent conflict. The conflict machinery has considerable inertia and is not easily dismantled even when its rationale has presumably been removed. It might be, however, that the conflict machinery is no longer so firmly targeted on the other party, being more continued as a potential, as a general capacity. Thus, distargeting rather than disarmament may be a more modest, but also in a sense a more realistic, goal that contains the most important component of what disarmament is supposed to be about.[33] After some time, disarmament or at least heavily reduced armament may then follow.

The fourth paradigm, the structural compatibility paradigm, leads us to much more complex types of disarmament thinking. A first idea might be to look for other institutions that could function like the military as a model 2 social formation. One suggestion is the police force: It is structurally not too different from the military and if sufficiently large, could serve the same function.[34] However, like the military, it may have extremely important negative and destructive effects, as when a police force is used as a major tool for internal surveillance or as the source of recruitment for staffing the chambers of torture.

A more innocuous such institution would be the fire brigade. When run as a volunteer association (as in rural areas of the United States and as in many other countries), it no doubt has performed this type of function. Still others would be peace corps, whether international or national, civilian service organizations, and so on—in general, William James's famous "moral equivalent of war." The Gandhian *shanti sena* is a typical example.

A more radical approach would be to question the use of the model 2 social formation as a development model. A model 3 formation in the military sector would, by necessity, consist of smaller units, and the experience, so far at least, is that they are used for defense rather than for attack. The whole modus operandi of guerrilla forces presupposes a home base, the famous fish in the water, and does not seem compatible with large-scale invasions abroad. In the future this situation may change, but at present invasions seem to be more easily made by highly vertically organized military formations whether of the model 1 or the model 2 variety, not by guerrilla forces.[35] As a consequence, a shift in the developmental model more toward model 3 social formations might be accompanied by a similar shift in military formations, and that in and by itself might be highly relevant to disarmament problematics. After all, it is hardly the numerous parts of the People's Liberation Army in China that are attached as small units to the people's communes that are considered a threat to neighboring societies; rather, it is the more conventionally constituted parts that are of concern.[36] On the other hand, if the word "commando" is used instead of the word "guerrilla," the argument might look less convincing as a high number of small commando units operating on the territory of a neighboring country, crossing the borders clandestinely at night, is not a pleasant prospect.

What about the fourth model, the idea of a pluralistic social formation, spilling over into the military system as plural forms of defense? It is probably in this direction that more definite answers to the problem of reducing military destructiveness are located, but this is certainly also the most difficult path to follow. A nonmilitary defense unit is usually considered as small and horizontal, like a guerrilla force, but in this case it is really hard to think of such a unit as a possible aggressive force. It would be much too easy for even a small conventional force to repel an international peace brigade that tries to cross the frontiers, because the former would be operating on home territory. Moreover, such a unit consists mainly of software, human beings and social structure, with hardly any hardware at all. Its way of operating is closely linked to the beta-structure aspect of a society,[37] to the small units rather than to the large hierarchical structures. It is nourished by these small units and, in turn, stimulates them and makes them more able to defend themselves against encroachment from the outside. It does not leave the population defenseless, and for this reason, a transition from military to nonmilitary forms of defense within a pluralistic mix is referred to as transarmament rather than disarmament, which is one reason why, in the present context, the goal has been the reduction of military destructive capacity rather than disarmament.

In conclusion, let only two things be pointed out. First, no efforts to deal with the phenomena of militarization/demilitarization, theoretical or practical, will be valid within the framework of any one of the four analytical frameworks alone. Second, the question of what mixture of the frameworks to use in a concrete case is very much in need of theoretical and empirical research.

Notes

This chapter, prepared as a paper for the Militarization/Demilitarization subproject of the Goals, Processes, and Indicators of Development project, was originally given as a lecture to a Danish peace research group in May 1977 and to the New Zealand Peace Society in June 1977. It is reproduced here in the original form, only with footnotes added. It should be noted that the word "formation" is used in the title to connote a structure in process.

1. That the figures for 1980 were more like $500 billion and $125 per capita cannot be explained away by inflation rates alone. The same applies to growth after that year.

2. The military would say the purpose is to save lives and guard values, but it seems fair to see institutions also in terms of heterotelic and not only autotelic values, as the latter tend to be almost identical for all major institutions (e.g., human "self-realization").

3. Thus, in terms of satisfaction of basic needs, the military sector is often quite self-contained. Even if it does not produce its own foodstuffs, textiles, and building materials, it orders and distributes according to its own very special and uniform designs. It also usually runs its own medical and schooling institutions as well as its own transportation and communication sectors.

4. For the actio-reactio and *Eigendynamik* categories I am deeply indebted to the seminal work by Dieter Senghaas. It is felt, however, that his line of thinking has had a tendency to focus too much on the military system as detached from its structural context, so this chapter may be seen as an effort to extend his framework for analysis.

5. The British meteorologist who certainly was a founding father of quantitative peace studies in this century, as witnessed by his *Statistics of Deadly Quarrels.*

6. Hence, the military would often be expected to present its claims, not in terms of being behind on all dimensions, but in terms of *profiles,* where they are seriously short on one or a few dimensions, thereby rendering the others inoperative. As a tactic this is, of course, the far better approach as it promises substantial returns for a relatively modest input.

7. The net result is, of course, expansion. I would tend to see this tendency as a mechanism fostering expansionism in Western economies generally, not just in the military sector.

8. This share is often pegged to national budget, GNP, or economic growth measures, meaning that in expanding economies/public sectors there will be expanding military systems regardless of the conflict context. The same principle does not necessarily hold for contracting economies, however.

9. This would mean applying demand-side economics, but it probably also works as supply-side economics—simply making the hardware available, i.e., putting it up for sale.

10. It should be noted that the two models do not exclude each other but, rather, should be seen as two components of empirical processes in which the proportion between the two factors may be changing over time.

11. For more on this point, see Johan Galtung, *The True Worlds: A Transnational Perspective* (New York: Free Press, 1980), chaps. 4–6.

12. This situation may change, of course, if a general world recession should put the internal and external proletariats more or less on the same footing.

13. See the articles by István Kende on local wars; "Twenty-five Years of Local Wars," *Journal of Peace Research* 8:1 (1971), pp. 5–22, and "Wars of Ten Years (1967–1976)," *Journal of Peace Research* 15:3 (1978), pp. 227–241.

14. With the invasion of Afghanistan December 27, 1979, it became clear that the Soviet North-South conflict is, in a very direct and real sense, not very different from the same conflict for the capitalist West.

15. The point is simply this: It is a question of where in the world many countries are in the gray zone between a private or a state capitalist road of development, and whether they are challenging superpower supremacy if they are already enrolled in a camp. At least until the formation of the Solidarity trade union in 1980 in Poland, the Third World had by far the higher number of both types of conflict.

16. I am indebted for this type of insight to an Eastern European high-level diplomat.

17. Indeed not: The "modernization" of nuclear arms, the long-range theater nuclear force (TNF), was accepted by NATO on December 12, 1979.

18. This part of the chapter was originally given as a presentation to the World Order Models Project meeting, Ibadan, Nigeria, in January 1976.

19. See Galtung, *True Worlds*, chap. 3, for an effort to spell out this type of a possible future society.

20. In the Nordic countries, this type of defense is being proposed once in a while, e.g., by socialist parliamentarians in Norway.

21. Discussion of the "mix" has been carried on by, among others, Bengt Höglund in Sweden.

22. The similarity between private and state capitalist countries becomes very clear at this point.

23. In the theory of why the Chilean military seemed less prone to intervene militarily in the 1960s, the idea of detachability between top officers and soldiers (a model 2 rather than a model 1 military) was prominent. It did feel called upon, however, when the pattern of U.S. imperialism and bourgeois privilege was really threatened, and it acted accordingly on September 11, 1973.

24. Cohesiveness in the top military echelons substitutes for vertical integration between the top and the soldiers. Thus, if the three branches of the armed forces concur, the military coup becomes a question of timing.

25. There has to be a written admission of defeat and the willingness to be placed under the administration of someone else.

26. These are essentially the key dimensions in cosmology analysis—see Johan Galtung, *Development, Environment, and Technology* (Geneva: UNCTAD, 1979), chap. 1.

27. It should be noted that according to this type of thinking, changing the model of development is not tantamount to demilitarization. The military may still be relevant in development, and in a positive sense, but for another development, hence, with another military.

28. Of course, all components have to be included, otherwise limitation on one will only be compensated for on the other dimensions of the military system. Cutting down the number of soldiers will make the system more capital intensive. Cutting down on research capacity may put some more basic limitations on the system, however—at least in present research-oriented societies.

29. No multilateral agreement is needed to make the spiral go upward according to the actio-reactio model, possibly a good argument that it may also work the other way—in other words, in favor of unilateral gradualism as an approach. But this idea presupposes a symmetry between armament and disarmament, and they are usually regarded as being asymmetric processes. There is a need for a theoretical and an empirical examination of the relative validity of the symmetry/asymmetry perspectives.

30. See Johan Galtung, "Two Approaches to Disarmament," in *Essays in Peace Research*, vol. 2 (Copenhagen: Ejlers, 1976).

31. This would be an important argument in favor of a more modest, self-reliant, use-oriented economic system.

32. Given this indicator, it is quite clear that the objective tension reduction in Europe, starting with détente in the mid-sixties to the Helsinki agreement in 1975, was far from reflected in any decreased size of the military machineries.

33. See Johan Galtung, *Co-operation in Europe* (Oslo: Universitetsforlaget, 1970).

34. Costa Rica might be an example.

35. Subversion is not a counterexample, it also presupposes a local basis—local water for the fish.

36. With the current change in China's social formation, the Soviet Union may have reason to feel more threatened as there is also a change in the military formation.

37. See Galtung, *Development, Environment, and Technology*, chap. 1.

Part 2

Global Militarization:
Crucial Trends and Links

Global Conflict Formations: Present Developments and Future Directions

Johan Galtung

Introduction

This chapter is divided into seven main sections and is an effort to integrate into some holistic, or at least relatively coherent, pattern a large number of the processes in the world of today, seeing them, essentially, as the workings of conflict formations. In other words, there are three basic perspectives that can be chosen for viewing the world.

1. The process, something that moves and changes, is the essential unit of analysis.
2. A process should be understood dialectically, as the expression of contradictions, and more particularly in many cases as the workings of conflicts with actors or at least parties.
3. All of these factors should be seen in a global and holistic context, not as applying to particular groups of people or groups of countries only, or to particular concerns or groups of concerns only.

Needless to say, it is impossible to carry out all these directives. However, it is important to indicate ways in which one might approach such ideals for discussion and further improvement. To do so, a point of departure has to be chosen: the key economic process in the world today, which for the sake of convenience might be referred to as the New International Economic Order (NIEO), although not quite in the UN sense. This, then, is seen as the "force motrice"—but in doing so, I am in no sense adopting a linear, causal, or economistic view.

The process is a highly contradictory one, replete with conflicts, and it makes sense to ask who are the winners and who are the losers globally. The second section deals with the contradiction between winners and losers in geopolitical terms (the descending North-West world as against the ascending South-East world); the third section, with the winners and the losers within the Third World; the fourth section, with a corresponding problematique in the Second, or state socialist, World; the fifth section, with the problematique for the People's Republic of China; the sixth section, for the First, or private capitalist, World; and the seventh section, for the conflict between the state socialist and private capitalist worlds, the so-called East-West conflict.

Still by word of introduction, I wish to add a prefatory note on conflict formation. It is often said that there is an East-West conflict and then there is a North-South conflict, and from the end of the 1960s until the end of the 1970s, the conventional wisdom was that the latter had become more important than the former. The position taken here is that *something* had become more important than the East-West conflict, but that something was not very well stated by reading the compass directions in such a simplistic manner.

Thus, I do not think there is any world North-South conflict formation, meaning a conflict based on economic issues with the more industrialized North as one actor and the less industrialized South as the other actor in that conflict formation (conflict formation, as usual, being defined in terms of issues and actors/parties).[1] It is absurd to assert that the private capitalist and state socialist countries, in the North-West and the North-East, respectively, participate in the global economy in the same way, as the latter cannot be said to have economic investments of any magnitude in the "South" and also seem to depend much less on the South for raw materials.[2] Furthermore, although the South, or the Third World, attains some coherence as a voting bloc in the United Nations and other intergovernmental settings, it would be highly misleading to see it as one economic actor with well-harmonized interests. It is cut through not only with continental, civilizational (including religious and linguistic), and major political divisions but also with purely economic divisions. Not only are some richer and some poorer, but relations of exploitation and dependency, which are usually analyzed as First World–Third World relations, are quickly being reproduced in the South, with internal cleavages.

More particularly, the South-East of the world, East and Southeast Asia, seems to be much stronger than the rest of the South, among other reasons because not only China but also Japan is a part of this region. In saying so, it is obviously understood that there is a dislocation in Japan's economic positioning in this world from the North-West corner, where it never belonged historically or culturally but gained some membership because of its strength, to the South-East corner, where it certainly does belong.[3] The economistic/conventional wisdom, trying to analyze the South in terms of newly industrializing countries (NICs),[4] is not very helpful because it lumps together countries in various parts of the South (and southern Europe) that have very different geographical locations, histories, civilizational profiles, and political orientations. But the NIC metaphor does point to the tremendous differences in the South in terms of economic growth, investment for industrialization, industrial output, and so on, although it misses contradictions, cleavages, and conflicts.

Thus, it is suggested here that the major economic conflict is not between North and South but between North-West and South-East, with the state socialist North-East and the greater part of the Third World— the South-West—largely spectators, marginalized by the North-West/South-East conflict-formation process. The map on the front page of the *Independent Brandt Commission Report* is highly misleading,[5] and not only because it does not reflect the class cleavages in all parts of the world—but in this respect, the commission was certainly not the only one to fail. "Industrialized versus nonindustrialized," "developed/developing," is not good enough. The North-West is much more dynamic than the North-East, and the South-East is much more dynamic than the South-West.

What, then, about the East-West conflict? First of all, it is not between East and West but only between the East and West of the Occident, and for that reason it should more properly be referred to as the North-East/North-West conflict. It should be noted, though, that this conflict also exists in one particular part of the Orient, the Korean Peninsula,[6] and also—in a very special form—around China. But let us stick to the words East and West since they are so often used in this context and instead ask the questions, Is it obvious that the conflict—for there is a conflict somewhere—is *between* East and West? Could it be that much of it is a conflict *within* the East that is paralleled by a conflict *within* the West? Might these two parallel conflicts now take the form of crisis in highly vertical, hierarchical systems, each headed by one of the two superpowers, which to some extent is expressed, even acted out, as if it were a genuine interconflict and not two parallel intraconflicts? In any case, the point should be emphasized that the East-West and North-South metaphors, which are so prevalent in the press, are not sufficient for a more serious analysis of the global conflict processes.

Conflict is over value, over something "worthy of being pursued or avoided." There is, however, an actor- and structure-oriented perspective on value.[7] Values held by actors, explicitly, may best be referred to as goals, or ends. But there are also implicit values (or value deprivation, value denials), the satisfaction or dissatisfaction of which is built into the structure. On the actor level these values show up as interests, and what these interests are becomes more clear when structures change, whether through deliberate action or not. What then shows up is that some actors/parties gain by the status quo and lose when there is change, whereas for others it may be the other way round. Under ordinary circumstances both parties may be so used to the way the structure distributes value that they take the process for granted. But the moment there is consciousness about the workings of the structure, the structure has already changed, and if this consciousness is translated into organization/mobilization, it may lead on to struggle through confrontation. Trivial and obvious, but this is some of the material out of which history is made, and the points that follow in this chapter are essentially variations on this theme. Occasionally, only occasionally, such processes even lead to some type of transcendence.[8] Several parts of the world may be in that kind of period now, and new national systems (capitalist, socialist, or something new?) or new international systems (concerts, like the Vienna Congress system; [con]federations; regional governments; or something new?) may be emerging. But most of those changes will occur beyond the horizon of the 1980s. The 1980s can probably best be described as a post–Second World War, postcolonialism period—with all the restructuring that those terms imply.

1. NIEO as World Capitalist Expansion: Two Winners, Two Losers

Let it first be stated unequivocally that in my view, the NIEO is a part of the world capitalist expansion process. It is in no way directed against capitalism as a way of running an economic system, even a world economic system,[9] but is directed against the near-monopoly of control that the North-West has had over the world capitalist system for nearly 500 years, and particularly for the last 200 years. Thus, the two theses "there is no crisis in the world capitalist system" and "there is a crisis in the North-West control of the world capitalist system" are not at all incompatible, except in the minds of the people who believe that only the North-West world is able to control the system. From the fact that the North-West has been able to do so, it does not follow that the North-West will always be able to do so. It does not even follow that it is in the best position to do so; others might be as good or even better at the capitalist game. It is this challenge of the North-West world—such as when the United States and Germany challenged Britain— that is basic in the NIEO.

The NIEO is seen here as a process that started with Japan's emergence in the world economic market from the early days of the Meiji Restoration (late 1860s) onward. Japan was the first country from the non-North-

West that "made it," that understood the workings of the world capitalist system sufficiently to be able to use the system to its own advantage. As it was the only country in the region to do so, Japan's emergence took place not only at the expense of other countries in the region[10] but also to the immense enrichment of Japan itself. There was a temporary setback as a result of the war in the Pacific, but today Japan is in a position to treat a former leader of the world economic system the way the United States has treated other countries: investing in the United States; marketing Japanese goods and building factories there; utilizing U.S. labor, which is reluctant to go on strike because of high unemployment figures; and sharing with the dependent country some technological secrets but by no means all.

Japan's example was then followed by other countries, most notably Iran when it, under Muhammad Mossadegh, tried to nationalize the oil corporations of the North-West and had to pay dearly for that attempt in 1953. However, that process was watched closely by a young Egyptian by the name of Nasser, who three years later seized a canal, a process that was watched very closely by a young Cuban by the name of Castro, who two years later seized a whole country. The resolutions passed at the Sixth and Seventh Special Sessions of the UN General Assembly in 1974 and 1975 (with corresponding resolutions in other branches of the UN system) should be seen, not as actions initiating a new process, but as an important acknowledgment that a process, as illustrated by the actions of the Organization of Petroleum Exporting Countries (OPEC) in 1973, was under way. The United Nations only rarely initiates a process; it usually endorses one and sometimes plays an important role in speeding it up. Most important in this connection was the adoption of the Charter of Economic Rights and Duties of States (CERDS) by the UN General Assembly in December 1974, which established a normative basis for what has followed. No doubt UNCTAD I, held in Geneva in 1964, was of key significance: Most of the NIEO—except that term—was contained in its resolutions. It seems possible today to distinguish between five important phases in the NIEO as a process, not necessarily presented here in historical order.

1. The *terms-of-trade phase*, in which higher buying power for raw materials and semimanufactured commodities in terms of processed goods and services (higher price ratios, not just higher prices) is requested.

2. *Expropriation/nationalization of productive assets in Third World countries*, meaning that these countries will internationalize what the First World used to consider as an external sector of its economy. The Third World will increasingly control its own natural

resources; its own capital resources, not necessarily recycling them back to banks in the First World; its own labor, for instance, by requesting that a tax be paid to Third World governments for each foreign worker trained abroad; corresponding measures to counteract the brain drain; and, of course, nationalization of factories, etc., that are located in free-trade zones, etc.[11]

3. *Increased trade and exchange in general among Third World countries*, what in UN jargon is called TCDC and ECDC (technical and economic cooperation between developing countries), or simply South-South trade/cooperation.

4. *Counterpenetration*, essentially meaning investment by Third World countries in First World countries, thereby treating the First World countries as an external sector of Third World economies.

5. *Conquest of world economic power positions*, starting with the Bretton-Woods system (the World Bank, International Monetary Fund, International Development Association, etc.) and the transnational corporations operating in a region, through national and regional takeovers, possibly also through some type of globalization whereby some of them (pharmaceuticals?) might be run somewhat like the ocean regime now taking shape through the Law of the Sea process.[12]

What only some years ago would have been totally unrealistic is today much more feasible because of changed power relations. With military intervention in most Third World countries a decreasingly available option, and with military regimes that are not necessarily friendly to the First World, the 1980s will probably witness the unfolding of exactly this scenario. It should be noted that the five points do not enter linearly. Too often, observers of contemporary history start their analysis with the OPEC action in 1973, which gives a great deal of emphasis to the first point on the list. However, the list should be seen more as a circle than as a line—starting anywhere, ending nowhere.

It is difficult to see where any of these actions differ from what the First World used to do when it was firmly in control of the system. Thus, to increase the price of oil was merely an exercise in elementary textbook economics. If there is something like an inelastic demand for a commodity over a certain price range, it would be stupid not to go to the upper end of that price range, possibly even somewhat beyond, in order to get the money the market can yield. The OPEC countries played the market and gained. If the First World countries did not like the situation it was not because the OPEC countries did something wrong, only because the game was less attractive when the other side proved to have the best cards. Unsurprisingly, the First World then tried to change the rules of the game by starting to talk about oil as something belonging to humankind in general, while having great reservations about this principle in connection with the ocean floor and its management or in connection with technology in general. The world game is still a predominantly capitalist one, meaning that the market sets the priorities for production, allocates resources and goods/services, and thereby also has a decisive influence on the consumption pattern.[13]

The game is the same: Capitalism is stronger then ever, now penetrating the most remote corners of the world. For reasons to be mentioned later, state socialism is not an antithesis to private capitalism. What is an antithesis is what usually is called a nonmarket, informal, or green economy—production for self-consumption and production for non-monetary exchange—and a local economy—production for monetary exchange but in very limited economic cycles. Such economies are, by definition, more use-oriented and less exchange-oriented; they may also be more need-oriented and less demand-oriented. Such an economy is often referred to as a subsistence economy in Third World countries, an economy that is now actually reemerging in certain First World countries, for reasons to be discussed later.

The thesis, then, is that these processes together are of the same magnitude as the decline and fall of the Roman Empire,[14] or the decline and fall of the Middle Ages,[15] and will have an equally profound impact. Less grandiosely, there will be winners, and there will be losers, both nationally and globally. The capitalist structure may not change much, but the point of gravity of the structure will change.[16] Since the capitalist system is based on inequalities that generate inequities,[17] countries that were in the center and have now become more peripheral will be losers according to the dynamics of the system, and those that were in the periphery and now are moving more toward the center will be winners. There is also a third category: those that previously were marginal to the system, running their own informal economies relatively untouched by colonialism (which was like a cat's paw compared to the lion's claw that is now making itself felt all over the Third World). They may also become losers, as they are moving from marginality to periphery.[18]

As the process now unfolds itself, two losers and two winners seem already relatively clearly defined.

Loser: the North-West, the old international economic order directorate; the United States–European Community (EC)–Japan triangle (Trilateral Commission, Organization for Economic Cooperation and Development [OECD]).
Winner: the South-East; the New International Economic Order point of gravity, the Japan–China–Southeast Asia triangle.

Winner: the elites in the Third World; the people running the bureaucratic-corporate-intelligentsia and the party-military-police complexes.

Loser: the people in general in the Third World; the rest of the population.

Of course, not all parts of the population will lose equally in the North-West, nor will all parts gain equally in the South-East. Not all people in the Third World will lose, nor will all elites gain. But these are the general perspectives that will be explored in the next sections.

2. Rise of the South-East, Decline of the North-West

The thesis is very simple—the NIEO is a strategy for unsaddling the North-West from its control position; it says nothing about where the new center is going to be. As a matter of fact, it sometimes seems as if the actors themselves think there is going to be no new center, but that is unrealistic. Whether by design or by the workings of the system, centers—more or less coordinated—will tend to emerge. Thus, if the point in the preceding section is that nothing is happening to challenge the capitalist structure of the world capitalist economic system, then the thesis of the present section is that there will be a new center and that center will be in the South-East part of the world. Five reasons will be given for this assumption.[19]

First, the China–Japan–Southeast Asia triangle has almost all the productive assets needed. Roughly speaking, it has 1.5 billion people, among them a 600-million-strong Chinese labor force; Japanese technology and capital (with the highest savings ratio in the world, 19 percent);[20] raw materials from all over the area, particularly Southeast Asia, including Indonesian oil (and also Chinese and Japanese offshore oil), and all of these resources together should satisfy a production function that is sufficient to meet a substantial portion of world market demands, particularly if the resources of Australia/New Zealand and Oceania are added.[21]

Second, the underlying ethos will contribute. China and Japan, and the part of Southeast Asia that is influenced by them, exhibit a particular characteristic of some oriental civilizations, an additive or eclectic nature.[22] There is a Confucian/Buddhist combination common to both countries, although the tonality is different when Daoism is added in the Chinese case and Shintoism is added in the Japanese case. This combination makes not only for a considerable cultural communality but also for a spirit of corporate endeavor, with Confucianism defining the vertical component (discipline and respect for authority, for nonmanual work, and so on) and Mahayana Buddhism the more horizontal, organic, solidarity aspect. But in addition, both of them are adding, in the usual eclectic manner, Western components: Christianity certainly, liberalism, and in the Chinese case, Marxism. The Western component makes for a universalism in space, combined with an idea of progress in time, that is not found in the more Asian components of these civilizations. It is difficult to see how all of these factors combined could fail to make for an almost perfect ethos for a world-encompassing capitalism. Weber has explained the significance of puritan Protestantism for the rise of capitalism, but at best his theory only gives a rationale for the capitalist entrepreneur; it offers little or nothing of comfort to the worker.[23] Marx explained what the workers' situation was and motivated the worker toward revolt and distribution, but he had very little to say that could inspire and justify entrepreneurial activity. The net result was, as we know, the two Norths with entrepreneurial growth without much distribution in the West, and distribution without much entrepreneurial growth in the East.[24] The contention here is that the whole South-East world, and not only Japan, is now transcending this apparent incompatibility because of its particular civilizational amalgam and will manage a very effective capitalism,[25] much more effective than that of the North-West.

The third reason, partly a reflection of the preceding theme, is the way the Chinese and Japanese are organized. A Chinese name like Tang, or a Japanese name like Tanaka, stands for millions of people. In the Chinese case, there is a certain amount of solidarity among the Tangs, the Lims, the Changs—a solidarity that borders on crystallizing them into one actor. To the extent that there are Chinese abroad—and this is considerable[26]—a Chinese family name may actually stand for a transnational corporation already. Whereas westerners tend to prefer to get away from very common names and have names that can better clothe their individualism,[27] Chinese and Japanese may prefer just the opposite, enjoying the sense of belonging to a greater collectivity as expressed by a very common name, although there are counterprocesses in the Japanese case. This preference can be seen as an expression of the famous collectivism of the Orient, which, among other factors, probably makes for less alienation in connection with the industrialization process than in the West. In a factory, the collectivity of workers and managers produces for the collectivity of customers, and both collectivities make sense in that particular non-Western setting. It is only in an individualizing culture that an individual worker producing for an individual customer in a direct individual-product-individual relationship makes so much sense,[28] and departures from that pattern create alienation, which may lead to some apathy, even withdrawal.

Fourth, the politics of the South-East triangle is taking shape. There are weak points, or points that have to be treated with great delicacy. China and Japan share the history of a terrible imperialist war only fifty years ago, and both of these big powers are looked upon with apprehension in the region. Chinese minorities everywhere may serve as points of contact, but they may also be seen as bridgeheads for expansionism. The people trained all over Southeast Asia by Japan during the *Dai-tō-ā* exercise (Great East Asia Coprosperity—the Japanese wartime slogan) learned to respect Japanese efficiency and patterns of organization in general.[29] Although the feelings of wartime animosity have by and large withered away, a scepticism may still prevail, welling up as incidents of Japanese cars' being burned in Bangkok and Jakarta.[30] Nevertheless, it may safely be said that business circles in Southeast Asia are heavily imbued with something Chinese and something Japanese, in addition to their knowledge of local and U.S. business practices. It should be noted, however, that both the Catholic Philippines and Muslim Indonesia are occidental in respect to civilizational belongingness and oriental only geographically, and the same applies to the Malay majority of Malaysia— a factor of some importance in the longer run. The countries that could be most easily integrated into this triangle would be the four mini-Japans: Singapore, Hong Kong, Taiwan, and South Korea; in the longer run, perhaps also North Korea and the countries of Indochina, even Buddhist Thailand. A great deal of highly delicate diplomacy would be needed, as witnessed by the 1982 textbook controversy, a major Japanese gaffe.[31] Crucial, however, is the Tokyo-Beijing axis that the Japanese apparently started forging the moment they discovered that the United States and China had rediscovered each other back in 1971. The match between Chinese labor and Japanese capital and technology, within a shared ethos and geopolitical potentiality, would seem perfect, but the details nonetheless have to be worked out. It had to take some time before Chinese workers could produce Japanese products, under license in the usual fashion, but that is now taking place (the case of Sanyo, for instance, "Made in the People's Republic of China").[32]

Fifth, in order to produce for the world market, and not merely for a national or regional market as would be the case for other NICs (Brazil and Mexico, for instance, possibly also India), something very persuasive is needed: products that are competitive both in terms of quality and in terms of prices. It is hard to see that relatively inexpensive Chinese labor coupled with Japanese and Chinese ingenuity should not increasingly be able to produce exactly this type of product.[33] At this point, some particular reasons why Japanese products seem to be so good should be mentioned. There has, of course, always been an element of truth in the Western countries' five standard techniques for debunking Japan and for comforting themselves: The products are imitations of Western products only and even the technology is "stolen"; the quality is shoddy; the prices are at the expense of an exploited proletariat; the prices are subsidized one way or another through dumping practices; and, the 1970s version, the products are all produced at tremendous cost to nature in terms of depletion and pollution. The elements of truth are decreasing, however. A sixth point, that Japan is not easily penetrated by foreign goods, remains true. Could it be partly because foreign goods are not that good—as the Japanese often claim?

Today's Japanese products are often highly ingenious combinations, in an additive, eclectic manner, of components also known elsewhere— as when one of the excellent Japanese watches is also equipped with a computer, or can be converted into a mini-TV just by pushing a little button and raising a small antenna. And the products are certainly far from "shoddy," given that the Japanese seem to have made use of the tendency of Western capitalism toward "planned obsolescence" and make products to last precisely because others do not. Moreover, the typical Japanese enterprise has low productivity when everybody engaged in the work is counted, because the products, in addition to being capital and research intensive, are also labor intensive: thorough, cooperative, no-nonsense, serious craftsmanship with every detail attended to by many people. Westerners may point out that the total productivity is low; the Japanese could point out that the quality is high but they seem to prefer that the customers do it for them—and the customers oblige. Japan has conquered the camera market to a large extent, and the television, radio, music machinery, and watch markets are now being increasingly taken over—just as in the sector of transportation the motorcycle market was the first one to be Japanized, now followed by personal cars, trucks, and so on.[34] Integrated circuits, computers—everything in that field is next in line—then airplanes and telematics.[35] Again, there is no reason to believe that these products will necessarily be inferior if they bear the stamp "Made in the People's Republic of China."

To the extent that all of this is becoming the case in the 1980s, obviously the economic conflict formation is not a North-South one but a North-West/South-East formation. It is, moreover, already perceived as such: Complaints about the penetration into the Western part of the classical triangle of the old economic order, United States–EC–Japan (the OECD and Trilateral Commission countries), are numerous. There is the usual admonition to "exercise restraint,"[36] but why should the Japanese or anybody else in the South-East do that when the North-West never exercised restraint? Of course, the interesting thing about Japan is that it is a member of both triangles, and this fact is used to communicate, forcefully, the apprehensions of the North-West.[37] Sooner or later Japan will probably have to leave the first triangle in favor of the second one, apart from keeping its links to the former as a listening post. But the initiative for this change would probably come from the North-West, not from Japan itself. When "exercising restraint" still fails to work, among other reasons simply because customers prefer Japanese products, the North-West response will have to be tariff and nontariff barriers. Psychological preparation for the latter may take the form of statistics about worse accidents with small Japanese cars than with big U.S. cars (albeit probably because they are small rather than because they are Japanese, and the Japanese answer may be to make bigger cars). Another preparation, obviously, is to utilize entrapment and racial prejudice, an old North-West practice.

To get into the question of what the South-East world will do in case of a trade war one has to ask the question why the South-East is engaged in this exercise at all. And the answer is probably very simple: Those countries know from experience how the North-West has been operating and that there are gains to be made if one can dominate the market; one can simply become very rich that way! Ultimately, domination has to do with one's own security, although it is well known that this road to security may become a road to insecurity.[38] Raw material sources and markets may be closed to the South-East world, hence one has to secure a minimum base of both, and the South-East triangle already has such a base. Even for the Japanese it will take time to saturate the Chinese market with Japanese goods made in China. Should everything else fail, there is always the *Dai-tō-ā*, the South-East world, the secure backyard. And should Japan decline and fall—not in the 1980s, but in the 1990s?—there might be little comfort in this fact for the North-West: The mini-Japans and China may take over.

About the rest of the world both Japan and China are probably relatively detached.[39] They do not have the Western view of their being in the center with the rest of the world's being a periphery to be converted into a second-rate copy of the center. On the contrary, to the Chinese, what is outside their own center are the "barbarians" of the northern (Soviet), eastern (Japanese), southern (Vietnamese, Southeast Asian), and western (the Occident) varieties. Of all of these, the northern barbarians are the most dangerous, and one should protect oneself against them by having their barbarian enemies as allies. The eastern barbarians are a nouveau riche, a slightly vulgarized variety of the Chinese. The southern barbarians are a mixed lot, many of them extensions of the Chinese, whereas the western barbarians are more like a lost cause, infantile but clever in their one-sidedness. Like children playing with matchboxes, one has to know how childlike they are, how dangerous are the matches, and how close the two are to each other. One has to be informed about the barbarians. To convert them is a hopeless and even meaningless task, however much they might need conversion.

For the Japanese, the world image is not that different: They are in the center, then outside Japan there is an East Asian zone, and outside that again the world as a resource. To evaluate the world purely in utilitarian terms, positively and negatively in terms of oneself, is by no means unknown in Western theories of state—after all, that is what the concept of "state interest" is about. But the Orient might go further than the Occident in not abiding by universal norms of justice or whatever if doing so would interfere with its own interests—not even seeing the world in universalist terms of Christian compassion or Roman-inspired law, or pretending to do so as Western powers often do. This propensity has the advantage for the non-South-East countries of the world in that there will be no attempts to convert them into talking Japanese or Chinese, into adopting the cultural patterns of either country or both, or anything else of the kind for that matter. All they are asked to do is to pay for the goods offered in terms of natural resources, capital, or technology.

South-East capitalism, on the world level, is much more specific, more contractual than the diffuse and all-embracing Western imperialism. The latter has left peoples all over the world with languages not their own and rooted in a political and spiritual capital that is not their own. China and Japan will neither attempt nor want to do anything of that kind. They *want* a distance, and they will get it.[40] As opposed to U.S. and French people, who feel flattered and confirmed when somebody far away speaks their own language perfectly, the Japanese and the Chinese feel uneasy when somebody is "getting under their skin" that way. It is like being spied upon, like having nowhere to retreat to.[41] It may be added that they have little reason to worry: Their languages are tremendously difficult to learn, taking at least five years of concentrated study. Those five years should preferably be at the very early stage in life—but in that case one *is* a Chinese or a Japanese. As the people speaking one of these two languages can understand the other up to 80 percent and can easily acquire the remaining 20 percent—in writing, that is—they have for all practical purposes a quite effective secret language with which to conduct their operations—an asset to be added to the others mentioned above. In addition, the sun rises earlier in Tokyo than in the West, which means that a Japanese can transact business before even a Zurich banker is in his office!

However, what would happen if the North-West adopted harsher measures? In the first run, doing so would mean a boycott, a tariff/nontariff wall that is unscalable, but may invite smuggling. The Japanese probably have no illusions that such a measure is not a possibility, and for that reason they are doing everything to create the best allies possible within the framework of a liberal economy, the consumers. Any such wall, low or high, would mean that the consumers would have to subsidize employment for the workers, and profit for the managers and stockholders, by buying more expensive cars than they otherwise could get; a dubious proposition from the point of view of a market economy. The Japanese might then call the bluff by its right name, but that would not decrease the agony of the dilemma.[42] In the meantime, countries in the South-East will have to secure markets for their goods all over the Third World and possibly also in the North-East world, in the state socialist countries that are still under the spell of North-West capitalism, oriented toward U.S., French, German, Italian, and even British products.[43] Needless to say, any trade embargo measure would be a blow to the South-East as the North-West is by far the best-paying customer, although the Third World bourgeoisie is now also coming up quite quickly. The question is whether the North-West governments are prepared to pay the price of having their citizens subsidize jobs in factories that otherwise are unable to stand up to South-East competition, with such obvious effects as a large-scale smuggling of South-East goods. It should also be noted that the Japanese government may organize a consumers' boycott of North-West goods even if Japan as a country should lower its tariff/ nontariff barriers. It is doubtful whether the North-West governments have a corresponding leverage on their own peoples.[44]

But what if this tension should be aggravated further and even lead to warlike measures? Let us analyze two possible scenarios. In the first scenario, the major loser in the expansion of the South-East, the United States, possibly followed by some Western European allies, initiates warlike measures against the South-East. Today this scenario may sound only hypothetical, even crazy, but one should remember that there are very real interests at stake and that such measures have been taken before, in the 1850s and the 1940s. It is also useful to comprehend what the Japanese would immediately do—establish closer ties with the Soviet Union and try to persuade the Chinese to do the same.[45] It is important to realize that Japan and the Soviet Union have a bargaining chip that they can push back and forth between the two of them—the Kuril Islands occupied by the Soviet Union after the Second World War. The Soviet Union might on some occasion hand them back, Japan might on some occasion recognize that they form part of Soviet territory; in either case, at a considerable price. Anyhow, the mere prospect of this type of triple concert—Japan–China–Soviet Union—is not one that would make the United States move far in the direction of this scenario— again one instance of how powerless "the most powerful nation on earth"[46] actually has become.

According to the second scenario, the United States and the Soviet Union one day both define the world in Occident/Orient, or even white/yellow, terms, finding that there is more to unite them than to divide them in the face of the "yellow peril." This second scenario has more equal balance: Demographically, the Orient would be superior; economically, the Orient and the Occident might be more even; militarily, the Occident would be superior. Against this scenario it may certainly be argued that all the Soviet Union now has to do is to sit on the sidelines and wait for the South-East to sufficiently outcompete the North-West economically so as to weaken it also politically and militarily. But it is not so obvious that the Soviet Union wants to wait for this outcome. The Soviets may fear that a militarily strong North-West on its way down economically may engage in some desperate action (and with good reason). They might want the North-West to remain strong, partly to scare their country's own population, partly to have a scapegoat, partly to continue to have something to "catch up" with and "surpass," and partly because they admire it as a source of technology and have not yet overcome the anti-Japanese prejudices referred to above. For such reasons this second scenario is not all that unlikely, and it has disastrous implications because of the civilizational and racial cleavages involved.[47]

The obvious Japanese-Chinese counterstrategy would be to see to it that the Cold War between East and West is kept alive. As there is such a heavy ideological and political investment on either side, this task should not be too difficult; in fact, what is needed is only something like one Afghanistan every five to ten years. The Soviet theories of Chinese provocation in this particular conflict may therefore not be that farfetched. And there is also another interesting speculation: Whereas the Chinese may produce an enormous amount of economic goods, they may prefer to use the Japanese as their economic agents abroad, their salesmen, thus turning Japan into a macro–Hong Kong for China's purposes, and the Japanese may prefer to let the Chinese do the political work for the South-East triangle. In this way, the Chinese remain economically pure and more free to pursue their internal zigzag course, and the Japanese are more free to look politically neutral, solely engaged in economic pursuits. This situation does not exclude the use of the Chinese abroad as a general network, but much more important, in this perspective, is Japan as a macro–Hong Kong.

One may now ask: If the South-East triangle is that strong, why did not all of this transition from North-West to South-East start earlier? For a very simple set of reasons:

1. China was down, weakened by internal processes and external imperialism, a worn-out country. Japan came out of Tokugawa

isolation as *the* modern and leading country in the Orient, was tempted into military adventurism, and now faces a choice between a symbiotic or a subservient relation to China. Japan obviously prefers the former—as dominance over China is out.

2. The occidentalization process (in the sense of adding occidental elements to the civilization) had not yet gone far enough to provide that forward and outward thrust that is so characteristic of the Occident.

3. The opportunity had not yet come: an Occident weakened by decolonization and by the part of the NIEO initiated by the Third World, particularly the OPEC action.

As a conclusion, the particular historical occasion had not yet presented itself; today it has, and the 1980s will show to what extent it is made use of. Let me only add that this is not a "Japanese twenty-first century" hypothesis. It is not about Japan only, and Japan may not last that long. Nor is it about the twenty-first century but about today. And it is a fact rather than a hypothesis, foreseeable for a long time about the South-East.[48] So let us call it the Fourth World and remember the Bible, "the last shall be the first."

3. The Third World: Processes and Counterprocesses

Most of the Third World countries (at least 100 of them) will be marked by aggravated internal gaps, class contradictions, and open class conflicts due to the NIEO factors mentioned above. The NIEO puts a premium on trade and then channels internal economic resources in that direction, which, given the structure of Third World countries in general, will tend to enrich the elites and impoverish the people who have productive assets taken away from them.[49] Coffee beans will be given priority over black beans; sugar for gasohol over sugar for nutrition. There are exceptions to this tendency, but they number fewer than a dozen countries: the socialist Third World countries; some countries in the South-East corner such as South Korea, Taiwan, Hong Kong, and Singapore (which is one major reason why they can be referred to as "mini-Japans"); and a few others. In these exceptional countries a new *intra*national economic order (accompanied or not by dictatorial repression) with some distribution preceded the new *inter*national economic order, which means that the latter does not have such detrimental consequences. But for the other countries, it is safe to predict that many of their NIEO dollars will be converted into police and military technology for surveillance of the population and suppression of revolts at any stage as international change precedes intranational change.[50] The repressive nature of the Taiwanese and South Korean regimes should probably be seen more in the context of the China and Korean wars than as simple class repression.

These are the obvious processes; the question is what the counter-processes might be. Iran might serve as a pilot country as the antishah revolt came from an unexpected corner. It had a clear economic deprivation/class character according to the Marxist scheme of analysis and was even formulated in Marxist idiom and with some Marxist leadership. But it also had another dimension: religious, fundamentalist, anti-Western, not in the sense of anti-imperialist but in the sense of antimaterialist.[51] It was the political genius of the Ayatollah Khomeini that was needed to weld those two dimensions into a working political coalition, and then later on to use the latter part to turn against the former. Translated to other Third World countries, this counterprocess would mean a search for fundamentalist, non- and anti-Western values on which to stand, a search for roots, for an endogenous platform.[52]

The basis for a more generalized anti-Western platform, not only anticapitalist but perhaps also antisocialist and anti-Marxist as well as antiliberal, is not difficult to find. All over the Third World after the Second World War, but particularly after decolonization in the early 1960s, two basic hypotheses have been tested: the road to growth and happiness through liberal private capitalism and the road to growth and happiness through Marxist state socialism, gambling on entrepreneurial activity in the former and revolutionary distribution in the latter. The only places where these experiments can be said to have had a positive result are some of the countries in the South-East, for the reasons mentioned, but there were so many special conditions in those countries that it is difficult to copy the example elsewhere. Hence, a generalized anti-Western attitude might also be a call to no longer listen to the false prophets. And here it should be noted that in the Khomeini scheme of thinking, there is the "great satan"—the United States, of course—surrounded by four lesser satans, of which the first is the Soviet Union followed by the United Kingdom, Israel, and South Africa—in that order. Thus, no attention is paid to the conception that the United States and the Soviet Union head two different ideologies, two different worlds for that matter (the "free" and the "unfree") between which one has to choose. Khomeini wraps them together—and in my view more or less correctly—by seeing one as subordinate to the other and rejects the whole package as "satanic" (his terminology has not caught on yet, though).

For a rejection of materialism in the 1980s there would be another factor of some importance. If the scenario hinted at in section 2 is anything like correct, the Third World by the end of the 1980s will more than ever look like a Japanese, and in general a South-East, trade fair (although "Made in the People's Republic of China" will be stamped on many of the products). It is my contention that these products will by and large be preferred to Western ones, not only because they are cheaper and better, but also because of the halo effect of Japan as being the first Third World country to become economically successful. Therefore, it is hard to believe that any but the most servile Third World country will join a U.S.-led economic boycott against the South-East. But that does not rule out the possibility of an antimaterialist revolt that might also hit Japanese products, although there seems to be a strange factor operating here: Somehow the U.S. Ford, not to mention a German Mercedes, looks more materialistic than a Japanese Toyota, even one of the bigger models. And the reason is perhaps not so difficult to find. It lies precisely in the specific character of Japanese capitalism abroad: product only, none of the connotations of an entire life-style that are always exported along with U.S. products. The Japanese remain anonymous, and prefer it that way.[53]

It is to be expected that these revolts will be unexpected; it is to be predicted that they will be unpredictable. The only continuity one can see would be a set of discontinuities. But there would be one common element if this scenario is correct: a revival of fundamentalist, non-Western religion, a purified Islam (and here the distinction between "fundamentalist" and "institutional" is probably much more important than the Sunni-Shia distinction some try to make the most of), fundamentalist Hinduism, purified Buddhism, and incidentally, a return also to the basic values of Confucianism and Shintoism.[54] In other parts of the Third World this revival may take the form of animism and animatism,[55] and in the Christian countries, the form of fundamentalist Christianity—such as the Moral Majority, the born-again Christians, and others.[56] Consequently, anyone who wants to understand the world, and not only the Third World, of the 1980s, had better start learning something about the religious faiths of the world and what they mean to the people who hold them. Power will be as important as ever, but the power basis in the Third World will be not only a carrot-and-stick power, based on economic factors (commodities) and military factors (weapons received in return for those commodities), but also normative, cultural power. More than ever this will be the decade of the "minorities"—a terrible misnomer as singly, and definitely combined, they usually are the majority. As a consequence, disintegration of some of the nation-state constructions is also to be expected, raising the need for new institutional frameworks after the nation-state. Third World dreams of penetrating First World markets will have to be tempered by the harsh reality of Fourth World efficiency, even penetration of Third

World markets. To service the ever-growing debt burden under such conditions would be close to impossible—debts that ultimately point to a small number of Fourth World and OPEC countries as creditors—but this is also a First World problem.

4. The Second World: Processes and Counterprocesses

In a sense the Second World is in a different situation than the Third World. It is less entangled economically with the Third World as it does not have major investments abroad or depend on the Third World for markets or raw materials to anything like the degree the First World does. However, the state socialist countries are so entangled with the private capitalist countries that any economic decline in the latter will have some contagious effect in the former. Unemployment and inflation will be exported to the extent economic interdependence provides for the conductivity of these phenomena, which means that they will be particularly predominant in Yugoslavia as that is the most "interdependent" country.[57]

However, there are other processes more endogenous to state socialist countries that should be pointed out in this connection, and they also seem to have an economic basis. The decline in production and productivity growth during recent years is important in this connection. It does to a state socialist economy what a decline in profit does to a private capitalist economy. Sooner or later there is a crisis because these economies have to move all the time, and the crisis is not least one of the spirit, a lack of faith in the system. However, the mechanisms are different for the two types of economy. In the state socialist countries it is probably more a question of overmobilization of productive resources in the capital, at the top inside the ministries, and in certain industries at the expense of an undermobilization of productive assets for the rest of the country, outside the ministries, and in less prominent sectors of the economy—for instance, agriculture. This concentration is seen also in terms of party power. Whereas the party at the center often has considerable talent at its disposal, the lower ranks and the party outside the capital are less flexible, more dogmatic, more afraid of the reactions of the center, and hence, less inclined to engage in anything like the entrepreneurial activity that characterizes not only private but also state capitalism (risk taking, hard work, ability to see opportunities others do not see, detection of new combinations in the production system, and so on).[58] This effect may be real, but the theory might also be misleading because revamping the party might be seen as the cure instead of a total revamping of the steep center/periphery gradients in general.[59]

Thus, as long as this situation exists, the dominant process, as far as one can see, will be for the production and productivity increases to decline toward zero, even negative, levels. At the same time, the nature of East-West trade has been, roughly speaking, goods on the lower levels of processing (including energy raw materials) moving from East to West (including compressors for pipelines). Thus, the terms of trade have by and large not favored the East, except for oil and gas and when countries there have been able to export some industrial goods, like ships. The gaps created could have been filled by productivity and production increases, but since this has not been the case, they have had to be filled with loans that then become increasingly difficult to service. The result is a situation in which productivity simply has to be increased, or the West gains too much power.[60] In general, that type of gap has a destabilizing effect—and makes social experiments difficult.

It is at that point the recent events in Poland become so significant. One may perhaps see them as an effort to arrive at a bargain between the workers in the periphery, Gdansk (later the workers all over Poland, due to the rapid spread of the Solidarity trade union), and the party and government authorities in the center, Warsaw: higher productivity, yes, but only in return for higher levels of freedom.[61] The twenty-one articles that came out of the dialogues among workers in Gdansk in the summer of 1980 essentially can be reduced to two components: more workers' control over the productive process, including free trade unions, and more attention given to the basic needs of the whole population. As these two points constitute a rather reasonable definition of socialism, the initial process may be referred to as "a socialist revolt in a state socialist country." As such, it is a rather important counterprocess, which also had as its goal the reduction of the tremendous gap between decision-making elites and the working class that produces the surplus on which the elites live. It should be added that in such countries, there is no question of converting NIEO dollars into military and police capability. The elites have this capability at their disposal already.

But the above is only part of the picture. State socialist countries are also cut through by other contradictions of no lesser magnitude, as can be seen from the following list of seven sources of opposition confronting the Soviet leadership.

1. The farmers and peasants want larger plots of their own and an opportunity to market their products in return for making more and better-quality products available; more genuine self-management.
2. The workers want free trade unions in order to protect themselves against exploitation by the apparat, in return for increasing pro-

duction through increases in productivity; more genuine self-management.

3. The intellectuals want both freedom of expression and freedom of impression in return for contributing a higher level of production of ideas and creativity in general; more geniune self-management.

4. The socialist bourgeoisie seems to want consumer goods and less homespun, more on the level available to the bourgeoisies in First and Third World countries and, increasingly, even in the People's Republic of China.

5. The minorities, including religious minorities, want autonomy, as has been demonstrated even in Estonia, inside the Soviet Union.

6. The periphery state socialist countries want autonomy, as has been demonstrated in many of them but practiced only by Romania.

7. The Communist parties want autonomy, as was recently demonstrated in the phenomenon of Eurocommunism (it should actually be called Latin communism as central and northern parts of Western Europe do not seem to have followed this lead).

With seven sources of contradiction and even open conflict, what keeps the system going is not so much the ability to control every one of the contradictions as the ability to fragment them, keep them apart, divide and rule. Disturbing in the Polish case must have been the extent to which workers and intellectuals came together (although the latter were largely the artisans and helpers for the former) and their substantial links to the farmers and peasants. There was also support from Latin Communist parties, but not open support from corresponding groups inside the Soviet Union, for instance. In short, there are many political ties still to be established and to be counteracted by the ruling elites, all of which will make the whole Second World a region of not only contradictions but convulsion in the coming decade.[62]

Imagine that all seven contradictions became manifest conflicts, working their way as processes: What kind of impact would that have on the Second World in the end? The net result might be some kind of state-controlled capitalism according to more social democratic formulas, with authoritarian elements and with many of the same problems the North-West countries have, except there would be less dependence on the South. The major positions in the economy would remain state controlled, but farming, small-scale production, construction work, and above all distribution would, to a much larger extent, be run by a private capitalist sector that might include elements of Yugoslav self-management (i.e., socialism in the sense of codecision on the microlevel within capitalism on the national market or macrolevel). The controlling position of the Soviet Union center in the formal sense would be considerably reduced, which might well mean that Soviet control would be enhanced, as it would be more informal, more based on achievement than on naked carrot-and-stick power.[63]

Why did such changes not occur earlier? Again, the historical situation was not there. Under Stalinism, for instance, none of the seven contradictions had the slightest chance of emerging into anything like visibility—from the point of view of the Soviet leaders, Stalinism had its advantages! Of course the contradictions were there, as latent conflict, but they were buried under terror. The system had to work its way through excessive optimism about the functioning of a centrally planned economy into a *credo quia absurdum* phase, from which it may now be emerging. There is also the possibility of a turn to the right, neo-Stalinism, even some sort of neoczarism with strong appeals to classical Russian Narodniki values, which view Marxism as a Western importation. We shall see.[64]

5. The People's Republic of China: Processes and Counterprocesses

It is as wrong to assume that China will follow the same social logic as Western countries as it is to assume that state socialist countries should have the same contradictions as private capitalist countries, or even more so. For one thing, the historical situation is different; for another, the cosmology underlying Chinese civilization is different, with that peculiar additive nature alluded to above. More particularly, there is no reason to assume that China should pursue its goal—a modern, socialist country by the year 2000—in the same way as countries in the Occident might. The instruments of modernity, economic growth through an ever-higher production and productivity of both goods and services, at ever-higher levels of processing and marketing, at ever-larger distances geographically and socially, might be about the same—with an emphasis on the importation of artifacts from the "modern" world so that China will no longer be in splendid isolation, on an island all by itself with the flood of history passing by on either side.[65] And the instruments of socialism might also be about the same: mechanisms whereby farmers and workers would keep more of the surplus through control on the bottom level, redistribution through welfare state mechanisms, better terms of trade between city and countryside, and better terms of trade between the secondary and tertiary sectors on the one hand and the primary sector on the other—all under the leadership of the party.

The difference seems to come in the way the different countries go about combining these two goals.[66] One hypothesis would be that the emphasis varies in China from period to period. From 1949 to 1958 the focus was on distribution in the countryside; from 1958 to 1966–

1969 the focus was on the first leap forward and economic growth; from 1966 to 1969 and onward to 1976 the focus was on distribution in the political system, the Cultural Revolution with all its shortcomings; and after the death of Mao Zedong in 1976 the focus has obviously been on the second great leap forward, the Four Modernizations (of agriculture, industry, science and technology, and the military). This zigzag in political emphasis shows up as a complex curve in economic production and trading patterns, with considerable lags as should be expected. But what we are concerned with here is politics more than economics; the political development ethos of any given period.[67]

It should follow that there may be a second turn, a second cultural revolution for that matter, but possibly without efforts to cut China off from its cultural heritage[68] and deprive the population of essential freedoms as well as to decrease productivity and, it seems, also production. Since each phase seems to last about nine years, this turnabout might come sometime in the middle of the 1980s and be accompanied by a return to fundamental Chinese virtues as enshrined in Confucianism and Buddhism, also Daoism. It may have an antimaterial tinge about it, and it may also be combined with the notions of reciprocal responsibility enshrined in Confucianism and organic solidarity enshrined in Mahayana Buddhism.[69] It should be noted that Confucianism and Buddhism legitimize growth and distribution, respectively, as do liberalism and Marxism, meaning that both segments of the zigzag course receive legitimation from both ancient and more occidental components of present Chinese civilization. It is also pertinent that Daoism legitimizes the very notion of zigzag itself through its highly dialectical view of life in general and social life in particular.

Thus, one conclusion that might follow would be that China makes use of its present situation to acquire the technologies it needs for continued growth and then switches once more to the distributive phase. China would, however, still need Japan just as Japan would need China, so it is difficult to see that this tendency in any way should impair their working relationship. But it would mean that the period in which there are non-Japanese partners in the Chinese developmental effort would come to a close—hence, they had better make their profits quickly if this scenario is correct! It would also mean that Japan has a great talent for not letting such rhetoric interfere with business. For Japan, China is the ultimate reserve, the final buffer if the Japanese economy becomes too sluggish. The Chinese know this and can strike good bargains with the Japanese if they want.

China has a dialectic of its own and will continue to. It is more complex than in the West because Chinese civilization is more complex and so is its history. The same might have applied to Japan had Japan not been so small and vulnerable; it certainly would have applied to Japan had that country been a part of China. China will continue to have a dim view of the Occident, both private capitalist and state socialist varieties, and will continue limiting its geopolitical control to the Chinese space, which, roughly speaking, is bordered by the tundra to the north, the Gobi to the west, the Himalayas to the south, and the China Sea. The former Indochina may be a gray zone in this connection, so may Mongolia and Korea. However, the hypothesis here is that China will encroach on neither and might also give more autonomy to Tibet, focusing on the genuine Han peoples. What China might request, however, is that the Soviet Union not step up its level of influence in the bordering territories. China will always work for the reduction of Soviet influence in these areas, meaning Vietnam, North Korea, Mongolia, and also—more significantly—the central Asian republics of the Soviet Union[70] (where China will probably work in its way for more local autonomy—see the corresponding point in the preceding section). It should be added, though, that the demarcation of the lines between Soviet and Chinese influence in Asia is only a part of the Sino-Soviet conflict, other parts of the total issue having such headings as "history of Soviet dominance from early 1920s until the late 1950s," "different conceptions of Marxism/socialism," and "collision course in the search for allies in the Third, Second, and First Worlds."[71]

What would be the net consequence if the dialectic continues to unfold as indicated here? Probably something like the goal stated but more "socialist" than "modern," more distribution than growth, and more so than in Second World countries because of China's collectivist heritage, not because of its assimilation of occidental socialism. And again the same can be said: The historical situation for all of this change was not ripe before. Only now have all these factors come together in a particular way—with the level of China's ability to control the Japanese economic invasion for its own purposes becoming the key factor.[72]

6. The First World: Processes and Conterprocesses

As a whole, the First World is now a region in relative and absolute decline. One does not emerge unpunished from living off the rest of the world for a long period of time when that rest of the world gets sufficient power to do something about the situation. This shows up as unemployment, inflation, personal and national debts, bankruptcies, etc. Metaphorically, two good noneconomic examples can also be given of this. The first is the reversal of the drug trade, as it is no longer Chinese youth and their parents who are poisoned, as was the case after the British "opened" China for the opium trade in the last century,[73] but the youth of the Western countries. The second is the Sun Myung Moon Unification church,[74] as it is no longer children and adolescents in the missionary fields in South America and Africa and Asia that are having their ties with their parents and their culture severed, perhaps forever, but youngsters in the United States and some other countries. In the colonies, cultural defense against missionaries was not that easy.[75]

All of this change must be seen in the light of what has been the basis of Western economy: exploitation of the internal proletariat (the working classes); exploitation of the external proletariat (the Third World); exploitation of nature; and an incredibly high productivity, which ultimately amounts to exploitation of the center of the First World itself.[76] This basis has ensured the bourgeois way of life (BWL), with its emphasis on nonmanual work; material comfort; privacy, whether in the nuclear or the extended family; and a predictable security. And the mode of production that has ensured this way of life has been the growth of bureaucracy, the growth of corporations, and the growth of the intelligentsia, all principally staffed by MAMUs (middle-aged men with university education). The problem is that all of these processes presuppose economic growth—and a great deal of it. What we now find is low, zero, even negative, growth and few—if any—reasons why that situation should change.

It is easily imagined what the strategy of crisis management will be. Most likely is the "brown," more or less fascist, scenario that will emphasize keeping the pillars of Western supremacy from crumbling by supporting them almost at all costs. Concretely, this scenario would mean increased exploitation of the working classes through interference with trade union practices (a reversal of the process that at present may be going on in state socialist countries); continued exploitation of the Third World by fragmenting it; propping up military dictatorships of various political colors—intervening militarily by rapidly deploying task forces if necessary; continued exploitation of nature, by not heeding the warning signals and also by banning ecological movements; and above all by stepping up productivity "to become more competitive abroad." The latter would be a minimum policy that could be agreed upon within the old triangle, by the OECD countries, unifying the less imperialist, nonfascist social democratic countries of the North with other countries.

But in so doing it is easily forgotten that increased productivity, meaning more output of goods/bads and services/disservices per human working hour, will always have to be obtained at a certain cost. More particularly, the cost can probably be seen in five terms.

1. A more top-heavy society: a higher proportion of bureaucrats, capitalists (private or state), and intelligentsia as research, capital,

and administration will have to substitute for labor in the production process. Incidentally, which costs less?

2. A much higher level of unemployment: possibly disguised as compulsory leisure time through the introduction of shorter working days, shorter working weeks, shorter working months, shorter working years, and shorter working lives; the last achieved by prolonging schooling and retirement, ultimately having the two meet in the so-called Danish solution, keeping people in school until they are forty-five and can retire. What is forgotten is that taking jobs away from human beings is also taking away from them the possibility of self-realization through some type of participation in the productive process, even a relatively alienating one, and making people socially useless since they do not enter the economic cycle except as the recipients of welfare and spenders of what they have received.[77]

3. Civilization disease no. 1: mental disorders, particularly among the unemployed because of the linkage between work and mental health.

4. Civilization disease no. 2: cardiovascular diseases, probably heavily stress connected and also closely related to the kind of products that people use, e.g., in their diets, in a society of high productivity.

5. Civilization disease no. 3: malignant tumors and cancers, which now kill 20 percent and affect 25 percent of the population in a country like Norway and is the second largest killer of children (the greatest being accidents). Their etiology probably also lies in the stress/pollution complex.

These are considerable costs, and costs that are already being paid.[78] The relationship between them and still higher levels of productivity is probably exponential rather than linear, meaning that higher productivity can only be recommended by people sufficiently blind to the "negative externalities" of this type, a blindness often found among economists. Consequently, the process of human decline that results from pressing for continued economic growth will probably be roughly proportionate to the economists' access to power, with their particular blindness to structure, culture, history, international politics, nature, and human beings.[79] They might like to learn from the South-East world how to recover, but that would be a rather vain enterprise since economists would not understand the civilizational background, and even if they did understand it, they would hardly be able to simulate a Confucian/Buddhist/occidental ethos. Besides, South-East labor productivity is not necessarily high; it is the cohesiveness and the goal directedness that are high.

It is for these and similar reasons that I would classify increased productivity among the brown alternatives; but that process attains, of course, a more human color when it is unaccompanied by the other three forms of exploitation. More interesting, however, is a second scenario, a counterprocess in terms of "the green wave." This scenario can be seen as a complete or partial negation of the structural elements considered above as basic to the North-Western construction.

1. A higher level of cooperative, communal production patterns with no distinction between labor buyers or labor sellers.
2. A pattern of coexistence with the Third World, possibly combined with less interest in the Third World as so much of traditional Western interest is linked to domination one way or another, for instance, through technical assistance practices.
3. The whole ecological movement—from which the green wave derives its name—coexistence with nature, humans as part of nature.
4. A lower level of productivity, limiting high productivity to some certain well-defined sectors of society and otherwise cultivating more highly labor-intensive and creatively productive forms of production. Being neither a "return to the Middle Ages" nor a "return to the Stone Age," this element, in many cases, would probably accompany research intensity, for instance, in the third agricultural revolution now taking place with its highly sophisticated utilization of bioenergy, biomass in general, sun collectors, wind collectors, local economic cycles of a new type, and so on.
5. More manual work for the class that, practically speaking, now engages in only nonmanual work, and vice versa.
6. Less material comfort, meaning more exposure to nature and more hard work but no dramatic change.
7. Less privatism and a more collective life.
8. A less predictable pattern of security, for instance, changing work, spouses, and places to live more frequently.
9. Less dependency on the state and more devolution, decentralization, and autonomy for local units.
10. Less dependency on capitalist production patterns; more green economy (often called the black or brown economy by social democrats and corporations); more production for self-consumption, for exchange on a nonmonetary basis, or for exchange on a monetary basis—in that case, in very local economic cycles.
11. Less dependence on intellectuals and a greater emphasis on self-reliance in the understanding of one's own situation (for instance,

women preferring to understand the condition of women themselves rather than having their role defined for them by men).
12. A general movement against MAMUs, the feminist movement
against the repression of women, and corresponding movements
for the very young, the very old, and the nonintellectuals (the
"hippie" revolt).

Roughly speaking, the green wave already has these components, ranging
from a full-fledged combination of all of them in an autarchic commune
to a very passive alternative way of life led by people who actually lead
a bourgeois type of life, but only with their body, not their soul. Such
people are today probably very numerous in the First World, and their
number will possibly increase. Gradually some of them will detach
themselves from the BWL and enter wholly or partly into other patterns.

Will the brown or the green alternative be stronger? An answer to
a question like this cannot even be attempted unless one is willing to
divide the First World into parts. For discussion here, it will be divided
into southern Europe, central Europe, northern Europe and Canada,
and the United States.

In southern Europe, one likely scenario might be that the problem
would not materialize, as this is the part of Europe that most easily
could enter into cooperation with a part of the Third World; from the
Maghreb countries and stretching into western Asia. Actually, this area
once composed the greater part of the Roman Empire. The economies
are quite complementary, and all these countries might have a shared
interest in keeping the superpowers out. They are also the countries that
still have the strongest informal economy to fall back upon. Efforts by
certain countries and groups to get southern Europe into the European
Community and NATO can be seen as efforts to prevent this type of
development.

In central Europe (England, France, Germany, and less so, Belgium,
Austria, and Switzerland), the economic crisis may certainly be severe,
and the possibility that the brown movements will be stronger there
than the green cannot be ruled out. One horrible sign is already there:
The tendency of Christians, when there is an economic crisis, to start
burning synagogues is probably one of the strongest indicators of
economic crisis there is.[80] An England under the Labour party would,
however, be less oriented toward brown scenarios than an England under
the Conservative party—or so it seems. Racial and ethnic issues centered
on foreign workers may serve as forceful catalysts, particularly as unemployment accelerates.

In the northern European countries and Canada, it looks as if there
is little social basis for a really strong brown movement, and also as if

the green movement, or wave, might be so much in line with the ethos of the populations that it might gain the upper hand. This would be particularly the case in the northern Scandinavian countries, perhaps a little less so in Denmark where people seem not so attached to nature, and in Canada if the crisis makes that country's economy less dependent on the United States.

Finally, there is the United States, of which, it is felt, nothing can be predicted. There are very strong brown tendencies, perhaps particularly rooted in USA 1 (the larger cities of New York, Washington, D.C., Houston, Los Angeles, San Francisco, and Chicago) when it comes to external affairs and in USA 2 (the rest of the country) when it comes to internal affairs. But there is also a strong green wave inclination based on volunteerism and localism. It seems hazardous to try to predict which one will win out; an oscillating pattern is also a possibility.

7. The East-West Conflict:
Processes and Counterprocesses

In the East-West conflict formation, at least the actors are very clearly defined: the two pyramids headed by the two superpowers—the United States and the Soviet Union—a military alliance headed by each, and some periphery countries.

(North-) West

US
NATO
Periphery

(North-) East

SU
WTO
Periphery

The structure of the two systems has been described ad nauseam, and similarly, the economic, political, and military capabilities as well[81] (although it would probably be wise not to believe any of the figures that are so frequently publicized as it would be strange if at this particular point in human history these actors would be unable to keep something secret from the data gatherers). The question is what the motivations might be. And that, of course, relates to the definition of the conflict issue.

To say that the conflict issue is like the old European adage, "My brother and I agree completely, we both want Milan," is probably to misstate the issue. Each group might like world domination in the sense of seeing its own system, (private) capitalism versus (state) socialism, prevail all over the world, but not so much that it would be willing to fight an all-out war. On the contrary, each might even believe that the wisdom of its own system is such that it will prevail by its own rationality, and by the progress built into the historical process. All that is needed is to be strong and to wait and see. However, this perspective might be more tenable for the Soviet Union than for the United States as world history after the 1917 revolution shows socialism, or rather state socialism, to be on the rise and private capitalism to be declining.[82]

Hence, a more correct reading of the issue would probably be something like this: The Soviet Union will intervene militarily (a) when a society is about to go "socialist" but needs some outside help; (b) to keep the process irreversible, in other words, to stabilize "socialism" and fight efforts to destabilize it; and (c) when the country borders on the Soviet Union. Analysis of Soviet behavior after the Second World War seems to confirm this broad notion, including analyzing the places the Soviet Union withdrew from after occupation (northern Norway; Bornholm, Denmark; Finland; Austria; and northern Iran).[83]

Correspondingly, if there is a chance that a country could turn "capitalist," the United States would do its best to help, and it would try to stabilize "capitalism" and fight its destabilization, regardless of where the country is located. However, given the basic trend referred to above, the Soviet Union might be on the offensive (task *a* as defined above) and the United States more on the defensive (task *b*). This situation might change, but so far there is nothing pointing in that direction, presumably mainly because private capitalism, advanced by Western colonialism and neocolonialism, has been such a dominant force, and such a negative force, in the world as a whole.

The conclusion to be drawn is that the conflict issue is located in societies in the gray zone between a clear articulation in one or the other of the two directions. An in-between society is also a society between the two pyramids, possibly to be lost by one, possibly to be gained by the other; or, equally important, possibly believed to be lost by one, possibly believed to be gained by the other.

Thus, the East-West conflict is located firmly inside the development problematique. For what is this transformation about if it is not about development? One may argue what constitutes a higher level of development, but it is unarguable that development is the issue. The East-West conflict is about the *type* of development in third parties—which of two narrow branches of human history to take. That there should be "development" is considered unproblematic.[84]

This issue is not about a piece of land, such as who should exercise authority on this or that island between Alaska and Siberia; in a sense, it is not even over who shall exercise authority in Berlin. The issue is about what kind of socioeconomic formation there should be in all places. It was also recognized in the Final Act of Helsinki that the geographical border issue is off the agenda, but the second and third "baskets" of those negotiations were exactly about the nature of the system, e.g., under what conditions can private capitalism from the West penetrate and under what conditions can human rights conceptions from the West penetrate, the two concessions being given in return for the first "basket" concession about the status quo over the borders.[85]

Immediately, then, an important problem is raised: What if countries opt for neither private capitalism nor state socialism but for something else, e.g., an undefined mixture agreeable to neither or a greater focus on green economies? And what if countries simply want to stay outside the two power blocks or pyramids? What happens if they want to have their development issues defined and their strategies developed autonomously, for their own sake, and not be treated as a pawn to be "gained by one" and "lost by another" power block? These are, or should be, the questions posed by the nonaligned movement,[86] and they also show the clear connection between nonalignment and development. But the answer to the questions is found within the framework of theories of imperialism: Most of these countries would have elites or counterelites firmly tied to either of the two superpowers, and in their struggle for internal change, these groups will invoke external "assistance," if for no other reason than they expect that the other side will make use of such assistance.[87]

But the analysis already points to what probably will become the major historical, perhaps even the only, way of ever resolving the East-West conflict: to extend the sphere of the countries that credibly declare themselves to be nonmembers of the conflict. This means more than nonmembership of a military alliance, i.e., nonalignment. It even means more than nonmembership of an economic bloc of countries that have reasonably similar economic systems—just as the OECD includes NATO countries but also some others, and the Council for Mutual Economic Assistance (CMEA) includes the WTO countries and also some others. What the statement actually means is that a society must make it clear and credible that it is going to choose its socioeconomic formation independent of what either superpower might think of it and defend its right to do so against any intervention by either of them. The problem with this position is that any country would be tempted to accept superpower assistance if it is in the direction the country wants but to reject it when it is opposed to the country's own will. (Let us for the sake of argument simply assume that there is an elite-people harmony in these matters, usually a highly unlikely assumption.) But in the former case, the other superpower will be present in one form or the other the moment the first superpower is, perhaps even before it appears on the scene lest it *should* appear. Consequently, only very strong or large, or both, nonaligned countries—such as Yugoslavia, India, and China—have so far managed to make their nonalignment relatively credible.[88]

That situation brings us back to the real world again, where the fact is that a number of countries are tied to systems that are neither military alliances nor economic power blocs but the type of structures that are referred to as "capitalist imperialism" and "social imperialism."[89] The net conclusion of what has been said in the preceding sections is that today, both of these systems are in crisis. This crisis is spelled out for the capitalist system, in the sense of the old international economic order as headed by the U.S.-EC-Japan triangle, in sections 1, 2, and 6, and for the "socialist" system in section 4. If this conclusion is correct, we are in the interesting situation that both superpowers may now be losing at the same time, simply because there is disenchantment with both systems. The two systems are still seen as mutually exclusive, in the sense that one cannot have them both at the same time or in the same place, but they are no longer seen as exhausting the range of possible socioeconomic formations.

Third World capitalism, for instance, with a strong public sector, will become increasingly important, if not a world economic power. Small-scale socialism, communal and cooperative, may also gain in significance. One point in this connection might be a hypothesis about the state socialist socioeconomic formation: It might also have reached or be reaching its climax. It seems very difficult today to find political leaders or groups willing to proclaim that the Soviet socioeconomic formation is the model they want to imitate. That does not mean that the U.S. socioeconomic formation stands up as a model either, except on the more private level where many people for a long time to come will still see the U.S. model as a stage that can offer them *personally* a better part in life. Extremely few people seem to perceive the Soviet Union's model that way, which may be precisely the problem in Afghanistan. The Soviet Union's effort to create some type of socialism in that country without including it in the Soviet power system is a very difficult option for a small country bordering on the Soviet Union to entertain. China has a border in common with the Soviet Union, but China is not small; Yugoslavia is small, but does not border on the Soviet Union. The situation is not quite symmetric, however, as it is almost meaningless for a country to run its own independent capitalist system.[90] Capitalism as defined today means participation in the world capitalist system, and a country has to be an advanced capitalist power in order to do this mainly within its own borders.

To recapitulate, the assumption is not that the two superpowers are striving at all costs for world domination. The assumption might be that they are striving at all costs to retain what they have and—if possible without heavy costs incurred to themselves—to expand a little. In other words, in a socioeconomic sense, they are here both conceived of as defensive powers that are no longer really hoping to expand their organic sphere of influence very much. At the same time, it is assumed that they are having great difficulties. They are "losing" countries on their own doorsteps, such as Nicaragua in the case of the United States (not quite on the doorstep but almost entirely lost) and Poland in the case of the Soviet Union (not quite lost but entirely on the doorstep). Both superpowers will try to destabilize the destabilization by all methods short of intervention, and possibly even resort to military intervention.[91] Both of them have scenarios for doing so: the destabilization of the Allende regime in Chile in the case of the United States (possibly practiced successfully in Jamaica)[92] and thirty years of experience in handling opposition in Eastern Europe in the case of the Soviet Union— in addition to the interventions into Hungary (1956), Czechoslovakia (1968), and Afghanistan (1979) and the more complex 1981 formula for Poland.

However, there is still a considerable distance to go before the struggle over socioeconomic formation inside countries, in other words, the struggle for social development, becomes detached from the systems headed by the two superpowers. For a long time yet, the superpowers will still assume that they have not only the right but also the duty to intervene,[93] although it may matter to them that the number of countries in general, and people in particular, who agree that they have a heavenly mandate of that type seems to be decreasing.

Having now defined the East-West conflict as essentially a conflict over development, we are in a position to move one step further to say something about the extent to which the East-West conflict is an interconflict, or two parallel intraconflicts. Essentially this is a question of the extent to which the two superpowers (and some of their trusted instruments) try to change the system of a society on the other side or of societies clearly committed to neither side versus the extent to which the superpowers are mainly concerned with preventing societies in their own sphere of influence from changing. As pointed out, the two activities are related to each other: The "superversion"[94] by one superpower may be a response to the subversive activity of the other. However, it may also be that this way of seeing what happens is a carry-over from the *inter*phase of the conflict to its more predominantly *intra*phase.[95]

This inter/intra dimension should be seen as a continuum, not as a dichotomy, and it might be worth an effort at operationalization combined with some empirical studies over time to get some grasp of the process. Such a viewpoint does not mean that the conflict is less dangerous or more amenable to solution. Particularly untractable may be a conflict that is more on the intra side but is treated like an interconflict, for reasons to be spelled out below.

Then there is the capability aspect of the East-West conflict: the horrendous arsenals of weapons, including 60,000 nuclear bombs with an explosive power corresponding to four or five tons of TNT for each human being on earth. There are many ways of analyzing this aspect, and the call for disarmament, for a reduction of the destruction potential on either side and lower-level balances, is more than understandable. However, disarmament—when there is an underlying, unresolved conflict with sporadic confrontations—will only lead to rearmament, even to an overshoot beyond the level from which disarmament was initiated. On the other hand, when there is no underlying conflict issue to speak of, armament in and by itself is not that dangerous—granted that there is always the possibility of technical and human error.[96] It seems equally clear that if there is an underlying confrontation, then arms races tend to lead to wars,[97] so from the proposition that disarmament does not necessarily lead to peace, it certainly does not follow that armament leads to peace. What does follow is simply that a confrontation in a setting saturated with the means of destruction is highly dangerous, and the more arms there are that can be employed destructively, the more dangerous the situation. Consequently, something has to be done about the problem, but this something is probably more on the conflict/issue side than on the armament side. This possibility also leads to some reasons for scepticism about the effectiveness of the two key arguments used against the arms race: (a) that it is tremendously costly and that the costs can be calculated as opportunity costs that could have been used to satisfy basic needs units (BNUs)[98]—the number of hospital beds, schools, human beings fed and clad and adequately sheltered, etc.—had there not been the diversion of resources for military purposes and (b) that wars are tremendously destructive in terms of lives lost and destruction to man-made and non-man-made environments.[99]

It is felt that it is not because of a lack of knowledge of these well-documented and deadly important facts that arms races and dangerous conflict articulation processes are a part of the contemporary scene. It may simply be that these two key arguments only scratch the surface and have about as much impact on the process leading to war as the argument about the opportunity costs of alcoholism—not to mention detailed descriptions of the evils of alcoholism—has on the alcoholic. This is not to deny, however, that such warnings might prevent others from embarking on similar courses.

There is a third argument in this connection that should also be mentioned. It actually goes beyond the opportunity costs argument and imagines that all the natural resources, capital, human labor, and research spent today on the military systems would be used for development purposes. This process would take the form of an effort to spell out positive peace, an attractive alternative that would be so appealing that it would create a motivation to divert human and social energy from the field of potential destruction to the field of potential development.[100] The difficulty with the argument, however, is that most of the productive assets are located in the North whereas the development problems are largely located in the South. If the program really were to be implemented, it would mean (a) a higher-than-ever penetration of North into South, as it is very difficult to imagine that all of the development assets would simply be given away, and (b) a type of development that would be highly capital and research intensive.[101] As this is the type of development that is wanted by the elites in most Third World countries, the conversion argument will carry some weight with them and will be pressed in the form of UN resolutions, and be picked up by people who oppose the armament process in the North. From the point of view of human and social development, this is not necessarily an advisable course of action, even though it may look progressive because it is against armament.

It is more important to look into the processes behind the armament process, and here again it looks as if the "arms race" metaphor is unfortunate because it is derived too much from an interconflict image of the situation. Again this dimension should be seen as a continuum and not as a dichotomy, but the important distinction made in armament theory between actio-reactio processes and *Eigendynamik* or autistic processes certainly enters the picture.[102] In a sense, the hypothesis was formulated by Eisenhower in 1961: the hypothesis of the military-industrial complexes (MICs). Related to this process is the idea that new weapons systems do not develop so much because politicians are watching the world scene—including the armaments on the other side—and ordering their military people to develop counterstrategies while they, in turn, put the research people to work. Instead, the systems develop because the researchers in the military laboratories around the world develop new weapons systems and ask the military people to develop a strategy that can put the systems to use, and the military people, in turn, demand from the politicians the necessary action, including appropriations, to go ahead.[103] There is some truth to both causal chains; the problem is how their relative significance changes over time.

Thus, we are concerned with two processes of internalizing the East-West conflict; one relating to the conflict issue itself, the other to the capability of destruction. These two processes also point to two possible approaches to conflict resolution. One relates to putting the brakes on the superpowers' tendency to intervene, both inside and outside their "sphere of influence," not by threatening retaliation by the other super-power, but through an increasingly powerful solidarity among third-bloc countries, the nonaliged against interventionism. The other possible approach would be to put a brake on the production of weapons systems in the only place where that brake really could be meaningful, in the military laboratories.

There are three reasons why this conflict resolution seems more urgent now than ever before in post–Second World War history. First, the changing character of the conflict issue, from interconflict between systems toward intraconflict within the two systems makes most efforts to bring the two parties to the negotiating table to regulate issues or arms rules irrelevant, since that table is part of the interconflict model. But old patterns of conflict behavior persist and will continue to produce irrelevant action, such as bilateral disarmament conferences, which are even presided over by the two superpowers![104] In general, it might perhaps be said that the interconflict pattern is used to conceal and mystify the intraconflict nature of the present situation, even to the point of making the parties less able to discover what is going on.

Second, because of the current emphasis on intermediate range land-based missiles, "theater missiles" (SS-20 on the Soviet side and Cruise and Pershing II on the U.S. side), Europe itself, more than the two superpowers, has become the most likely nuclear battlefield. Moreover, these arms are located in the "gray zone" between the SALT/START (Strategic Arms Reduction Talks) system of negotiations, which discusses intercontinental nuclear weapons, and the MBFR (Mutual Balanced-Force Reduction) system of negotiations, which discusses the conventional forces (neither system has been successful). Whether deterrence in the sense of each superpower's disinclination to launch a war when the result could be the annihilation of its own population really worked before, or whether nuclear war has been avoided for some other reason, we do not know. But it seems clear that at present, a much higher proportion of the nuclear missiles would now be spent in the European theater of war, thereby cutting down on one barrier to a nuclear war between the superpowers.

Third, and related to the second point, presidential directives 58 and 59 (from the Carter administration) and the defense guidance proposal of May 1982 (from the Reagan administration) both seem to indicate the codification of a transition in strategic thinking from the use of nuclear arms to *deter* to the use of nuclear arms to *win* a war, whether by striking first or not. Targeting on the weapon system of the other side, and on the administrative centers and points of gravity in the economic system, which is indicated in presidential directive 59, cor-responds to the emphasis on bunkers for the decision-making elites in presidential directive 58. Evidently, one would expect the other side to develop the same kind of strategy for protracted warfare, limited or not, and should such a war break out, then there is no reason to worry about the preceding six sections in this chapter.

Conclusion: An Even More Difficult World

Dividing the world into North and South, West and East, gives the four worlds on which this analysis is based: North-West, North-East, South-West, South-East:

	WEST	EAST
NORTH	*First World:* Private capitalism	*Second World:* State socialism
	OECD countries	CMEA countries
SOUTH	*Third World:* NIEO	*Fourth World:* Ichi-ban
	South America, Caribbean, Africa, Arab world, West, South Asia	China, Japan, Korea, Taiwan, Hong Kong, Singapore, Southeast Asia (ASEAN), Indochina, Australia, New Zealand, Oceania

To get at some of the dynamics of this scheme, let us for a moment try to capture the world situation from the U.S. point of view. The general thesis is that the United States is deeply involved in four conflicts, each of a different nature and each of them deep and extensive and intractable. To wit, conflict

- with the Second World: a military-political conflict with the Soviet Union over basic values and basic interests, with an accompanying arms race that absorbs more than 30 percent of the domestic capital formation—possibly much more. There has been no success in curbing the race, and the probability of a major nuclear confrontation is far from zero.
- with the Third World: an economic-political conflict of liberation from networks of neocolonialism, some of it fought in an institutionalized form in UN fora, some of it in open international defiance. Much of this conflict takes the form of guerrilla movements fighting both the United States and local governments linked to the United States.
- with the Fourth World: an economic competition that, by and large, the Fourth World has won[105]—not yet in the sense of topping the

world statistics but in the sense of having dynamism, initiative, and growth.[106] If Japan fails, the mini-Japans may take over; if they fail, the People's Republic of China may take over—all of them using the rest of the Fourth World as a reserve for capital, labor, raw materials, and markets.[107]

- with the First World: resulting from the other three conflicts, an increasingly visible estrangement between the United States and its allies in the First World—the United States being seen as less overpowering in its strength (relative to the Second World), less straight in its international morality (relative to the Third World), and less unbeatably rich in its capital accumulation (relative to the Fourth World). The strong, rich, and moral aspects of the United States are in the process of transformation toward their own negation—in First World eyes. No other country in the world is being exposed to a process of status erosion that is so profound, and so dangerous, so quickly.

Economically these conflicts cannot but lead to the prediction of a continuing decline in the relative position of the First World. The question, however, is how this decline is absorbed inside the society: by elites pushing it on the people through unemployment and decreasing purchasing power or by elites and people going down that difficult and unexplored road called economic decline together? Obviously, these are the conservative and social democratic approaches, respectively, but the First World is badly prepared for this situation, not even having a theory of economic decline, much less a management of decline.

In the Second World, it is hard to imagine large economic changes for the better given the international situation and the static nature of the economic structures. It is also difficult to imagine major differences in the distribution between elites and people in the years immediately ahead, particularly after the defeat—at least so far—of the Solidarity approach in Poland. Political changes might be more likely than major economic ones.

In the Third World, the NIEO gives such advantages to the elites that they should be able to capture most of the growth of each country as a whole, leaving the people (75–95 percent of the population) in a period of stagnation or decline. In the Fourth World, the ability to distribute is an important asset. There will be growth, less spectacular for Japan, more so for the countries next in line, and parallel for elites and peoples.

What kind of world does this situation leave us with? A very problematic and dangerous one, to say the least. The economic point of gravity changes, from the North-West to the South-East corner of the world.

The political point of gravity slides toward the Third World to the extent that UN votes are important. The military point of gravity, in an old-fashioned and badly working balance-of-power formula, remains in the North, divided between West and East. This is not to say that the old formula, with all three types of power firmly anchored in the North-West world, was better, as it conferred much too little power to the rest of the world and much too much to the few who used it badly to exploit and repress and fight among themselves and are now suffering some of the consequences of their maladapted behavior in a world that is increasingly becoming a world system. Without any sort of world government with sufficient power over these forms of power, a much better formula would have been a balance of power along all three dimensions.

As it now stands, three already discernible patterns may become much more pronounced. One, the First World will react with the military power it has in excess and abundance, e.g., in the form of rapid deployment forces, against the militarily weak, i.e., the Third and, to a lesser extent, the Fourth Worlds. The condition for concerted action is that there is a general dependence in the First World on commodities, particularly oil and gas, and efforts to become independent, or dependent on the Second World, will be frowned upon as that would provide less reason for wielding military power. By and large, efforts to use military power will be accepted, even applauded, by a population that is in general economic decline (as in the Falklands/Malvinas exercise). The First World will also use economic embargoes against the Fourth World.[108] The Second World may engage in similar actions but more regionally, mainly toward border countries (as in Afghanistan), and with more of a military motivation.

Two, the Third World will continue to decry such actions, and the elites there will use strong anti-imperialist rhetoric to make people believe that the old enemy is still the major force responsible for the cleavages inside their country. There being neither force nor money behind these (strong) words, they will tend to pass largely unnoticed.

Three, the Fourth World will continue to push forward economically, and since it is composed of countries with highly uneven levels and types of development, there are many surprises still to come—particularly for the First and Second Worlds, which, because their thinking is steeped in racism and white supremacy, will always be late in understanding how they are overtaken by other parts of the world. The general world economic decline will, of course, also affect the Fourth World, but it is assumed that even if the First World closes itself to much of the trade, there are sufficient markets in the Second World, among the Third World elites,[109] and in the Fourth World itself for some time to come.

But much time will still be required before this leap forward is accompanied by the usual panoply of global political manipulation and military pressure tactics.

This means too much change, too soon, for a world that has adjusted badly to the change it has already undergone. And yet the drives of private capitalism for profit, of state socialism for control, of the NIEO for a fair share in the world capitalist system, and of the South-East world to beat them all at their own games are strong and will tend to continue unabated, at least on the elite level in all worlds. But what about the people? They will probably be more interested in the other two possibilities, state capitalism and private socialism, and will probably demand the former through elections, and/or through elite efforts to imitate Japan and the *japoncitos*, and the latter by taking refuge in collectives, communes, interfamily cooperation, etc., as people will do in a crisis. The governments will decry the later choice as withdrawal from the formal (and controllable) sectors, but it is hard to deny people the right to defend themselves. And yet those acts of self-defense, local and self-reliant, may well become models and precursors of what elites will have to do on the more national levels: increase self-reliance in an increasingly problematic world.

Notes

1. A "conflict formation" is actually the same as a conflict, if the latter is defined as actors pursuing goals (or parties with interests) that are incompatible. The word "formation," however, draws more attention to the social organization of the conflict, and particularly to how it is embedded in the structural context. The "issue" is the incompatibility; a more diplomatic word that is often used is "situation."

2. This situation, of course, has to do with the magnitude of the Soviet Union as a territory. One might also say, however, that czarist Russia incorporated areas of what otherwise would have been considered part of the Third World in a territory that later was expanded and consolidated as the Soviet Union, thereby making the relationship different because of contiguity.

3. For an attempt at analyzing Japan's position, see Johan Galtung, "Japan and Future World Politics," chap. 6 in *Essays in Peace Research*, vol. 5 (Copenhagen: Ejlers, 1980).

4. This terminology is particularly used by the OECD and draws attention to certain economistic similarities in line with Rostowian thinking, but that perspective is inadequate from the vantage point chosen here as it is much too mechanistic.

5. See Johan Galtung, *The Brandt Report: Old Wine in Old Bottles with New Labels* (Bonn: Friedrich Edert Stiftung, 1981), an essay collection on the Brandt Report.

6. See Johan Galtung, "Divided Nations as a Process: One State, Two States, and in Between: The Case of Korea," chap. 5 in *Essays in Peace Research*, vol. 5 (Copenhagen: Ejlers, 1980). I am particularly indebted to Glenn Page and Yoshi Sakamoto for pointing this out so clearly in many discussions about East Asia.

7. These concepts are developed in some detail in Johan Galtung, "Two Perspectives on Society," chap. 2.1 in *The True Worlds: A Transnational Perspective* (New York: Free Press, 1980).

8. For a more complete description of this type of political process, see Galtung, *True Worlds*, chap. 4.3; also see the excellent analysis by George Lakey, *Strategy for a Living Revolution* (New York: Grossman, 1973).

9. This type of thinking, of course, would be in line with the highly seminal works by Immanuel Wallerstein on the world economic system: *The Modern World System I* and *The Modern World System II* (New York: Academic Press, 1974 and 1980).

10. The list includes the Sino-Japanese war over Formosa 1894–1895, the attack on Korea 1910–1911, the Manchurian "incident" 1931, not to mention the war in the Pacific—certainly not unprovoked—from 1941 onward, and before that, the war against czarist Russia 1904–1905.

11. For more on the theory of this phase, see Johan Galtung, "World Economics in the Near Future: Some First- and Third-World Scenarios," GPID Papers (Geneva, 1980).

12. See Johan Galtung, "On the Future of Transnational Corporations: Two Scenarios" (Paper prepared for the Center for the Study of Transnational Corporations, New York, November 1980).

13. In short, it is definitely not an informal, "green," subsistence-type economy that the OPEC countries are interested in!

14. See Johan Galtung, Tore Heiestad, and Erik Rudeng, "On the Decline and Fall of Empires: The Roman Empire and Western Imperialism Compared," GPID Papers (Geneva, 1978).

15. The basic point here is that the Middle Ages should also be seen as something that declined and fell. It was a social formation in its own right—the medieval social formation (with its manorial and feudal phases)—and it declined and fell in the period, say, 1250–1350 (ending with the Black Death).

16. In a sense, this process is analogous to a card game. The game that is played is the same, or almost the same, but the distribution of the cards is different. The best cards are where they usually were not. Or, cards formerly not considered so good are now among the best.

17. That is the famous Leninist principle: the law of uneven development.

18. Probably this situation is to a large extent the story of the "minorities," the indigenous peoples, now gradually being incorporated.

19. The reasons given are good reasons why the South-East triangle is a strong one, but there is a deeper underlying assumption: that a world economic system organized in a capitalistic way will have to have some kind of center; it cannot be really polycentric. This assumption is explored to some extent in Johan Galtung, "A Structural Theory of Imperialism Ten Years Later" (Millennium

Lecture, London School of Economics, January 1981). A center is based on the law of uneven development: By and large, it has more of what is needed than is found in other regions, above all control. At the same time, there is probably also a mental gestalt at work: a notion among a sufficient number of people that this type of activity begs the question of where the center is, and then they consciously and unconsciously look for the indicators as to where that center is. It's a little bit like a sports competition: Given the patterns of individualism and competition, it would be very difficult for most people raised with that mental configuration not to feel dissatisfied, incomplete, unless a clear answer is given to the question, Who won?

20. Corresponding saving ratios in the Western world might be between 3 and 7 percent; for the United States, 6 percent—see *Newsweek*, August 2, 1982, p. 48.

21. Australia and New Zealand enter as rich dependencies to be maintained adequately by the center, the South-East triangle. Historically and culturally, racially and ethnically, they are different. I am indebted to Reginald Little, an Australian diplomat with much experience of Tokyo and Beijing, for information about how China and Japan may look from Australia and New Zealand, and vice versa—see Reginald Little, "Economics, Civilization, and World Order" (Thesis, Institut universitaire d'hautes études internationales, Geneva, 1978).

22. See Johan Galtung, "Five Cosmologies: An Impressionistic Presentation," GPID Papers (Geneva, 1980), and "Western Civilization: Anatomy and Pathology," *Alternatives 7* (1981), pp. 145–169. It is a surprise to westerners that the Japanese and the Chinese combine orientations that do not combine in the West.

23. In fact, it is almost surprising how little Weber has to say about workers in his famous book on the spirit of capitalism—it is as if they simply do not exist. Weber's work was a rebuttal of Marxism, or intended as one—certainly not an adequate one when the problems Marx points to are left uncovered.

24. This point is explored, to some extent, in Johan Galtung, "On Human-Centred Development," GPID Papers (Geneva, 1980).

25. And yet Max Weber, in his book *The Religion of China* (Glencoe, Ill.: Free Press, 1951), predicts that there is not much possibility of capitalism in Japan!

26. I am indebted to Professor Ungku Aziz for pointing out so clearly the importance of this particular factor during a seminar in Kuala Lumpur, September 1979.

27. Of course, a westerner with a very uncommon name might find protection, a source of solidarity, and a focus of identity in a group of people with the same name. But this is hardly the case for the Smiths and the Joneses in the Anglo-Saxon world, for the Hansens and Jensens in the Nordic countries, and so on.

28. It should be noted that it is in that context that the theory of alienation is developed; one more example of how culture bound a theory may be.

29. It is very difficult to ascertain how many people in Southeast Asia in fact were collaborators with the Japanese during the occupation, but the number

must be considerable. Today, one can still find later-middle-aged Southeast Asians serving the Japanese war machine. What one finds above all is the sprawling growth of the Japanese economic machine, no doubt making use of the groundwork laid during the occupation. For some impressions about this point, see N. I. Low, *When Singapore Was Syonan-To* (Singapore, 1973).

30. Both Thai and Indonesian students seem to be good at organizing ritualisitc burnings of Japanese cars and flags. The question is, How much real resistance to Japanese consumer goods (better than others, cheaper than others) is there in the population? At any rate, the Japanese fear such incidents.

31. See the *Daily Yomiuri*, August 15, 1982, for an excellent summary.

32. There is some feeling of déjà vu that might emerge if one discovers that type of gadget in Mongolia, for instance.

33. It should be pointed out that this type of cooperation is not the same as trade between Japan and China, nor is it exactly the same as the Japanese building a factory in China under a limited-time contract. It should rather be seen as a long-lasting partnership, as a type of transnational corporation with all kinds of transfers within the corporation and a high level of coordination when it comes to relationship to the outside.

34. As an example, see the article "Welche Autos kaufen die Deutschen?" *Die Welt*, January 30, 1981, with the following table giving in percent which brands of cars were doing better than the year before and which were the losers:

The Winners (%)		The Losers (%)	
1. Mitsubishi	+100.7	1. Lada	−43.7
2. Toyota	+81.1	2. Leyland	−42.6
3. Datsun	+61.0	3. Alfa Romeo	−35.1
4. Honda	+50.0	4. Volvo	−31.7
5. Mazda	+44.2	5. Talbot	−20.4
6. Mercedes	+2.6	6. Ford	−19.9

35. For an excellent article on this particular subject, see "Integrated Circuits Industry: How Japan Bred a Winner," by the *Financial Times* Far East editor in Tokyo, Charles Smith, *Financial Times*, January 29, 1981. The article, as usual, points to the excellent bureaucracy-corporation-intelligentsia cooperation in the Japanese system and the Japanese genius for "improving on the original." For an emphasis on "low-noise and energy-saving aircrafts," see *Asahi Evening News*, February 1981.

36. For example, some quotes from articles in the Western press: "Japan must alter its trade role, disillusioned U.S. advisors agree—Japanese leaders will find that to try to continue upward mobility of their people through excessive penetration of others' markets is risky" (*International Herald Tribune*, January 5, 1981) and then some slightly contradictory headlines about the same mission: "EEC Sees 'Glimmer of Hope' Over Japan Trade" (*Financial Times*, January 29, 1981) and "Lawine aus Japan rollt weiter: Mission der EG gescheitert" (*Die Welt*, January 30, 1981).

37. It would be interesting to have a clearer view of what the Japanese role in the Trilateral Commission has been; some of that role has now been analyzed in *Trilateralism*, ed. Holly Sklar (Montreal: Black Rose, 1980).

38. The question, of course, is how well they do know that. Giving a talk about international political economics in general and the Japanese situation in particular to the editors of a leading Japanese newspaper early in the 1970s, I concluded that there would be considerable tension in Southeast Asia, and rightly so, because of the relationship that was emerging. The conclusion of the editors, and they were not right wing, was that this assessment was probably correct; for that reason, Japan should rather move to Africa.

39. See Galtung, "Five Cosmologies." It should be pointed out very clearly that the Japanese attitude toward East and Southeast Asia is very different from their attitude toward the rest of the world—in a sense, it is a more occidental attitude. It is not my impression that the Chinese have a corresponding trichotomy; the concept of barbarian seems to start right outside China's doorstep, although there are barbarians of various shades and degrees.

40. What is being said here is that the distance between the internal sector and the external sector is greater in China and Japan than in the West. The external sector is even more remote, even less the object of empathy; and the internal sector is even more consolidated and at least potentially more an object of internal solidarity—although more in the Japanese case (Shintoism) than in the Chinese case.

41. The paradigmatic example is the Western room in so many Japanese homes: a room with Western furniture in which westerners are received—so far, but no further.

42. In this dilemma there is something corresponding to another famous case in U.S. history: the contradiction between norms of equality and mobility and the practice of prejudice and discrimination against nonwhites, which Gunnar Myrdal referred to as an "American dilemma"; the Japanese challenge to this is likely to become "American dilemma II." One may also recall the history of the famous Navigation Act in British history.

43. It should be remembered that in state socialist countries, the Marxist blind spot still applies: The enemy is private capitalism in its international formations, capitalist imperialism, and it has its center in the North Atlantic area. This is the enemy to be beaten, not something emerging from a nonwhite, nonoccidental corner at the other end of the world. The model for the North-East is in the North-West, not in the South-East. It is the North-West one has to "catch up" with, even overtake. That this task may become considerably easier because of the way in which the North-West is being shaken by the emerging South-East will create tremendous problems ideologically, politically, and psychologically. The racial/ethnic dimension of these problems should not be underestimated either.

44. It is possible that the U.S. government might have that type of leverage on its people: In times of crisis, that country has a tremendous ability to respond collectively. The same might apply to the British and to the French, but does it apply to the Italians? Will they forgo some individual advantage just because the government tries to persuade them to buy cars made in Italy?

45. Thus, it is my contention that what today looks like some kind of working triangle, the U.S.-China-Japan connection, in fact is a very weak alliance. The United States would do well not to underestimate the kind of wound left on the Japanese soul by the Second World War, what happened before it, its aftermath, and particularly the nuclear genocides in Hiroshima and Nagasaki, with the racial overtones of those particular acts. The Chinese have suffered even more humiliation at the hands of the West.

46. Of course, it is not wise of a country to use such expressions about itself, nor to refer to the U.S. president as "the most powerful person on earth." The contradiction between such expressions and the reality during, for instance, the hostage crisis with Iran becomes only too tangible.

47. See Galtung, "Japan and Future World Politics," and Galtung, *True Worlds*, chap. 6.4, particularly p. 292.

48. I am thinking of the book *Emerging Japanese Superstate: Challenge and Response* by Herman Kahn (New York: Prentice-Hall, 1971).

49. This problem is discussed in some detail in Johan Galtung, "Poor Countries Versus Rich; Poor People Versus Rich—Whom Will the NIEO Benefit?" pt. 2 of *Toward Self-reliance and Global Interdependence* (Ottawa: Canadian International Development Agency, 1978).

50. This inclination to call general attention to the time order of development strategies is a key point in Irma Adelman's analysis, and it is also developed in Johan Galtung, "Weakening the Strong and Strengthening the Weak," GPID Papers (Geneva, 1979).

51. See M. Taghi Farvar, "Aspects of the Iranian Revolution," GPID Papers (Geneva, 1979).

52. The cosmology approach adopted in Galtung, "Five Cosmologies," is an effort to try to systematically trace relations between religious conceptualizations and highly concrete politics.

53. Strictly speaking that statement is not quite correct. In a setting of Western imperialism, combining economic penetration with political, military, cultural, and structural aspects, the Japanese penetration stands out precisely because it is so single-mindedly economic. It is "one-legged imperialism" as opposed to "five-legged imperialism," and in a company of five-legged entities, the one-legged one becomes highly conspicuous in spite of the fact that its imperialism is so curtailed. Thus, the Japanese will never forget, it seems, the expressions, so popular in the 1960s, referring to Japan as an "economic animal" and to the prime minister as a "transistor salesman" (attributed to de Gaulle).

54. In the case of Confucianism this would basically mean more discipline, more power to the older, the educated, and to men. In the case of Shintoism this might mean more emphasis on the Japanese as a chosen people. The synergistic combination of these two in the case of Japan could very well spell militarism once again.

55. Thus, in the Caribbean, the rastafari and shango movements might be cases; and in several African countries the search back to their own religions will probably accelerate wih the fallacy of Project Economic Growth. The Sendero Luminoso guerrillas in Peru invoke Inca values.

56. See Monica Wemegah, "The Spiritual Quest of AWL," GPID Papers (Geneva, 1980).

57. However, looking at the data in note 34, it is quite clear that the Soviet Fiat, Lada, is loser no. 1. The explanation given in the article in *Die Welt* is *Qualitätsprobleme*.

58. See Silviu Brucan, "A Strategy for Eastern Europe," GPID Papers (Geneva, 1980).

59. For something more about this idea see Johan Galtung, "On the Future of the Eastern European Social Formation," GPID Papers (Geneva, 1981).

60. On the other hand, if productivity is increased, it is probably because of more capital- and research-intensive forms of production, and the technology for that is, in turn, likely to come from the West. In other words, it looks like these countries will lose either way as long as that particular game is being played. It is also interesting to note how this thinking drives a wedge between the technocratic and partocratic elites in these parties and the people in general as the latter do not reason in terms of servicing national debts, increasing productivity, and so on, but in terms of their own level of living.

61. For more on this aspect see Johan Galtung, "Poland August–September 1980: Is a Socialist Revolution Under State Capitalism Possible?" *Journal of Peace Research* 17:4 (1980), pp. 281–290.

62. But not necessarily for the reasons indicated by the late Andrei Amalrik in his famous book, *Will the Soviet Union Survive 1984?* (New York: Harper and Row, 1970), as relations with China were seen as the key factor. The direction of analysis taken here is more internal, based on characteristics of the system itself.

63. For an analysis of power in international relations in such terms, see Johan Galtung, "Power and Global Planning and Resource Management," in A. J. Dolman, ed., *Global Planning and Resource Management* (New York: Pergamon, 1980), pp. 119–145.

64. It should be pointed out that this is not the convergency thesis. That thesis has as its major point that the countries in East and West, state socialist and private capitalist, will become increasingly similar. Although I believe that countries having the bourgeois way of life as the major goal for their citizens and technocracy (with more or less developed elements of partocracy) as the major structural element in obtaining this goal will tend to develop the same kinds of phenomena in general and problems in particular, the countries of East and West are so out of phase with each other that it is exactly for this reason that they may sometimes converge, sometimes diverge. Thus, the problems in the overdeveloped countries have only just started becoming problems in the East, whereas in the West, many people are already working for basic change. This situation makes for divergence rather than convergence.

65. This factor, simply to be *in* it, be *with* it, should not be underestimated, and it is hardly ever taken adequately into account in development theory.

66. For more details, see Johan Galtung, "Is There a Chinese Strategy of Development?" *Review* (Fernand Braudel Centre) 5:3 (1982), pp. 460–486.

67. The concrete manifestation of that ethos may actually come in the next period, which might even have the opposite ethos. The results of the economism

of the great leap forward may have shown up in the Cultural Revolution period when the dominant theme was "politics in command"; the results of that period might well show up in the second great leap forward, the period China is currently in, with people pressing demands more strongly, and so on.

68. What happened was evidently very non-Chinese, even anti-Chinese: a disrespect for the additivity of civilizational elements. Mao himself was a much better Chinese than his wife, or so it seems; and his writings are filled with references to the old masters, to the Chinese tradition.

69. It should be noted that this possibility is in line with the predictions for the Third World in general: a revival of fundamentalist orientations (the word "religion" should not be used in connection with Confucianism and Shintoism; it may also be doubtful whether it can be used in connection with Daoism or Buddhism).

70. Although racially related to China (the "Mongolian race"), these republics are culturally different. All five—Uzbekistan, Tadzhikistan, Turkmenistan, Kirgizia, and Kazakhstan—are Muslim. Today, almost every fifth Soviet citizen is Muslim; with the population growth, Soviet Muslims may number 100 million by the year 2000.

71. This point is developed to some extent in Johan Galtung and Fumiko Nishimura, *Learning from the Chinese People* (Oslo, 1975; also in Norwegian, Swedish, Danish, and German editions), chap. 6.

72. When discussing this situation with Chinese officials the response is usually the same as in Eastern Europe: Before we were weak; now we are strong, and we can control such factors. This may prove to be an underestimation of the penetrating power of the capitalist system.

73. The first opium war was between Britain and China (1839–1842); the second, Britain and France against China (1856–1860). The British had already started smuggling opium grown in India into China at the beginning of the nineteenth century.

74. I am indebted to Ali Mazrui for pointing this out during the Lisbon meeting (July 1980) of the World Order Models Project.

75. An excellent book in this connection is *How Europe Underdeveloped Africa* by the late (political murder 1980) Walter Rodney (London: Bogle L'Ouverture, 1972) because it also develops the cultural aspects.

76. This theme is developed in Johan Galtung, "Expansion/Exploitation Processes: A Multi-dimensional View," GPID Papers (Geneva, 1981).

77. In a sense, we are already in the process depicted by John Maynard Keynes in his famous essay "Economic Possibilities for Our Grandchildren," in J. M. Keynes, *Essays in Persuasion* (London: Macmillan, 1931), pp. 358–373. The only problem is that Keynes failed to take into account the negative aspects of the future he depicted so brightly.

78. Thus, all of these five points are already at the top of the list of social concerns, if not of governments, at least of broad popular movements in the most "advanced" industrialized countries.

79. A statement like this might sound hostile to economists, and that is one intention. But it should be pointed out that this statement does not necessarily

refer to economics as an academic discipline; a certain one-sidedness may be necessary for the type of scientific approach pursued in the Occident (itself a subject of critique, though). It is when such people have political power that they become dangerous. On the other hand, economists who have realized this problem and gotten out of their predicament can become extremely valuable social critics in their position of "former economists." It should be noted how this particular list of blind spots covers the four types of exploitation and the five problems of high productivity.

80. Such actions took place in France and Germany at the end of 1980.

81. I am thinking of the publications from the International Institute of Strategic Studies in London, the Arms Control and Disarmament Agency in Washington, D.C., and the Stockholm International Peace Research Institute in Stockholm.

82. See the paper by Mihai Botez and Mariana Celac, "Global Modelling . . . Without Models? Theory, Methodology, and Rhetoric in World Modelling" (Tokyo: United Nations University, 1981).

83. This point, of course, in no sense means that Soviet pressure on neighboring countries and direct intervention should not be seen as expressions of social imperialism. In the days right after the Soviet intervention in Czechoslovakia, I had the occasion to discuss precisely this point with the Hungarian Marxist philosopher, G. Lukács, who was deeply upset by the invasion. To him, the invasion was profoundly anti-Marxist because it was antidialectical. Contradictions within a given unit, in this case Czech society, would have to work themselves out and be solved or surpassed within that unit itself, which is precisely the Chinese argument in connection with social imperialism. But the situation in Czechoslovakia does mean that the Soviet Union has withdrawn when there was no hope of a state socialist regime—and has had to be forced out when there was (such as in Iran).

84. The idea of progress is one of the many themes shared by Marxism and liberalism—see Johan Galtung, "Two Ways of Being Western: Some Similarities Between Marxism and Liberalism," in Chair in Conflict and Peace Research, *Papers* (Oslo: University of Oslo).

85. See Johan Galtung, "Europe: Bi-polar, Bi-centric, or Co-operative?" and "European Security and Co-operation: A Sceptical Contribution," chaps. 1 and 2 in *Essays in Peace Research*, vol. 5 (Copenhagen: Ejlers, 1980), particularly chap. 2.

86. See, for instance, the book by Peter Willetts, *The Non-Aligned in Havana* (London: Frances Pinter, 1980). The book deals with "how demands are aggregated in the world's largest, most comprehensive diplomatic organization outside the United Nations"—in other words, a rather important organization.

87. Such has been world history since the Second World War: One side calls in one superpower as a governmental adviser, to establish bases, to have forces permanently stationed in the country; the political opposition calls on the second superpower to bring in weapons and agents, secret services, large-scale smuggling of arms, subversive know-how in general, and so on. The consequences are "local wars."

88. The other nonaligned countries are either very weak or not very nonaligned. It should also be noted that the third founding country of the nonaligned movement, Egypt, recently seems to be interpreting nonalignment as an oscillation between alignment now to one, now to the other side.

89. See Johan Galtung, "A Structural Theory of Imperialism," chap. 13 in *Essays in Peace Research*, vol. 4 (Copenhagen: Ejlers, 1980), and "Social Imperialism and Sub-imperialism: Continuities in the Structural Theory of Imperialism," in Chair in Conflict and Peace Research, *Papers*, no. 22 (Oslo: University of Oslo); also published in Galtung, *World Development* (1976).

90. This point is true only if expansionism is seen as being inherent in capitalism.

91. This is the major topic of the article referred to in note 61 above, which gives a reason why the Soviet Union would be tempted to intervene and a number of reasons why it should/would not. In early 1982, the latter seemed by and large to outweigh the former.

92. That there was U.S. intervention in Jamaica in the usual form of economic sticks to Michael Manley and economic carrots to Edward Seaga before the elections of October 30, 1980, is obvious. Whether the intervention went beyond that is less obvious. The consensus in the region among political observers seems also to be that Manley would have lost anyhow because he never was able to get on top of the Jamaican pattern of violence and also was less than successful in economic management.

93. The Monroe and the Brezhnev doctrines for the Western Hemisphere and the "socialist countries," respectively, have exactly this point built into them. See the comparison between the invasion of the Dominican Republic in 1965 by the United States and that of Czechoslovakia in 1968 by the Soviet Union in Johan Galtung, "Big Powers and the World Feudal Structure," in *Essays in Peace Research*, vol. 4 (Copenhagen: Ejlers, 1980).

94. I apologize for this neologism, but if there is a word—"subversion"— for what is done from below in order to manipulate a structure, then there should also be a word for what is done from above, and "superversion" might be just as good as any. Or could it be that the English language is biased in favor of the status quo?

95. In other words, if a conflict formation presupposes actors and an issue, then it might simply be that one has just the actors and no longer a real issue. One way of looking at the last fifteen years or so of East-West system history would be to say that in the period beginning when de Gaulle really launched détente in the mid-sixties until the Final Act of Helsinki in 1975, there was not much of an issue left (see Galtung, "Europe: Bi-polar, Bi-centric, or Co-operative" and "European Security and Co-operation"). But after 1975 something happened—in my analysis, very serious strains started developing inside the two pyramids. As if this were an interactor conflict, issues had to be found, and they were found. We are in that phase now. For the sake of systematics, let it only be added that there is also such a thing as a conflict formation only with issues, not with actors. This is a contradiction, or a latent conflict, in which the actors have not yet crystallized with their goals. (Hence, one should talk instead about parties with interests.)

96. This point is developed in some detail in Galtung, *True Worlds*, chap. 5, particularly 5.4.

97. See the articles by Michael Wallace, "Arms Races and Escalation," *Journal of Conflict Resolution* 23:1 (1979), pp. 3–16, and "Old Nails in New Coffins: The Para Bellum Hypothesis Revisited," *Journal of Peace Research* 18:1 (1981), pp. 91–95.

98. As an example of this type of analysis consider the following from *Women and Technology in the Industrialized Countries* by Maria Bergom-Larsson, (New York: UNITAR, 1979), p. 19.

With only 5 percent of the world's annual military budget:

- all the children in the underdeveloped countries could be vaccinated against the most common diseases;
- 700 million people could get instruction in writing and reading;
- great portions of the third world could get preventive health care;
- 500 million people could get enough land to support themselves;
- 300 million people living in the slums today could get new housing;
- 200 million under- and malnourished children could get extra food rations;
- 60 million pregnant women suffering from undernourishment could be helped;
- 100 million more children could be sent to school;
- everybody could have pure water by 1990.

All this for only 5 percent of the world's annual military appropriation. In order to make the problem even more concrete, Inga Thorson demonstrates that one nuclear submarine costs as much as it costs to keep alive 16 million children under one year of age.

99. This destruction, incidentally, lasts long after the war is over. Thus, UNITAR, in cooperation with the Institut universitaire d'hautes études internationales in Geneva and the Institute diplomatique in Tripoli, organized a conference in Libya on war residues in May 1981:

Alors que les pays européens sont parvenus à débarasser leur territoire de ces reliquates, des pays en voie développement d'Afrique et d'Asie sont encore affectés par ce problème. Les mines, les bombes et autres explosifs encombre toujours leur sol et, partant, constituent un grave danger pour les êtres humains, gênent le développement du pays et entravent largement manifesté en Afrique de Nord. La Libya a été choisie comme exemple pour étudier ce problème. [Memorandum, January 1981]

Although European countries have managed to rid their territories of these war relics, developing nations of Africa and Asia still contend with this problem. There continue to be mines, bombs, and other explosives on their soil. These represent a significant danger for people and hinder certain development efforts, a problem that is particularly manifest in North Africa. Libya has been chosen as a case study. [Translation by M. Nincic]

100. Peace research has not been good at developing this argument, at least not so far. One reason may be that this type of thinking has been developed further in development studies for the low-income countries and in future studies for the high-income countries, thereby creating a division in three transdisciplinary

research activities (peace, development, future) that actually should go hand in hand.

101. Exactly why and how is developed in some detail in Johan Galtung, *Development, Environment, and Technology* (Geneva: UNCTAD, 1979), which is an effort to analyze the impacts of different technological styles.

102. This way of thinking, of course, is associated with the excellent work by the leading German peace researcher, Dieter Senghaas.

103. In short, weapons in search of strategy rather than strategy in search of weapons. This emphasis puts a major source of the dynamism of the arms races in the research laboratories and with the researcher and the think tanks.

104. Hence, one obvious strategy would be simply to cut the superpowers out of such conferences, even more so as they seem to do it themselves anyhow in their bilateral SALT negotiations and other processes. To include them, even as copresiders, is the joke of the century; unfortunately a rather bad one.

105. The Japanese Economic Council, an advisory body to the prime minister, predicts that the Japanese GNP per capita will be far ahead of the U.S. GNP per capita by the year 2000—$21,200 as against $17,000.

106. The picture given by world trade statistics is relatively clear. The share of the United States in world exports of manufactured products decreased from 22.6 percent in 1955 to 12.3 in 1977; that of the EC remained rather stable— from 46.4 to 45.0 percent in the same period; Japan's increased from 4.0 percent to 11.9, and that of the four mini-Japans from almost nothing to 4.5 percent. If we focus on the developing countries alone and look at the share countries and groups of countries in that category have, then the four mini-Japans stand out with an increase from around 20 percent in 1955 to 58.2 percent in 1977. Next in line are India with 6.7 percent (for 1976, less than tiny Singapore which had 6.0 percent the same year) and Brazil with 6.1 percent.

107. So, the general thesis about the Fourth World is that of a three-wave pattern, or maybe four. First, of course, there is Japan. Then, there are the "4 'New Japans' Waiting in Wings to Pose a Fresh Economic Challenge to West":

> During the 1970s the economies of rapidly industrializing Taiwan, South Korea, Hong Kong and Singapore grew at an average annual rate of more than 9 percent, while Japan posted a yearly growth rate of 6 percent. For the United States, the rate was just 3 percent. To be sure, growth has slowed for the East Asian economies during the current worldwide recession. But most economists expect that once the world picture brightens a bit, the East Asian economies will bounce back with a vengeance. They predict that in the 1980s, Taiwan, South Korea, Hong Kong and Singapore will increase the size of their economies by 7 percent to 9 percent a year while Japan's more mature economy shows annual gains of 4 percent. [*International Herald Tribune*, August 25, 1982]

"Singapore Prime Minister, Lee Kuan Yew started the Seek-Inspiration-From-Japan campaign several years ago. Malaysia adopted a 'Look East' policy, which includes South Korea as well as Japan, after Dr. Mahathir Mohamad became prime minister nine months ago. Vice president Adam Malik of Indonesia says his country has much to learn from Japan's giant trading firms" (*Daily Yomiuri*, April 29, 1982). The latter article has an interesting sidelight on Dr. Mahathir

Mohamad in Malaysia: "the first Malaysian prime minister not educated in Britain coupled his Look East campaign with the deliberate deemphasizing of relations with Britain." Third, there is China, in a different phase: "China's post-Mao movement toward a mixed economy already permits Special Economic Zones where foreign businessmen can set up factories, hire and fire workers and make early profits. Now leaders of the People's Republic have made yet another concession to capitalist ways—individuals who are in business for themselves will be allowed to hire up to seven employees" (*Time*, December 7, 1981).

108. The best example of efforts to block Japanese car imports is probably in France where the French minister for industries, André Giraud, declared in February 1981 that for each five Japanese cars imported one French car industry worker becomes unemployed. As a result, Japanese cars were blocked in the harbors (*Dagbladet* [Oslo], February 6, 1981). But penetration has gone far: It is a telling sign of the superiority of the Fourth World, in this case and so far of Japan, that trade unions insist on Japanese investment. "The Northern Region TUC [Trade Union Council] has offered a total breakdown of traditional job demarcation in an attempt to lure the new Datsun car factory to the region. . . . An end to restrictive trade union practices was thought to be the best offer which the TUC could make to ensure that Datsun came to one of three possible North-east sites" (*Guardian*, June 16, 1981). A corresponding story from Italy, although it referred to England again, "O rientra lo sciopero o Leyland ai giapponesi" (*Corriere della sera*, October 20, 1981)—referring to a *Sunday Express* article of October 18, according to which the president of British Leyland threatened that unless British workers suspended their strike, the whole firm would be up to sale—to the Japanese. In view of the situation, it is debatable whether that constituted anything like a credible threat.

One of the clearest symbols of Japanese industrial supremacy was reported in the *Daily Mail*, November 11, 1981, and witnessed by millions of people before that: "the installation of a 25-ton, 36,600 square foot advertisement, containing 10 miles of wiring, for Fuji film has consolidated the Japanese dominance of the neon New York Times Square. By the end of the year, 22 of the Square's 30 incandescent ads will promote Japanese goods. The Fuji hoarding is the most elaborate since the Winston cigarette man used to halo the square with smoke rings."

109. Thus, Japan won the important competition for the production of "the third car" in India—in addition to the Morris Oxford and the Fiat 1100. "Suzuki clinched the deal with Maruti after months of patient negotiation beating better-known competitors such as Nissan, Renault, Fiat, BL and Volkswagen. The 800 cc subcompact offered by Suzuki scored over its rivals in fuel consumption (about 65 mpg) and price ($5,500) inclusive of taxes, which at the moment constitute 40 percent of vehicle prices in India" (*Daily Yomiuri*, April 30, 1982).

3

War and the Power of Warmakers in Western Europe and Elsewhere, 1600–1980

Charles Tilly

The Rise and Fall of Civilian Government

Once, it seems, armed conquerors personally ran almost every government worthy of the name anywhere in the world. Conquest created government, and armed might held it in place. Then, fitfully and painfully, rulers fashioned civilian government: Warriors dismounted; kings, priests, and their lieutenants fought less or not at all; vassals and hirelings carried on the work of conquest and control. Over the centuries after 1500, European sovereigns brought these processes to their paradoxical height. The making of war created the structures of national states. Yet as big, destructive wars called forth the mobilization of ever-more men, food, weapons, ammunition, uniforms, horses, lodgings, and cash, corps of nonsoldiers arose to manage that mobilization. Thus, the very changes that permitted states to wage war on a previously unimaginable scale and to extend their military conquests throughout the world also created bulky, powerful civilian staffs as well as armies subordinate to the holders of land and capital. Within limits, large-scale war civilized Western states.

The twentieth century compounded the paradox. On one side, open military conquest of one government by another declined. Although twentieth-century wars wreaked incalculable damage and displaced people as never before, the race for direct territorial expansion slowed. Although economic control of land, labor, and capital in one country by people in another country may well have increased, it became unusual for one government to pass formally into the control of another.

As the twentieth century moved on, the great colonial powers stabilized their overseas rule, shifted toward the establishment of civilian government in their colonies and dependencies, then—however reluctantly—participated in the creation of formally autonomous states in place of their former empires. What is more, those new states typically emerged with formal structures that greatly resembled those of their former overlords: constitutions, representative institutions, civilian bureaucracies, non-military executive officers, subordinated armies. Even those states in which soldiers ruled directly justified their rule as a transition to stable democracy. Almost everyone honored civilian rule in principle.

Yet the long-term trend toward civilian government reversed itself. In the former colonial areas of Latin America, the Middle East, Africa, and Asia, the coup d'etat became the standard form of governmental succession. In those regions, professional soldiers—often men trained in the military schools and armies of the great colonial powers—increasingly took direct control of the state. Models of westernized civilian control such as Nigeria and Burma moved into the ranks of military states. As of 1981, by one count, armed forces dominated 54 of the world's 141 independent states. Those states were concentrated almost entirely in Latin America, Africa, the Middle East, South Asia, and the Pacific (Sivard 1981, 7). By Samuel Finer's more stringent criteria for military rule, 35 states qualified as of the late 1970s; those 35 followed essentially the same geography as Sivard's 54 (Finer 1982).

After World War II, the great Western powers became more and more heavily involved in shipping arms to the new states, in training their armies, and in influencing their military policies. Between 1960 and 1980, world arms exports tripled. The Warsaw Pact countries and NATO powers ended up shipping about the same quantity of arms to the rest of the world; between them, they accounted for about nine-tenths of the world's arms exports (Sivard 1981, 6). Over the same two decades, NATO and Warsaw Pact armed forces declined slightly in number, and their combined military expenditures in constant dollars increased by less than 50 percent. In the rest of the world, armed forces increased by about half, and military expenditures roughly quadrupled.

Three crucial changes occurred during those decades. First, the whole world shifted to using more expensive varieties of armament. Second, armed forces grew disproportionately outside of Europe and North America. Third, European and North American powers specialized increasingly in arming other states. They not only shipped arms but also organized and trained national armed forces.

The United States and the USSR, in particular, became the great entrepreneurs of armed forces throughout the world. No other states came close to their efforts. Military support, at a price, became an even larger part of great-power foreign policy. These reversals threatened to remilitarize the great powers themselves. As Table 3.1 shows, the regions of the world with very high military expenditures per capita were North

Table 3.1. Military expenditure per capita and as percentage
of GNP, 1978 (U.S. dollars), by world region

Region	Military Expenditure Per Capita	Military Expenditure as Percent of GNP
North America	468	4.9
Latin America	22	1.5
NATO Europe	237	3.6
Warsaw Pact	311	8.2
Other Europe	121	2.3
Middle East	250	12.2
South Asia	5	2.8
Far East	30	2.7
Oceania	156	2.4
Africa	22	3.6
World	97	4.5

Source: Ruth Leger Sivard, World Military and Social Expenditures
1981 (Leesburg, Va.: World Priorities, 1981).

America, the Warsaw Pact region, the Middle East, and NATO Europe. In terms of proportion of the gross national product (GNP) spent on military activity, the Middle East led the rank order, but the Warsaw Pact and North American regions followed. Rich countries were spending more on military might, both absolutely and proportionately. However, they were spending it increasingly on arming the rest of the world.

Since these matters are easily misunderstood, let me state clearly what I am saying and what I am not saying. Above all, I am *not* proposing a contrast between an "orderly," "gradual," "peaceful" path toward the creation of the state in Europe and a "rapid," "turbulent," "violent" path elsewhere. On the contrary: European states took shape through external war and internal coercion. After 1500 or so, the national states of Western Europe and its extensions became the world's most powerful organizations. Within those powerful states, the armies were long the most extensive, costly, and powerful structures. The states competed with each other by means of war followed by economic exploitation, and by means of economic exploitation backed by the threat of armed force. From around 1500 to 1900, the survivors of the competition in Europe increasingly extended the same combination of conquest and commerce to other parts of the world.

Building armed forces involved the managers of national states in struggles to wrest the wherewithal of war from a generally reluctant population within their own territories. In the process, more or less inadvertently, the managers of national states created most of the apparatus we now think of as being central to those states: the apparatus of tax collection, of budgeting, of supply, of surveillance, of control. The struggle also hammered out bargains between state makers and the subject populations: some limits on the state's power to tax, some forms of representation vis-à-vis the sovereign, some reinforcement of the local institutions—assemblies, systems of landholding, courts, guilds, communities—that played a part in the state's extraction of resources for war.

Thus formed strong, centralized national states with at least a modicum of popular participation. In that sense, war making created national states as we know them. From beginning to end, then, the creation and use of armed force remained central to the activity of states. By the twentieth century, successful state makers were waging ferocious wars on an international scale. Yet, paradoxically, the creation of support structures for a state's armed forces civilized domestic political administration. Increasingly, the day-to-day operation of the national state on its own ground fell into the hands of nonmilitary people. The dominant classes and the managers of the state withdrew more and more from personal involvement in war and in the display of armed force; more and more they entrusted those activities to specialists, to the professional soldiers. Soldiers, however, became ever-more dependent on their civilian supporters for the wherewithal of war. The net effect of these changes was not to diminish the importance of war or armed force but to decrease the autonomy and personal power of the men who actually wielded armed force.

In that light, the twentieth-century experiences of Latin America, the Middle East, Africa, and South Asia look strange, for in those parts of the world, military men have not lost autonomy and personal power. If anything, they have gained strength. As Table 3.2 shows, both the frequency of coups and the success rates of coups increased in almost all Third World regions between 1945–1959 and 1960–1972; by 1981, the majority of governments in most Third World regions were run by the military. If anyone still believes that Third World states are essentially recapitulating the state-making experiences of Western Europe and its extensions, the increasing visibility of soldiers in the politics of those Third World states should give the believer pause.

Why might that be? Let me confess at once that I know too little about Third World history and social structure to offer a convincing answer to such a large question. Let me concede immediately that the proper way to search for an answer passes through soundly documented historical comparisons. Let me grant without complaint that the nations of the Third World vary far too much in wealth, size, and history to permit any single explanation to cover most of their experiences. Let me admit without delay that I write as a student of Western European

Table 3.2. Coups d'etat in Third World regions, 1945–1972

Region	Number of States	1945–1959		1960–1972		Percent of Military Governments in 1981
		Number of Coups	Percent Success	Number of Coups	Percent Success	
Central America	9	8	12.5	23	47.8	55.5
Caribbean	6	2	0.0	2	50.0	33.3
South America	9	19	21.1	27	40.7	66.7
Mainland Asia	18	12	41.7	21	42.9	61.1
Pacific	8	4	75.0	5	60.0	25.0
Middle East	16	20	35.0	57	52.6	25.0
Sub-Saharan Africa	38			78	59.0	60.5

Source: Compiled from lists in Gavin Kennedy, The Military in the Third World (London: Duckworth, 1974).

history confronting a perplexing fact: The rest of the world is not recapitulating Europe's experience. Why should the world be so uncooperative?

The point of my speculations, then, will be to see whether variation within Europe, properly understood, provides any insight into variation in the contemporary world. My main speculation will follow this line: To the extent that a state builds up its military power through the direct wresting of military means from its own subject population, it creates barriers to military rule; to the extent that a state depends on other states for its military organization and personnel, it becomes vulnerable to military rule.

Creation and Extension of the
European System of States

Let us consider an organization to be a national state to the extent that it (a) controls the principal concentrated means of coercion in a bounded and contiguous territory larger than a single city and its hinterland, (b) claims the right to control the movement of people and goods across its boundaries, and (c) is formally centralized, differentiated, and autonomous. In a full-fledged national state, by such a definition, there is a fairly clear distinction between "internal" and "external" political arenas. At the beginning of the sixteenth century, by such a definition, none of the larger European powers had become a full-fledged national state. On one side, every nominal monarch in 1500 faced great lords who operated their own private armies, police forces, and systems of justice, and whose cooperation the monarch had somehow to enlist in order to carry on repression within the territory and war with other monarchs outside it. On the other, so-called national territories were commonly discontinuous, divided by enclaves of alien power, and bounded only approximately.

Over the next 200 years, royal conquests—both "inside" and "outside" the national territory—deeply altered that situation. By 1700, most of the map of Western Europe showed bounded, contiguous territories within which a single relatively centralized, differentiated, and autonomous organization controlled the principal concentrated means of coercion. The sixteenth and seventeenth centuries, then, brought about the heyday of state making in Western Europe.

As that process went on, the managers of different states regularized their relations with each other, increasingly differentiating their treatment of other people according to whether they were (a) citizens of their own state, (b) citizens of another state, (c) officials or representatives of their own state, or (d) officials or representatives of another state. One can reasonably say that not merely an aggregation but a *system* of interdependent national states, confirming each other's sovereignty, came into being.

Three kinds of relations linked the system of states. First, there were flows of resources in the form of loans and supplies, especially loans and supplies devoted to war making. Second, there was a competition among states for hegemony in disputed territories; although that competition obviously divided particular pairs of states, other states acted to contain the conflict and to influence its outcome. Third, there was an intermittent creation of coalitions of states that temporarily combined their efforts to force a given state into a certain form and a certain position within the international system. The war-making coalition is one example, the peacemaking coalition another.

Peacemaking coalitions were probably the more important. After 1648, with the settlement of the Thirty Years' War, all effective European states coalesced temporarily to settle on the boundaries and rulers of the recent belligerents—especially the losers when one state clearly had defeated another. From that point on, the major reorganizations of the European state system came in spurts, at the settlements of widespread wars. From each large war, in general, fewer national states emerged than had entered it. An international compact of interested states, having negotiated the new boundaries and rulers, acquired a commitment to maintain both, or at least to defend them against the maneuvers of other states.

This statement does not mean that states developed a commitment to peace. On the contrary, war became the normal condition of the international system of states. War became the normal means of defending or enhancing a position within the system. Why war? No simple answer will do because war, as a potent means, served more than one end. But surely part of the answer goes back to the central mechanisms of state making: The very logic by which a local lord extended or defended the perimeter within which he monopolized the means of violence, and thereby increased his return from that monopoly, continued on a larger scale into the logic of war. Early in the process, external and internal rivals overlapped to a large degree. Only the establishment of large perimeters of control, within which great lords had checked their rivals, sharpened the line between internal and external. Then the existence of a system of states became a greater advantage, since in the process of conquest a ruler could bargain for not only the acquiescence of the people in the conquered territories but also the assent of those who ran the adjacent states. Thus developed the practical definition of legitimacy that prevails among states today: the willingness of subject populations to accept a state's commands coupled with the readiness of neighboring states to enforce those commands when asked.

Whether they contested or assented, furthermore, the interaction of those adjacent states with a conquering state tended to make them more similar to the conqueror. Either they adopted some of the same organization for war, or they borrowed models of administration for peace, or both. When states agreed among themselves, in peace or in war, they tended to force upon other states that fell within their zones of control the form or forms of government they preferred. Therefore, a transition occurred: From a situation in which states took shape mainly through a great lord's own efforts to conquer or check adjacent competitors, Europe moved to a situation in which existing states, in concert, played a large part in creating or reorganizing other states. Roughly speaking, there was a transition from internal toward external processes of state making.

With due recognition that the distinction between internal and external processes is fragile and arbitrary, we might schematize Europe's state-making history into three stages.

1. The differential success of some power holders in external struggles establishes the difference between an internal and an external arena for the deployment of force.
2. External competition generates internal state making.
3. External compacts among states influence the form and locus of particular states ever more powerfully.

With caution, we might then think of France and England as states that took shape mainly during the first stage; of Norway and Austria as states showing significant effects of the first two stages; and of Finland, Czechoslovakia, Poland, and the two Germanies—despite their glorious earlier experiences of pristine state making—as states whose current structures show clear effects of the third stage, of compacts among many other states.

In this perspective, state-certifying organizations such as the League of Nations and the United Nations simply extended the European-based process to the world as a whole. Whether forced or voluntary, bloody or peaceful, decolonization simply completed the process by which existing states acted together to create new ones.

Does Europe Predict the Third World's Future?

As a model for the formation of national states in the rest of the world, it turns out that the European experience offers an ambiguous lesson. On the one hand, along with generations of Western political analysts, we might consider the pristine European state-making experiences—those of France, England, Spain, and perhaps of Brandenburg-Prussia or Sweden—the proper and probable models for the rest of the world. On the other, we might reason from the same experience that (1) the forms of particular states tend to crystallize at well-defined moments of strenuous organization or reorganization, then change only slowly and in secondary ways between such heroic moments; (2) when the last such moment appears with respect to the development of the whole system of states deeply affects the states' present form; and more precisely, (3) since 1500 or so, the more recent that heroic moment of crystallization, the stronger the impact of other states' bargaining on the form of the state in question. Although I began my own explorations of European state making with a naive hope that some version of the first might be true, I now think that if the European experience in forming national states has any relevance for the current experience of the Third World, it must be through the second and third lines of reasoning.

Certainly the extension of the Europe-based state-making process to the rest of the world did not create states in the strict European image. Broadly speaking, internal struggles in Europe, such as the checking of great regional lords and the imposition of taxation on peasant villages, produced important organizational features of states: not only the relative subordination of military power to civilian control but also the extensive bureaucracy of fiscal surveillance, the representation of wronged interests via petition and parliament, and the reinforcement of the local community as a fundamental unit of government. Some European states lay far outside this process and proved vulnerable to military takeovers. Portugal, Spain, and Greece are the prominent twentieth-century examples. One might likewise make a case for the France of 1958, although the final result of de Gaulle's arrival in power was another round of civilianization.

On the whole, states elsewhere developed differently. In general, the more recent a state's creation, the more likely that other states fixed and guaranteed its external boundaries and played a direct part in the designation of its rulers and the less likely that those rulers faced well-organized internal rivals other than their own military forces. An initial coalition government such as that of Zimbabwe is the exception, not the rule.

The most telling feature of that difference appears in military organization. European states built up their military apparatuses through sustained struggles with their subject populations and by means of a selective extension of protection to different classes within those populations. Agreements on protection constrained the rulers themselves, making them vulnerable to courts, to assemblies, and to withdrawals of credit, services, and expertise.

Table 3.3. Types of state by sources of military organization
and resources

Source of Military Organization	Dependence on Exports to a Single Country for Military Resources	
	Dependent	Independent
External	client states, e.g., Honduras	clones, e.g., South Korea
Internal	merchants, e.g., Iraq	autonomous states, e.g., China, South Africa

To a large degree, states that have come into being recently through decolonization or through reallocations of territory by dominant states have acquired their military organization from outside, without the same internal forging of mutual constraints between rulers and ruled. To the extent that outside states continue to supply military goods and expertise in return for commodities, or military alliance, or both, the new states harbor powerful, unconstrained organizations that easily overshadow all other organizations within their territories. To the extent that outside states guarantee their boundaries, the managers of those military organizations exercise extraordinary power within them. The advantages of military power become enormous, and the incentives to seize power over the state as a whole by means of that advantage becomes very strong.

The apparent exceptions are those states, such as Angola, that achieved independence through coalitions of guerrilla forces, each supported by different external powers and each retaining a degree of autonomy past the moment of the state's independence. Within a new state, a unified military organization gives its commanders enormous leverage. Despite the great place that war making occupied in the making of European states, the old national states of Europe almost never experienced the great disproportion between military organization and all other forms of organization that seems the fate of client states throughout the contemporary world.

In our own time, not all states entering the European-based system of states have been clients, and not all have been equally vulnerable to military control. As a first attempt to reason from possible lessons of the European experience to alternative means in the contemporary world, let me propose a simple fourfold classification (see Table 3.3). As usual, the four categories result from arbitarily cutting each of two continua in half. The continua are (a) the extent to which a state's military organization is created, trained, staffed, and supplied by other states, internal versus external, and (b) the extent to which the resources to support a military organization are generated directly by the export of labor or commodities to another country, dependent versus independent.

In general, states that acquire their military organization, training, personnel, and supplies from outside powers are less likely to have struggled through to having civilian constraints on their own armed forces. A state that depends on exports to a single destination for the funds to pay for its armed forces is deeply vulnerable to outside influence because fluctuations in the target country's economy affect its own ability to sustain its armed forces directly, and because the receiving state can so easily influence the sending state's welfare by manipulating the terms of trade. If we take the European experience seriously, we should expect client states to follow signals from their patrons, clones to be especially vulnerable to military coups, merchants to wax and wane with the vigor of the market for their commodities or labor, and autonomous states to occupy positions similar to those of the old members of the European state system.

Over the last century or so, the world has seen a decisive net shift from the lower right-hand corner of the table to the upper left-hand corner: from internal creation, staffing, and supplying of military organizations by states that depend only a little on exports to a single trading partner toward a situation in which military forms, personnel, and supplies flow into a state while exports flow out to a single destination and pay for the military wherewithal. The twentieth-century drive of great powers to surround themselves with rings of poorer and militarily dependent states fosters just such a shift.

Tables 3.4 and 3.5 display some outcomes of that process. Their categories, regrettably, do not correspond to those of Table 3.3; for that, we would need information about export dependency and about the sources of military organization and training. They do, however, provide a preliminary indication of the dependence of states in different parts of the Third World on arms imports for their own military organizations. The first fact to note is that three-fifths of the states with military rule in 1981 also relied on a single supplier for the great bulk of their arms. Latin America, where the United States had eight clients while the USSR supplied Cuba, led the pack. Middle Eastern states, although great consumers of arms, managed to diversify their sources of supply; both their oil revenues and their geopolitical position probably helped in that endeavor. Asian states, nevertheless, were the ones most heavily involved in international military networks. Over 55 percent of all Asian states had military rulers, and almost 70 percent had either military rule, or

Table 3.4. Distribution of Third World states by military type, 1981

	Region				
Type	Middle East	Asia	Latin America	Africa	Total
Military rule, one large supplier	23.5%	34.8%	37.5%	27.3%	30.6%
Military rule, several suppliers	5.9	21.7	16.7	25.0	19.4
Nonmilitary rule, heavy arms imports	29.4	13.0	8.3	6.8	12.0
All other states	41.2	30.4	37.5	40.9	38.0
Total	100.0	99.9	100.0	100.0	100.0
Number of states	17	23	24	44	108

Definitions:
   One large supplier: One state supplies at least 75 percent
of the state's arms imports.
   Heavy arms imports: State imports at least $0.5 billion
worth of arms in a year.

Source: Ruth Leger Sivard, World Military and Social Expenditures
(Leesburg, Va.: World Priorities, 1981).

Table 3.5. Military expenditure per capita in Third World regions, by type of regime, 1981 (in US dollars)

	Region				
Type	Middle East	Asia	Oceania	Latin America	Africa
Military rule, one large supplier	114	32		20	31
Military rule, several suppliers	52	22		40	7
Nonmilitary rule, heavy arms imports	402	25		28	44
All other states	574	142	80	13	19
Percent of GNP in military expenditure	12.2	2.8	2.4	1.5	3.6

Source: Ruth Leger Sivard, World Military and Social Expenditures
(Leesburg, Va.: World Priorities, 1981).

heavy arms shipments, or both. In terms of per capita expenditures for military activity, the Middle Eastern states overshadowed all the rest. On the average, nonmilitary states outspent military states, a fact that suggests that states with military rulers benefited more significantly from the protection and subsidy of the great powers than did their civilian-led neighbors. Not the sheer level of military expenditure but the relationship between military forces and other organizations appears to have forwarded or checked military hegemony.

If the building up of circles of dependents around the great powers were the only trend, the world would be divided neatly into autonomous states and clients; clones and merchants would not exist. But the world actually contains some clones and plenty of merchants. Competition among the great commercial and military powers has made it possible for some states to use their strategic locations to bargain for extensive military support from another power, and thus to become clones, while states that have their own military establishments as well as a valuable export have bartered the export for military supplies, thus becoming merchants. Japan, Taiwan, and South Korea, all of which enjoy extensive military protection while spending exceptionally low shares of their national incomes on military might, show some of the advantages of cloning.

In light of the European experience, the situation of the merchants—especially, in our own time, exporters of oil—poses some especially interesting questions. To the extent that their buyers band together to form a single bloc, these countries become as vulnerable as a country that has only one destination for its exports. Their situation most resembles that of Spain when riches were flowing into that country from the New World. On the one hand, when demand for their exports is high, they avoid much of the state-making effort, and the consequent hammering out of agreements with major classes in their own territories, that so marked the European countries' preparation for war. That side of the equation suggests the possibility of an acquiescent population and a relatively peaceful exercise of power by the people who control the essential commodities. On the other hand, the military organizations of the merchant states acquire a fearsome power in relation to other organizations within the same countries. When it is technically possible for the same small group to seize control of the military apparatus and the sources of exports, there will probably be an incentive to stage a military coup that will outshadow the petty maneuvers of the clones.

When the export is extremely valuable, as in the case of oil, we might expect the great powers themselves to support military factions that (a) show promise of being able both to seize control of the state and to assure the continuation of the export and (b) are willing to barter a promise to export to the great power for support from that great power.

What will happen if and when the merchants' incomes rise? Two complementary dangers arise. The first is that merchant states will build their military might to unprecedented levels, thus increasing the stakes in domestic struggles for power and the destructiveness of international war. The second is that their demand for arms will feed the military industries of the great powers, thereby promoting the remilitarization of the great powers themselves. Today's large shipments of U.S., Soviet, and French weaponry to various Middle Eastern states augur ill for peace—domestic or international—in that troubled region. Increased military power there and elsewhere in the Third World provides no guarantee of stable government or a nonviolent settlement of international disputes.

Notes

This is a revised version of "Speculations on Warmaking and Domestic Military Power," Working Paper 280, Center for Research on Social Organization (CRSO), University of Michigan, December 1982. I have also borrowed a few passages from my "Warmaking and Statemaking as Organized Crime," CRSO Working Paper 256, University of Michigan, February 1982. In lieu of a documented general argument, I am providing an extensive bibliography of the reading that has led me to the positions presented in the paper.

References

Ames, Edward, and Rapp, Richard T. "The Birth and Death of Taxes: A Hypothesis." *Journal of Economic History* 37 (1977):161–178.

Ardant, Gabriel. "Financial Policy and Economic Infrastructure of Modern States and Nations." In *The Formation of National States in Western Europe,* ed. Charles Tilly. Princeton: Princeton University Press, 1975.

Badie, Bertrand. *Le développement politique.* 2d ed. Paris: Economica, 1980.

Badie, Bertrand, and Birnbaum, Pierre. *Sociologie de l'Etat.* Paris: Bernard Grasset, 1979.

Bean, Richard. "War and the Birth of the Nation State." *Journal of Economic History* 33 (1973):203–221.

Braun, Rudolf. "Taxation, Sociopolitical Structure, and State-Building: Great Britain and Brandenburg-Prussia." In *The Formation of National States in Western Europe,* ed. Charles Tilly. Princeton: Princeton University Press, 1975.

———— . "Steuern und Staatsfinanzierung als Modernisierungsfaktoren: Ein Deutsch-Englischer Vergleich." In *Studien zum Beginn der modernen Welt,* ed. Reinhard Koselleck. Stuttgart: Klett-Cotta, 1977.

Busch, Otto. *Militarsystem und Sozialleben im alten Preussen 1713–1807: Die Anfänge der sozialen Militarisierung der preussisch-deutschen Gesellschaft.* Berlin: de Gruyter, 1962.
Calvert, Peter. *A Study of Revolution.* Oxford: Clarendon Press, 1970.
Carneiro, Robert. "Political Expansion as an Expression of the Principle of Competitive Exclusion." In *Origins of the State,* ed. Ronald Cohen and Elman R. Service. Philadelphia: Institute for the Study of Human Issues, 1978.
Chapman, Brian. *Police State.* London: Pall Mall, 1970.
Cipolla, Carlo. *Guns, Sails, and Empires: Technological Innovation and the Early Phases of European Expansion, 1400–1700.* New York: Pantheon, 1965.
Clark, Sir George. "The Social Foundations of States." In *The New Cambridge Modern History.* Vol. 5, *The Ascendancy of France,* ed. F. L. Carsten. Cambridge: Cambridge University Press, 1969.
Dickson, P.G.M. *The Financial Revolution in England: A Study in the Development of Public Credit 1688–1756.* London: St. Martin's Press, 1967.
Duffy, Michael. "Introduction: The Military Revolution and the State, 1500–1800." In *The Military Revolution and the State, 1500–1800,* ed. Michael Duffy. Exeter Studies in History, no. 1. Exeter: University of Exeter, 1980.
Elton, G. R. "Taxation for War and Peace in Early-Tudor England." In *War and Economic Development: Essays in Memory of David Joslin,* ed. J. H. Winter. Cambridge: Cambridge University Press, 1975.
Finer, Samuel E. *The Man on Horseback: The Role of the Military in Politics.* London: Pall Mall, 1962.
_____ . "State-building, State Boundaries, and Border Control." *Social Science Information* 13 (1974):79–126.
_____ . "State- and Nation-Building in Europe: The Role of the Military." In *The Formation of National States in Western Europe,* ed. Charles Tilly. Princeton: Princeton University Press, 1975.
_____ . "The Morphology of Military Regimes." In *Soldiers, Peasants, and Bureaucrats: Civil-Military Relations in Communist and Modernizing Regimes,* ed. Roman Kolkowicz and Andrzej Korbonski. London: Routledge & Kegan Paul, 1982.
Fueter, Eduard. *Geschichte des europäischen Staatensystems von 1492–1559.* Osnabruck, West Germany: Zeller, 1972. Reprint of 1919 edition.
Gooch, John. *Armies in Europe.* London: Routledge & Kegan Paul, 1980.
Hale, J. R. "Armies, Navies, and the Art of War." In *The New Cambridge Modern History.* Vol. 2, *The Reformation, 1520–1559,* ed. G. R. Elton. Cambridge: Cambridge University Press, 1968.
_____ . "Armies, Navies, and the Art of War." In *The New Cambridge Modern History.* Vol. 3, *The Counter-Reformation and Price Revolution, 1559–1610,* ed. R. B. Wernham. Cambridge: Cambridge University Press, 1968.
Hamilton, Earl J. "Origin and Growth of the National Debt in France and England." In *Studi in onore di Gino Luzzato,* vol. 2. Milan: Giuffre, 1950.
Hintze, Otto. *Staat und Verfassung: Gesammelte Abhandlungen zur allgemeinen Verfassungsgeschichte,* ed. Gerhard Oestreich. Göttingen: Vandenhoeck & Ruprecht, 1962. First published in 1910.

Howard, Michael. *War in European History.* Oxford: Oxford University Press, 1976.

Janowitz, Morris, and Van Doorn, Jacques, eds. *On Military Intervention.* Rotterdam: Rotterdam University Press, 1971.

Johnson, John J. *The Role of the Military in Underdeveloped Countries.* Princeton: Princeton University Press, 1962.

Jones, Colin. "The Military Revolution and the Professionalization of the French Army Under the Ancien Regime." In *The Military Revolution and the State, 1500-1800,* ed. Michael Duffy. Exeter Studies in History, no. 1. Exeter: University of Exeter, 1980.

Kennedy, Gavin. *The Military in the Third World.* London: Duckworth, 1974.

Kidron, Michael, and Segal, Ronald. *The State of the World Atlas.* New York: Simon & Schuster, 1981.

Lane, Frederic C. "Force and Enterprise in the Creation of Oceanic Commerce." *The Tasks of Economic History.* Supplemental Issue of the *Journal of Economic History* 10 (1950):19–31.

———. "Economic Consequences of Organized Violence." *Journal of Economic History* 18 (1958):401–417.

———. "The Economic Meaning of War and Protection." In *Venice and History: The Collected Papers of Frederic C. Lane.* Baltimore: Johns Hopkins Press, 1966.

Luckham, Robin. *The Nigerian Military: A Sociological Analysis of Authority and Revolt, 1960-67.* Cambridge: Cambridge University Press, 1971.

Lüdtke, Alf. "Genesis und Durchsetzung des modernen Staates: Zur Analyse von Herrschaft und Verwaltung." *Archiv für Sozialgeschichte* 20 (1980):470–491.

Lyons, G. M. "Exigences militaries et budgets militaires aux U.S.A." *Revue française de sociologie* 2 (1961):66–74.

McNeill, William H. *The Pursuit of Power: Technology, Armed Force, and Society since A.D. 1000.* Chicago: University of Chicago Press, 1982.

Modelski, George. "The Long Cycle of Global Politics and the Nation-State." *Comparative Studies in Society and History* 20 (1978):214–235.

O'Donnell, Guillermo. "Comparative Historical Formations of the State Apparatus and Socio-Economic Change in the Third World." *International Social Science Journal* 32 (1980):717–729.

Peacock, Alan T., and Wiseman, Jack. *The Growth of Public Expenditure in the United Kingdom.* Princeton: Princeton University Press, 1961.

Pounds, Norman J. G., and Ball, Sue Simons. "Core-Areas and the Development of the European States System." *Annals of the Association of American Geographers* 54 (1964):24–40.

Rapoport, David C. "The Praetorian Army: Insecurity, Venality, and Impotence." In *Soldiers, Peasants, and Bureaucrats: Civil-Military Relations in Communist and Modernizing Societies,* ed. Roman Kolkowicz and Andrzej Korbonski. London: Routledge & Kegan Paul, 1982.

Redlich, Fritz. *The German Military Enterpriser and His Work Force.* 2 vols. Vierteljahrschrift für Sozial- und Wirtschaftsgeschichte, Beiheften 47, 48. Wiesbaden, West Germany: Steiner, 1964–1965.

Rosenberg, Hans. *Bureaucracy, Aristocracy, and Autocracy: The Prussian Experience, 1660–1815.* Cambridge: Harvard University Press, 1958.

Russett, Bruce M. *What Price Vigilance? The Burdens of National Defense.* New Haven: Yale University Press, 1970.

Singer, J. David, and Small, Melvin. *The Wages of War, 1816–1965: A Statistical Handbook.* New York: Wiley, 1972.

Sivard, Ruth Leger. *World Military and Social Expenditures 1981.* Leesburg, Va.: World Priorities, 1981.

Stein, Arthur A., and Russett, Bruce M. "Evaluating War: Outcomes and Consequences." In *Handbook of Political Conflict: Theory and Research,* ed. Ted Robert Gurr. New York: Free Press, 1980.

Stone, Lawrence. "State Control in Sixteenth-Century England." *Economic History Review* 17 (1947):103–120.

Wijn, J. W. "Military Forces and Warfare 1610–1648." In *The New Cambridge Modern History.* Vol. 4, *The Decline of Spain and the Thirty Years War, 1609–48/59,* ed. J. P. Cooper. Cambridge: Cambridge University Press, 1970.

Wolf, Eric R. *Europe and the People Without History.* Berkeley: University of California Press, 1982.

Zolberg, Aristide R. "Strategic Interactions and the Formation of Modern States: France and England." *International Social Science Journal* 32 (1980):687–716.

4
The Urban Type of Society and International War

Keiichi Matsushita

Introduction

In order to seek a peace policy, it is essential to examine, in a sociological sense, what are the underlying assumptions of international war. By itself, the deductive theory of peace (i.e., a normative approach) is quite insufficient in building peace policies in actual terms.

Certainly, it is natural and important to consider the military-technical conditions of war, the politico-economic structures of each government in particular, and international relations in general. However, it appears to be urgent in the contemporary context to create a new type of sociology of war in order to make peace research more productive and meaningful than ever before. Without such a vigorous effort, peace research will not become a policy science in the strict sense of the word.

As is often said, military experts tend to have a strong psychological characteristic that is demonstrated in the saying, "Generals are fighting past wars." Even at the time of World War II, developed nations had not fully developed an urban type of society, and this type of society was still immature. As a result, theories drawn up by military experts, and ideas held by statesmen and commentators drawing upon those theories, have not taken sufficient account of what the maturity of the urban type of society means in the contemporary context. It is indeed the responsibility of people in the social sciences and policy sciences to try to clarify the substance of the sociological assumptions about peace and war as well as the degree of maturity of the urban type of society observed in developed nations. Hence, they should radically criticize the existing military theories, and the purpose of this chapter is to tackle this task as objectively as possible.

Maturity of the Urban Type of Society
in Developed Nations

It seems that little concern has been shown for the sociological underlying assumptions of war within the contemporary context. When the salient differences in sociological conditions between developed and developing nations are noted, however, it is of great importance to pay a great deal of attention to the conspicuous contrast between urban and rural types of societies. Because of this structural difference, sociological considerations are in fact very significant for the foundation of peace research. Why is this so? Because at the time of World War I and even during World War II, the characteristics of a rural type of society still existed in Europe, the United States, Russia, and Japan. In other words, in these countries, an urban type of society was then not as fully matured as it is today.

When we consider the mature stage of an urban type of society, an important question must be posed, What will be the logic of international war? One cannot predict with certainty what the logic will be in actual terms, so it is urgent that efforts be made to build a model of peace based on the urban type of society. The earlier theories of peace and war, whose focal points were based on a rural type of society, clearly must be replaced by a new one.

It is well recognized that the use of nuclear weapons, if only for regional defense, would lead to total nuclear war between the two superpowers and then to the global annihilation of mankind. If we consider the occurrence of conventional wars (even in this case, the use of nuclear weapons cannot be excluded as a possibility), the logic of war within the context of an urban type of society would appear to be very different from that in the context of a rural type of society. This difference would certainly be clear if, for example, European countries and Japan, whose populations are quite dense, were contrasted to the Soviet Union or the United States.

What characterizes the transition stages from a rural to an urban type of society? As I see it, the first indicator is a decrease in the population employed in primary industries (particularly in the agricultural sector). I would define the transition stage from the rural to the urban type of society as the period in which the share of primary industry drops to less than 30 percent of the total population. Then I would regard an urban type of society as mature when the population employed in the primary industries reached a level of less than 10 percent of the total population. The second indicator, the concentration of the population in cities, is related to the first, as is the formation of a megalopolis.

Table 4.1. Agricultural population of major countries (1910–1977)

Great Britain	7%(1921)	5%(1951)	4%(1960)	2%(1977)
France	30%(1911)	20%(1951)	22%(1960)	10%(1977)
Italy	45%(1911)	35%(1951)	31%(1960)	13%(1977)
United States	32%(1910)	12%(1950)	7%(1960)	3%(1977)
Soviet Union	71%(1928)	40%(1958)	42%(1960)	19%(1977)
Japan	52%(1925)	48%(1948)	33%(1960)	14%(1977)*

Sources: Kuznets and World Bank; Miyazaki, Okumura, Morita, *International Comparative Statistics* (Tokyo, 1981), p. 17.

*The agricultural population of Japan today is less than 10 percent.

As is shown in Table 4.1, the United States, Western Europe, and Japan were in the transition period at the time of World War II and are now in the mature state. On the other hand, the Soviet Union is still in the transition stage from a rural to an urban type of society, and it will take time for this country to reach the mature stage.

Since 1945, there have been three types, or possible types, of war.

1. War between developing nations—Indo-Pakistan War, Vietnam-China War, wars between African states, and the Iraq-Iran War
2. War between developed and developing nations—the United States vis-à-vis North Korea, the United States vis-à-vis Vietnam, the Soviet Union vis-à-vis Afghanistan
3. War between developed nations

Of these types of war, there has been no occurrence of the third type, and both the first and the second types of warfare have tended to be, by and large, limited to the rural type of society. If this is actually the case, it is now most necessary to replace the earlier logic of war with a new logic of war based on the context of a mature urban type of society.

If the sociological underlying assumptions of war in an urban type of society are not considered, peace research in developed nations will lose its basic significance. This theoretical effort will conversely lead to a clarification of the sociological underlying assumptions of war within the context of the rural type of society in developing nations. The first objective is to consider through sociologically based assumptions what the dynamics of peace are and what the dynamics of war mean, and then I shall propose some relevant hypotheses that can be considered as logical consequences of war in a mature urban type of society.

Significance of Development (Democratization and Industrialization) and Military Ambivalence

Development processes are most likely to produce, whether under capitalism or under socialism, transition dynamics from a rural to an urban type of society, on to the maturity of the urban type of society. As is often the case, theoretical concerns have been primarily with the processes of industrialization. However, one must note the fact that industrialization processes have of necessity produced—through urban concentration of the population—liberalization, equalization, and democratization, the last in the "formal" sense of the word. Quite interestingly, both democratization and industrialization have ambivalent effects on the dynamics of war and peace.

Democratization

What is the main result of democratization? Apparently, it is the formation of a mass democracy. It is this democracy that has led to bureaucratic controls and mass manipulation on the part of governments, in other words, conditions for mobilizing people for international war. Mass democracy is really a prototype of wartime totalitarianism, which is exactly what happened during World War II.

As we will see later in more detail, mass democracy simultaneously brings about conditions that produce a great deal of criticism of governmental policies on the part of people and conditions that produce antiwar and resistance movements, even revolutions. There is a likelihood that these movements could transcend national boundaries to create new international linkages between peoples of different countries. In this sense, it is very clear that the impact of democratization on war is ambivalent.

Industrialization

Progress in industrialization first implies a growth in national productive power. Industrialization is most likely to provide countries with techniques for war management because the military industries and communication techniques are fully developed by this dynamic. Byproducts of these processes are even more profound. For instance, automobile industries and tractor industries can be converted at any time to the production of tanks. Progress of motorization will make it easy to train a large number of tank personnel, and computers are also likely to enable many military personnel to operate weapons systems. As with the case of the democratization process, industrialization leads to the intensification of potential power to move toward militarization.

And as I will analyze later, industrialization can also have a negative effect on militarization processes.

Industrialization is also likely to complicate the domestic and international division of labor more than ever before, making nations more and more interdependent. With interdependence being expanded in scope, international war will cause crisis situations in the national economies of the small and middle-sized developing nations. The same will not be the case for superpowers such as the United States and the Soviet Union because they are continental powers. Also, the possibility of a panic occurring in a megalopolis should be considered.

The characteristics of industrialization have, therefore, indefinite and sometimes contradictory effects on the dynamics of war. In democratized and industrialized societies, war in an urban type of society will lead to the expansion of militarily negative factors. Therefore, the classic theory of war by Karl von Clausewitz, which emerged with the birth of the nation-state system in international relations, will lose its original significance, because this classic theory has presupposed demarcated national boundaries, independent national economies, the continuation of central governments, and the monopoly of military forces by central governments.

Military Issues in Democratization

Transformation of Personality Types

With the process of urbanization through industrialization, democratization appears to transform human beings from a traditional type (i.e., rural) to a citizen type (i.e., urban). What is clear is the change in the human personality (i.e., ethos). With this personality change, physical appearance will be transformed largely by improvements in nutrition and in labor conditions.

First, perseverance, stoicism, diligence, and self-sacrifice are virtues of soldiers in every country, and these virtues are widely believed to be the ethics of a rural type of society. People who are highly urbanized will lose the substance of virtues developed in the rural societies.

Second, rural people have been circumscribed by the traditional community in their way of life. Accordingly, they tend toward a closed type of feeling and a sort of chauvinistic nationalism. By contrast, the urban type of people tend toward cosmopolitanism (or *Weltbügertum*). As a result, they are going to be transformed into a citizen type of human being. Such people are likely to be critical of chauvinistic nationalism, arguing that international exchanges must be expanded, and they may have many "friends" in "enemy" nations. Thus, a human confederation will appear in civic daily lives that transcends national boundaries or nationalism between different peoples. This process seems to be similar to what occurred among European aristocrats in the Middle Ages.

So, in the urban type of society, soldiers may escape from the battlefield, and individuals may try to seek refuge not only within their own country but also in foreign countries as well. Others may involve themselves in antiwar movements that extend beyond national boundaries. The last has been already demonstrated as an embryonic case in international civil movements with respect to the nongovernmental organizations in the United Nations. U.S. citizens who were against their country's Vietnam War policy are considered to be such an urban type of person. At the time of the Vietnam War, even a minimum standard of war ethics was virtually lost. It had been corrupted. And yet, one would have to say that there was a distinction between the rural type of Vietnamese and the urban type of American. The Vietnam War should be examined from the perspective of personality type.

The Birth of Articulated Democracy

Democratization processes that are realized ultimately as mass democracy have contributed to the growth of centralized bureaucratic institutions and military organizations, which are the institutional prerequisites of military mobilization. On the other hand, they also produce a multipolarization of societies. This process will lead to the birth of articulated democracies, which are characterized by having the following:

1. Civil liberty and the guarantee of liberty
2. A variety of civil movements and the emergence of pressure groups
3. Operationalization of a multiparty system
4. Expansion of the right of self-government by local governments
5. Independence of parliament and the establishment of a court of justice within the central government

To put it differently, democratization processes have been associated with the progress of articulated democratic institutions, as has been observed in the dynamic tensions between totalitarian and articulated principles.

The multipolarization of society, and therefore the articulation of politics, will, in fact, make the image of "total war" more and more unrealistic. This image of total war was a utopia once dreamed of by military generals like General Erich Ludendorff who dreamed of a military state.

As was noted earlier, both democratization and industrialization, whether under capitalism or socialism, bring about conditions for totalitarianism. At the same time, however, these factors are conducive to the institutionalization of articulated democracy. In matters of war and peace, articulation principles are realized in the following forms: peace movements, antiwar movements, and formations of resistance; policy confrontations among political parties concerning war; countermovements by local governments, for instance, in the declaration of free cities; and a high priority on constitutional procedures with respect to war preparations, war declarations, and war mobilization. When nations cannot appropriately deal with political situations, central governments are certain to be reactionary in their behavior. Without reactionary policies, governmental actors cannot execute war against adversary nations, but in the long range this reactionary quality will produce a chance for revolution.

Difficulties Involved in Military Organizations

In the contemporary military establishment, whose basic premise has been democratization, it is almost impossible for ruling elites to monopolize the posts of the higher staff officers. Although military leadership and diplomacy were once a part of the king's secret art, the institutionalization of civilian control is today appearing as a matter of policy in military leadership as well as in diplomacy. This situation implies that constraints on the military establishment have been more or less effective. The traditional feature of the military is reflected in the privileged thought of closed groups, and that thought is concerned with excessive militaristic statism.

Difficulties in the Execution of Conscriptions and the Maintenance of Discipline. Who today is considered as being subject to conscription by governments? Unlike in the rural type of society, the youth who are subject to conscription in the urban society are high in intellectual standard. And yet, they are blessed with a civic feeling of "freedom" and with a civic type of critical mind. Not only in peacetime, but also particularly in time of war, governments have to think about how to deal with conscientious objectors, internal or external refugees, deserters, etc. If they are not dealt with properly, the legitimacy of conscription policies would be apparently lost. In countries in which political party confrontations are always salient, one can assume that there must also be factionalism within the army. These factors will each contribute potentially to the slackening of the army.

Even if one cannot expect the army to be broken up, the governments may not be able to force soldiers to obey orders through blind loyalty, simply because these soldiers are highly intellectual in thought as well as in behavior. Therefore, officers in the army will often be criticized by soldiers. Presumably, the right to resist illegal orders and the right to surrender will also become important issues within the military.

Indeed, these issues were widely discussed by international military courts after World War II.

Openness of Military Intelligence. Today, military intelligence is gradually becoming open in countries in which freedom of speech and freedom of the press are guaranteed by the government, through a variety of media. On the international level, we have witnessed during the past few decades an increased mutual interaction between nations and an increased exchange of information between governments, and reconnaissance satellites (satellites spying from new heights of altitude and sophistication) are now gathering intelligence daily. As a result, the degree of openness of military intelligence is being expanded in scope. Military secrecy is only effective for the time being, and in this sense, even confidential military matters are transitory in nature as almost all confidential matters are certain to be exposed to the public eventually. Moreover, openness is likely to be an issue for public argument, and requests for openness of information will continue to increase. The prestige of the army—the core of which lies in military secrecy—will be in all likelihood downgraded because of the politicization of the military intelligence issue.

Certainly, under the totalitarian system, these issues are likely to be suppressed by one-party dictatorship and by the privileged military establishment. Such suppression, however, can be only temporary, and it may lead to the accumulation of human energy by which revolution can one day be triggered, depending on what military situations are prevalent. Defeat in war may lead to social revolution. Therefore, we must emphasize that such regimes cannot be easily involved in total war, apart from localized war. Even developing nations with totalitarian political systems are beginning to be transformed into an urban type of society, and a wave of liberalization has begun to emerge through the proliferation of the urban type of personality.

Military Problems in Industrialization

Expansion of the Domestic and International Division of Labor

In a rural type of society, people are able to sustain themselves in small-sized villages or regions, and autarky is possible. However, industrialization has transformed this primitive type of subsistence into a national economy, which has led to the international division of labor. "Interdependence" has increased in contemporary world politics, and as a result, society itself has been greatly internationalized. The national economies of developed nations in which the urban type of society is full-fledged should be characterized only as national frameworks that are simultaneously a part of the domestic and the international networks of the division of labor.

With greater industrialization, the division of labor is being expanded not only on the domestic but also on the global political level. With this structural transformation, economic planning has progressed, whether in a market economy or in a controlled economy, but this increased division of labor at different levels has contributed to the breaking up of economic mobilization in times of war.

Disturbances in the international system of the division of labor caused by war appear to have a direct impact on the national economies of developed nations in particular. A principal reason for this situation lies in the fact that although the continental powers (i.e., the United States and the Soviet Union) are exceptions, European countries and Japan continue to be heavily dependent on foreign countries for raw materials, especially oil. Quite evidently, tanks, fighter airplanes, and ships would all have to be scrapped if there were no oil. Moreover, industrial and agricultural production would have to be stopped if oil were not available. Any sophisticated means of production would become meaningless, and such primitive means as hoes and hammers would again be necessary. Urban life would be destroyed, and this destruction would be accelerated by an unwillingness to sell or by a hoarding of goods on the part of business firms and individual citizens.

It is true that both European countries and Japan have increased their political voices vis-à-vis the two superpowers, but even so, they are militarily very vulnerable. We should recall that during World War II, the destruction of civilian lives and military production was very apparent among the "have not" countries (Germany, Italy, and Japan), which had many of the characteristics of a rural type of society. Even victorious Britain had to face almost the same problem, though it was economically supported by the United States, and since urbanization has accelerated in Britain, the situation of that country is becoming more and more serious.

Emergence of Megalopolises

The emergence of megalopolises implies that the domestic and international division of labor is deeply rooted in societies. A megalopolis, meaning a combined group of cities whose population each amounts to more than 1 million, is not a legally institutionalized large city. Today, there are megalopolises with a population of more than 10 million; for instance, the population of the Tokyo megalopolis is 28 million, and that of the Osaka megalopolis is 13 million.

People in a megalopolis can survive only when the daily supplies of food and essential resources are provided without interruption. If the

Table 4.2.   Comparison of Japan and Western Europe

	Japan	Britain	West Germany	Italy	France
Population	100	27.4	38.5	25.5	14.3
GNP	100	22.0	56.4	16.2	19.0
Energy consumption	100	39.3	62.3	23.6	17.1

Source: Yano Institute, *A Survey of Japan 1979*, based on UN sources.

Note: Index relates variables to area and population.

supply route were disturbed, or if it is only predicted that it could be, the people in the megalopolises would certainly panic. Families in cities generally hold food stocks for only few days, and since the sense of crisis would result in an unwillingness to sell and a hoarding of goods, clashes would naturally occur. In addition, a great portion of the population, possibly 1 million to 10 million people, would begin to flee from the megalopolises in a state of panic. Rural districts and small-sized cities do not have enough capacity to absorb such huge numbers of people, so the people who escaped from the megalopolises would very likely become "boat people." In one way or another, some groups of them would also turn into mobs.

Self-destruction of the megalopolis would soon bring civilian lives and national economies into bankruptcy, which would have many adverse effects if the megalopolis was the capital of a country. These effects would certainly be associated with the breakup of the central bureaucratic organizations and with the overthrow of the military. No matter how much the military, police, and the people's police tried to strengthen domestic security measures, they could not keep the people of the megalopolis from falling into a state of panic.

In particular, one should note the case of Japan (Table 4.2). In terms of size, Japan roughly corresponds to the U.S. state of California or to such European states as West Germany, Norway, Italy, or Poland, and yet, 70 percent of the land in Japan is uninhabitable mountain land. Since the population of Japan is about 124 million, it seems quite natural for us to characterize Japan as a overcrowded society. If the Tokyo megalopolis were to be combined with the Osaka megalopolis, the population total would be more than 40 million. In addition, there are five other Japanese cities with a population in excess of 1 million, so a little less than 50 percent of Japan's population is concentrated in the megalopolises. One can say, therefore, that Japan is now at the stage of an over-mature urban type of society. If the people of the megalopolises were to flee to the provinces, for instance, during a war, the rural population would double in number. The rural areas would not be capable of sustaining such an increase in population.

The politico-economic structure of Japan especially differs from that of West Germany, as well as from that of France. While West Germany is characterized as having a decentralized system, France has had a tendency toward centralization, but Japan is much more centralized than France (with all political and economic activities being centralized in Tokyo). All essential supplies of food, energy, and water are structured in Tokyo through a huge system, and if only a part of that system were disturbed for a limited period of time, Tokyo would probably be thrown into a state of panic.

Individual gardens in the Japanese megalopolises are disappearing because of the high price of land, and when compared with European cities, Tokyo is critically weak in terms of a supply of vegetables. In addition, Japanese houses would be very vulnerable in time of war because they are primarily made of wood. These factors would result in serious problems in time of war or a large earthquake. However, these problems are not yet fully recognized in Japan, nor have they been fully recognized as an important factor in the sociology of war. In my opinion, Japan represents an appropriate model for the formation of a "sociology of crises" in general, which would include a sociology of war.

Factors That Disturb Military Actions

Breakup of Military Logistics

Unlike in the cases of continental powers, the United States and the USSR, both civilian lives and national economies are structurally quite vulnerable in European countries and Japan. These countries, as discussed earlier, have a very mature urban type of society, and the deepening of the domestic and international division of labor has enhanced their structural vulnerability.

During World War II, European countries and Japan rapidly lost military capability when their stocks of strategic weapons and goods were exhausted. At the same time, this loss was indicative of the destruction of national production power and the willingness to continue fighting. Moreover, for both Germany and Japan, access to resources, especially oil, had been a major objective of their military operations. These factors are becoming even more conspicuous in European countries and Japan today. Present technology does not permit the operation of tanks, airplanes, and ships without oil, and a vast amount of oil is also required for a variety of weapons. The military mechanism is being expanded and is inclined more toward an exhaustive war. Factories are highly sophisticated and could not operate sufficiently without their normal supplies of raw materials and energy. Soldiers and labor often come from the cities, and a breakup of civilian lives might mean that city-born soldiers and laborers would return to rural areas. As a result of any of these factors, the wartime mobilization system would break up.

Problems of Boat People

Wars are certain to produce numerous displaced people because of occupations and the destruction of cities and rural areas. Even if nuclear weapons were not used in a future war, the present level of military destructive power far exceeds that of the conventional weapons used in World War II. As was mentioned earlier, if a megalopolis broke up, millions of boat people (refugees) would result. Under such circumstances, an army could not execute its military operations because it would be hindered by the large number of boat people.

Possibilities of Domestic Turmoil

If civilian lives and national economies were actually disturbed and if the legitimacy of war were totally lost, one can assume with high probability that domestic unrest would occur. In the case of the Vietnam War, we have to pose the question of whether the U.S. forces were defeated by the Vietnamese people or whether they were defeated by domestic unrest and the peace movement at home.

An expansion of domestic turmoil would certainly spread to the military, bring about its self-destruction, and eventually result in a revolution. When the battle became domestic, soldiers could easily take off their uniforms and run away from the army. Even if only a small percent of the soldiers deserted, it is likely that the military would break up.

Factors That Hinder an Invading Army

Preparations for Invasion

When one country is planning to invade another, there must be a long period of preparation with respect to the gathering of a huge army and to logistics. Such preparation will be, in all likelihood, detected by intelligence activities or by reconnaissance satellites, which means that the invading army will suffer greater losses.

Continuity of Logistics

In a war of attrition, an invading army will have a difficult time putting a large force into operation with an expectation of concentrated effects as the national economy of the invaded country will be destroyed. Procurement of supplies for a small army was once possible in a battlefield area, but today this is unthinkable. It is therefore now particularly difficult for an invading army to preserve and maintain a long-range logistical supply line from the military base to the battlefield.

Policy Measures for Citizens in the Invaded Areas

Even if physical force is not used by an invading army, civilian lives will still be destroyed. In European countries and Japan in particular, there would be a large number of displaced people because of the high population densities of those countries. Caring for these refugees would be costly for the invading army.

An invading army will suffer from the uncooperativeness or resistance on the part of local people, along with a lack of legitimacy for a military intervention. Especially if an army with a relatively low cultural standard tries to intervene in a country with a high cultural standard, the army cannot expect that the citizens will cooperate with the invading divisions. Thus, the invading army will face much pressure in trying to keep such an occupied region secure.

As mentioned, in Japan almost half of the population lives in a megalopolis, and the country is a highly mature urban type of society. I would like to add to these facts the following points that would hinder any army that would try to invade that country. First, Japan is an island country, and an army would have to have a great number of warships before it could invade it. It would also be essential for the army to retain control of a sea-lane for logistical purposes. Compared with an invasion of a neighboring country, invasion of an island country is difficult, which is historically shown by Hitler's failure to invade Britain during World War II. Landing in Normandy or on Okinawa was possible only because of the overwhelming industrial power of the United States at that time.

Second, more than 70 percent of Japan is mountainous, and most of the agricultural areas are paddy fields. Therefore, it would be difficult for a large number of tanks to engage in mobile operations. Mountainous lands with abundant bushes and trees are advantageous for guerrilla warfare, as was demonstrated in the Vietnam War.

Third, there is a serious deficiency of resources, including essential foods, in Japan, so the country must depend on external trade. An invasion of Japan implies a suspension of industrial production, and the

Japanese national economy would also sustain great damage. Japan does not produce petroleum, and rice is an essential part of the country's food supply. Instead of being able to take advantage of Japan's industrial power and agricultural productivity, an invading army would have to depend largely on imported oil and food supplies.

Policy Sciences and Peace Building

If peace research is to actually have some kind of significance, it will not be enough to deduce theories from peace principles. The relationships between the logic of war and the maturity of the urban type of society in developed nations must be examined, and so far, there have been very few studies of this important point. One must say that a theoretical distinction between the rural type and the urban type of society is in fact an essential sociological premise in considering dynamics of the military, technology, economics, and politics. Examining the sociological underlying assumptions is of great importance, and it is really beyond ideologies. It is essential for either defensive or offensive policies. If peace researchers try to propose policies without having a scientific methodology of distinguishing the urban type of society from the rural type of society, they will certainly fail; indeed, they will make a grave mistake. This methodology is also significant in considering the place of guerrilla warfare in the contemporary typology of war.

With respect to proposals for peace policies, it is naturally necessary to have peace diplomacy based on peace principles, not only on the government but also on the citizen level. However, at the same time, domestic reorientation is an important step in creating peace policies. A reorientation of domestic structures necessitates the realization of peace principles through the application of the original constitutional requirements, but domestic structures must be further decentralized politically and economically. I have already referred to the possibility of an articulated political system, and I should now like to make some suggestions concerning strengthening the independence of local self-governments, a topic that has more or less been overlooked by many people.

In order for local self-governments to be independent of the central government, they must expand the scope of peace policies so that they allow for

1. direct reflection of citizens' opinions,
2. criticism of the war policies of central governments,
3. development of peace diplomacy between local governments,
4. protection of citizens by the declaration of free cities.

Furthermore, local governments must transform themselves from centralized to locally decentralized systems within the political and economic structure of the nation, which will work in such a way as to constrain the excessive development of an urban type of society.

In summary, local self-governments must expand their mechanisms for crisis management, not only during peacetime, but during times of war as well, which will create a so-called civil minimum for freedom and security. From this point of view, Japan's national security measures should not move toward a military buildup but toward the breakup of the Tokyo megalopolis since Japan is indeed an over-mature urban type of society. In this context, a peace strategy for developed nations, whether socialist or capitalist, must seek internationalization or decentralization depending on the structural characteristics of each nation.

What I have noted here is not a direct policy proposal to specifically respond to current international affairs. It is in fact a peace proposal drawn from a consideration of the sociologically important factors of war. This sort of sociological understanding should not be irrelevant in the contemporary context, for military experts in each developed nation have not paid enough attention to this problem. They tend to be overly concerned with the rural type of society in proposing policies of defense and invasion, and military theorists have not concerned themselves with the essential differences between urban and rural types of society. Bearing this situation in mind, I am confident that this sociologically developed argument will indeed contribute to an understanding of the real politics in the world. It will contribute to the deterrence of aggressive military behavior on the part of certain countries, and it will work for changes in domestic and foreign policies. Formation of a policy science of peace is therefore an urgent objective for our social scientists.

Notes

The original version of this chapter was delivered in part as a paper at the Fourth Hiroshima University Symposium on Peace Studies, October 10–11, 1979, and a later version was presented at the militarization workshop held in Oslo in May 1981. Its Japanese version was published as an article in *Chuo Koron* in 1981; also Research Report no. 8 from the Institute for Peace Science, Hiroshima University, 1982.

Part 3

Local Experiences:
Historical Dimensions

5

Militarization in Thai Society

Chulacheeb Chinwanno

One of the most important developments in world politics in recent years has been the militarization of many countries of the Third World, including Thailand, a small country in Southeast Asia. Thailand seems to have become increasingly militarized since the Second World War, as the Thai armed forces have not only intervened in politics and ruled the country but also have expanded and dominated the society vertically and horizontally.

This militarization has probably been caused by several factors, internal as well as external. Conflicts within society, especially the challenge of the Communist party, or the perceived threat from neighboring countries can accelerate the militarization process. Militarization in a society can manifest itself in many forms and in many arenas—political and economic as well as social. This chapter is an attempt to investigate the militarization in Thailand, especially its causes and manifestations.

Definition of Militarization

Militarization is a concept that is very much related to the military or the armed forces. Although the term "militarization" is frequently used, it has rarely, if ever, been defined, theoretically or operationally, in the literature on military organization.

Moreover, militarization can be defined differently or mean different things to different people. Some may define militarization as the expansion of the size and role of the military, while others may define it as the domination of the military sector over the civilian sector. In my view, militarization refers to the process of transformation of society from a civilian to a military orientation. Therefore, "militarization" is defined here as "the process by which norms, institutions, and other aspects of society are penetrated, dominated, or influenced by the military establishment."

It has been argued by Hermann Heller, a noted social scientist, that the greater the physical danger to the state from within or without, the more intensive the development of the military organization will be. Militarism thus arises only when increases in military power relative to the political sector are out of proportion to the actual exigencies of the domestic or international situation. The same is true in the case of militarization. Militarization will increase as the armed forces penetrate into and dominate the civilian society.

The Military in Thai Society:
A Historical Perspective

Traditionally, Thailand was not a militarized society and had a rather small standing army. The traditional government and the farming masses were rather poor and existed in subsistence economy with little surplus. Hence, the soldiers were recruited only in time of war, and no training was required because the way of fighting was primitive. In peacetime, the soldiers were demobilized and returned to their former occupations while military commanders and officers were reassigned to civilian or administrative posts.

This simple defense system was inherited by the Thai monarch, Rama I, who founded the present Chakri dynasty in 1782.[1] Shortly after the founding of Bangkok as the new capital of Siam (the old name of Thailand), the Chakri monarchs came under severe pressure from European colonizers. Burma, a traditional rival to the west, was gradually subjugated by the British, and the French began their conquest of Indochina (present-day Vietnam, Laos, and Kampuchea). At first, the Chakri monarchs responded with an isolationist policy, closing the door even to trade, but they later realized the weakness of their armed forces and other vulnerabilities.

The closed-door policy followed by the first three Chakri monarchs was reversed by Rama IV, or King Mongkut (1851–1868), who recognized the need to accommodate Siam to European imperialism. King Mongkut thus negotiated treaties that formalized relations with Britain and other European countries, opened the country to commercial interaction with the West, and initiated several reforms to adapt the traditional bureaucracy to these changes.

However, it was King Mongkut's son, Rama V or King Chulalongkorn (1868–1910), who began to modernize systematically. The traditional feudalistic bureaucracy gave way to new organizations based on Western administrative principles, and the royal rule was extended into the bordering provinces, where local chieftains had until then been virtual sovereigns. Thus, the Thai kingdom was consolidated, and power was tightly centralized. Unlike their neighbors, the Thai people were able to enter the modern era of the twentieth century with their independence preserved, with their traditional authority symbol intact, and without the agony of colonial rule.[2]

The traditional system of defense also changed during the reign of Rama V as he felt that it was necessary to modernize and professionalize the armed forces to protect the country from imperialism and the gunboat policy of the European powers.[3] Therefore, the military establishment was reorganized and modernized. In 1870, Rama V organized a European-style military troop among his pages and recruited princes and sons of high officials to serve in it.[4] In 1887, a royal cadet school was established in order to train young officers, and a number of young Thais were also sent abroad to study modern military science. By the early twentieth century, a corps of professional officers with modern military knowledge had been created, and the military had become an institution that was differentiated from the rest of the royal bureaucracy. The armed forces then probably formed one of the most modern institutions in the Thai polity.

Thus, it was ironic that in 1932 the Thai absolute monarchy system was overthrown by these foreign-educated military officers and their civilian counterparts.[5] The breach between the Thai monarchy and the military was illustrative of the dilemma in any transitional society in which the ruler or the monarch seeks both to preserve authority and to modernize the country. The modernization of Thailand involved the centralization of political power in order to advance needed social and economic reforms. These reforms, especially the educational and bureaucratic ones,[6] resulted in a westernized and foreign-educated civil service and military officer corps, whose growing autonomy as social organizations gave them corporate identities and interests that were increasingly distinct from those of the monarchy. Education in Europe made many of these young officers and civilians acquainted with democratic ideas and representative government. The 1932 "revolution" changed the Thai absolute monachy into a constitutional monarchy and established the military as the dominant actor in Thai politics.[7] Since 1932, the military has intervened in politics several times, and the Thai society has become increasingly militarized.

Military Intervention:
A Manifestation of Militarization

Military intervention in politics through coups d'etat is a form of militarization. One study has estimated that more than two-thirds of the countries in the Third World have experienced some degree of military intervention in politics since 1945,[8] and another study has calculated that more than one-third of the governments represented in the United Nations in 1974 had come to power through a military coup.[9]

In many countries, this form of militarization has occurred so often that it has become institutionalized as a way for the military to participate in politics. However, scholars have not agreed on what motivates the military to intervene. Some cite regime vulnerability,[10] while others emphasize the organizational strength of the military.[11] Still others consider the socioeconomic or circumstantial factors,[12] and some distinguish between precondition and precipitant factors.[13] No matter what motivates the military to intervene in politics, military intervention through a coup d'etat as a form of militarization seems to be widespread in the Third World.

Thailand has been mostly ruled by the military in the fifty years since the absolute monarchy was overthrown in 1932, and it has achieved power as a result of coups d'etat and intervention. There have been nine successful coups d'etat (June 20, 1933; November 8, 1947; April 6, 1948; November 15, 1951; September 16, 1957; October 20, 1958; November 14, 1961; October 6, 1976; October 20, 1977) and seven abortive ones (October 11–27, 1933; January 29, 1938; October 1, 1948; February 26, 1949; June 29, 1951; March 26, 1977; April 1–3, 1981).

The military has consequently penetrated and controlled Thai politics on the national level. This aspect of militarization has been extensively analyzed by foreign and Thai scholars[14] and will be briefly discussed here. Several factors induced the Thai military to intervene and seize power. Although the generals have often claimed that they intervened in order to "protect the throne and the nation," they were in fact protecting their own political and financial interests, whether individual, factional, or corporate. The political ambitions of some military officers and the rivalries among different cliques were also important factors; weakness of the civilian regime and instability and disorder in the society, as perceived by the military, also prompted interventions.

After a successful coup, a new cabinet consisting of military and civilian leaders was usually set up to rule the country. Although most of the cabinet members were civilians, key positions, such as those of prime minister and ministers of defense, interior, foreign affairs, industry, and communication, often went to the military elites. The coup leader himself would head the cabinet or, in a few instances, entrust that power to a civilian puppet. As a result, from 1932 to 1982, there were forty-two cabinets and sixteen different prime ministers in Thailand, ten of whom were civilians and the rest, military officers. It is important to note that the ten civilian prime ministers combined occupied the office only nine years while the six military prime ministers were in power for forty-one years.

The repeated coups d'etat and threats or rumors of a coup have destabilized the legislative system. The Thai Parliament is a rather weak institution and is sometimes dominated by the military. It became usual that after a coup, a new legislature would be appointed by the military and a new constitution drafted, providing for a Senate, whose members were appointed, and a House of Representatives, whose members were elected. The majority of the appointed senators were military officers from the three services of the armed forces; army, navy, and air force—to make sure that the legislature would not act contrary to the wishes of the military-dominated regime.

Parliament at the time of writing was composed of the House of Representatives and the Senate. Members of the House had been elected in 1979, and the members of the Senate had been appointed by General Kriangsak Chamanand, then the head of the military junta and later prime minister. About 81.3 percent of the members of the Senate appointed by Kriangsak were military officers.[15] The dominance was somewhat reduced in 1981 when Prime Minister Prem Tinsulanon, Kriangsak's successor, appointed one-third of the Senate members to fill seats vacated by constitutional requirement, but the military-dominated Senate still played a crucial role in supporting the coalition government headed by General Prem Tinsulanon. The general elections in 1983 strengthened the parties critical of military rule in a new coalition government, again led by General Prem.

External Threats and Militarization

Thailand at present has the third largest armed force in Southeast Asia, after Vietnam and Indonesia. The size of the armed forces in 1982 was estimated at 233,000 men, excluding 500,000 trained reserves and about 600,000 paramilitary forces. The size of the armed forces represents an increase of more than seven times the size ten years previously, when Thailand had about 30,000 military men.

The defense budget has also increased significantly, rising from US $639 million in the fiscal year of 1976 to US $940 million, $1.09 billion, $1.28 billion, and $1.31 billion in the fiscal years of 1979, 1980, 1981, and 1982, respectively, roughly 16.7 percent, 19.5 percent, 19.9 percent, and 19.5 percent of the respective annual budgets for those fiscal years. Those figures do not even include the purchasing of weapons from the United States under the foreign military sale on credit program. Such credits and loans to Thailand totaled US $30 million, $36 million,

$50 million, and $80 million in 1979, 1980, 1981, and 1982, respectively, and in 1983, Thailand expected to receive as much as US $100 million for the purchase of arms and ammunition from the United States. In real terms, then, Thailand's defense budget is probably more than 20 percent of the country's national budget. The armed forces' expansion and budget increase further enhance the domination and influence of the military in Thai society.

The military leaders have argued that the armed forces and the budget need to be larger so as to strengthen the defense and protect the country from external threats. The Thai military officers have been deeply anticommunist and sensitive to developments and changes in neighboring countries, and Thailand's geographical location has also enhanced their concern about security problems. China, after being taken over by the Communists in 1949, has been perceived as an ambitious great power and a threat to Thai security, and the conflict in Indochina, where the Communist Vietminh was fighting the French for independence, was considered by the Thai military as the expansion of communism into Southeast Asia.

The military regime then decided to ally Thailand with the United States for protection against perceived external threats,[16] so the Military Assistance Agreement was signed in 1950 and a collective security treaty with the United States was signed in 1954. Military assistance, equipment as well as training, has strengthened the Thai armed forces, especially the army, and the alliance has made Thailand a partner of the United States in the Cold War between East and West.

In the 1960s, the Thai military collaborated even more with the United States in the latter's war effort in Vietnam. The military benefited a great deal from this close relationship, as the United States continued to support the military regime. The Thai generals also believed that fighting a war against communism outside their country was better than fighting one inside it. However, the situation started to change in 1970 when the United States, condemned by public opinion and nationwide protests, decided to withdraw its troops from South Vietnam and reduce its involvement in Southeast Asia. The war in Vietnam ended in 1975 when the Communists took over South Vietnam, Laos, and Kampuchea. Thailand tried to negotiate for peaceful coexistence with its Communist neighbors and decided to establish diplomatic relations with the People's Republic of China in 1975.

However, Thailand's external threat significantly changed in nature in the late 1970s as a consequence of violent conflicts among Communist states in Indochina. Vietnam, allied with the Soviet Union, invaded and occupied Kampuchea in 1979,[17] and the presence of 200,000 Vietnamese forces in Kampuchea and another 50,000 soldiers in Laos has created tension along the border Thailand shares with Kampuchea (798 kilo-meters) and Laos (1,750 kilometers) as well as instability in Southeast Asia. Since 1979, the Vietnamese forces have often staged summer military campaigns to eradicate the Khmer resistance forces near the Thai border, and they have sometimes crossed into Thailand, as happened in Non Mark Moon village in June 1980. Many Thai soldiers were killed in that incident, but the Vietnamese forces were also forced to return to Kampuchea. Foreign military incursions into Thailand occurred more often in 1982, and more shells were dropped inside the Thai border. The Thai military has used these incidents to pressure for more money, men, and equipment. Moreover, such events have also revived the fear of a Vietnam backed by the Soviet Union and have created an atmosphere favorable for the military to continue the militarization of and domination over Thai politics and society.

Internal Conflicts: Rural and Urban Unrest

The military in Thailand is also very much concerned about conditions in the rural areas where 80 percent of the Thai people live. The majority of these rural people are poor farmers and are not adequately provided for by the government. Moreover, they have sometimes been subjected to injustice or taken advantage of by government officials because of their innocence and illiteracy. The northeastern region, probably the poorest region in Thailand, is also the area where Communist insurgents have been most active. The Communist party of Thailand (CPT), formally established on December 1, 1942, spent several years building up its cadres and infrastructure, especially in the Northeast. The military regime under Field Marshal Pibul Songkram then enacted the Anti-Communist Act in 1952 and arrested several leftist politicians. From then on, the military embarked upon massive and repressive anticommunist campaigns. The suppressions by the military seemed to make things worse, as many innocent people were killed or arrested, so the Communist movement expanded and grew. With assistance from the Chinese Communist party and North Vietnam, the CPT insurgents were able to start a people's war, and their first armed clash with the government occurred in August 1965 in Nakorn Panom Province in the Northeast. Since then, more armed clashes have occurred, and from 1966 through 1972, the frequency of these clashes increased markedly from 155 to 680, with government troops suffering heavy casualties.[18]

In the 1970s, the military encountered opposition, not only from the Communist insurgents in the rural areas, but also from intellectuals and university students who demanded democracy. The intellectuals, including university instructors, were mostly foreign educated and quite progressive, and they spread the Western ideas of democracy, freedom, and equality and encouraged their students to pay attention to and participate in politics. University students thus organized into the National Students' Center of Thailand (NSCT), demonstrated and protested against military dictatorship, and demanded democratic processes and government. The military tried to suppress these mass-supported demonstrations but failed to do so.

The demonstrations turned into a student uprising that successfully overthrew the military dictatorship on October 14, 1973. The generals fled into exile, elections were held, and a civilian government ruled the country.[19] During the democratic interregnum, Thailand was quite unstable as the farmers, workers, and other interest groups demonstrated and protested for higher rice prices or higher wages. Strikes, labor unrests, and farmer protests were widespread. The military, disliking the instability, staged a coup on October 6, 1976, after a bloody massacre at Thammasat University in Bangkok,[20] and students and intellectuals fled to the jungle and joined the Communist party. After ruling the country for three years, the military junta decided to permit a general election in 1979 in order to gain legitimacy. Thus, the military has learned several lessons, the most important of which is that the role of the masses is important in contemporary Thai politics.

Militarization of Thai Society

In response to the rural unrest and the internal Communist threat, the Thai military authorities first set up an agency called Headquarters for National Safety (Kaw Raw Paw Klang) to coordinate the counterinsurgency activities. In 1965, the powerful Communist Suppression Operation Command (CSOC, later changed to Internal Security Operation Command, ISOC) was established to step up the Communist suppression campaigns while the Kaw Raw Paw Klang was put in charge of civic action programs in the remote areas. The military regime was using both military and socioeconomic means to combat the Communists in the rural areas.

The Kaw Raw Paw Klang set up many mobile development units to carry out such activities as road building and socioeconomic development projects such as water supply and sanitation projects in the rural and remote areas. These socioeconomic projects benefit the rural population and have provided an opportunity for the military to have a presence in the countryside, to gain access to the rural people as well as to earn their trust. Through this channel, the military has succeeded in penetrating and controlling the population of certain remote areas.

However, the most obvious manifestation of the militarization of Thai society is the proliferation of paramilitary forces, which were organized by the military in the late 1970s. In the rural, especially the "sensitive," areas, the villagers have been organized into National Defense Volunteers, or Thai Asa Pong Kan Chart units. The age of these volunteers ranges from eighteen to fifty years, and schools in the rural areas are used as training sites. These rural people are trained and controlled by the military, and their duty is to defend the villages from Communist insurgent attacks.

The urban population and the people in "nonsensitive" areas have been organized into another form of paramilitary organization called Look Soue Chao Baan, or Village Scouts. These people receive less military training but get more indoctrination into military values and nationalism. It is alleged that the main reason these paramilitary units in the urban areas were organized is so they can be used to counter mass organizations organized by progressive elements. The activities of the Village Scouts and Defense Volunteers receive extensive coverage in the national media, and generals often preside at mass gatherings and training ceremonies to give their blessing and support. It is obvious that more and more Thai people are being organized, influenced, and controlled by the military through these paramilitary organizations.

The military values, norms, and ideas are communicated not only to these organized paramilitary organizations but also to the general masses through the radio, television, and other mass media. It was estimated that in 1982, there were 235 radio stations in Thailand, more than half of which, or about 117 stations, belonged to the three services of the armed forces (91 belonged to the army; 22, to the air force; and 4, to the navy). There are also four television stations in Thailand, two of which belong to the army. These stations have been used by the military to promote ideas and transmit messages to influence public opinion.

The Thai armed forces, in addition to expanding their roles and penetrating into the political arena on the national as well as the grass-roots levels, have also penetrated into the economic realm by appointing senior military officers to be the chairmen or members of the boards of directors of many public enterprises—such as the State Railway Organization, the Port Authority of Thailand, the Thai International Airline, and the Telephone Organization of Thailand—in order to control and gain access to the economic resources of these enterprises. Membership on such boards represents one of the mechanisms of military penetration and control. The available economic resources can be allocated to the military's clients and supporters, which enhances the capability for further military influence and control.

Problems and Prospects

At present, the military seems to have gained control of and access to all sectors of Thai society. By virtue of the organizational strength of the military vis-à-vis the organizational weakness of the political parties and other pressure groups, the military is destined to maintain its pervasive power in society and to dominate Thai politics.

Militarization of the Thai society has been manifested in several forms: military interventions by coups d'etat, military rule, expansion of the rule of the military into economic and development arenas, and the proliferation of paramilitary organizations. Military norms and values have been promoted and have penetrated society through the armed-forces-operated media.

The process of militarization of Thai society has been caused by both internal and external factors. Conflicts within the society, especially the challenge of the Communist movement and the emergence of progressive mass organizations, have alarmed the military leaders, who have responded by setting up their own mass organizations in rural as well as in urban areas in order to combat the potential enemies. Externally, the events in Indochina, especially the perceived threat from Vietnam after its occupation of Kampuchea and the presence of Vietnamese forces along the eastern border of Thailand, have provided justification for further militarization.

Since neither the internal nor the external factors are likely to disappear, Thailand will continue to be militarized and dominated by the military. It is quite clear that as militarization increases, the influence of the Thai armed forces and their domination of Thai politics and society will also increase. Consequently, freedom is likely to be restricted, and different opinions on political, economic, and social issues may not be tolerated in the future by the military or the military-dominated regime. As a consequence, a stable and uninterrupted democratic process is likely to be an "impossible dream."

Notes

1. Chula Chakraponse, *Lord of Life: The Paternal Monarchy of Bangkok, 1782–1932* (London: Alvin Redman, 1960), pp. 4–7.

2. David J. Steinberg, ed., *In Search of Modern Southeast Asia* (New York: Praeger Publishers, 1971), pp. 176–179.

3. Paradi Mahakan, "The Genesis and the Role of Professional Soldiers in the Reign of King Rama V," in Kanala Sukpanich, ed., *The Military and Politics: Comparative Analysis* (Bangkok: Social Science Association of Thailand, 1980), p. 122.

4. Ibid., p. 123.

5. See Thawatt Mokarapong, *History of the Thai Revolution: A Study in Political Behaviour* (Bangkok: Siva Phorn, 1972).

6. David K. Wyatt, *The Politics of Reform in Thailand: Education in the Reign of King Chulalongkorn* (New Haven: Yale University Press, 1969), p. 78.

7. David A. Wilson, "The Military in Thai Politics," in John J. Johnson, ed., *The Role of the Military in Underdeveloped Countries* (Princeton: Princeton University Press, 1962), p. 259.

8. Eric A. Nordlinger, *Soldiers in Politics: Military Coups and Government* (Englewood Cliffs, N.J.: Prentice-Hall, 1977), p. xi.

9. Claude Welch and Arthur K. Smith, *Military Role and Rule* (North Scituate, Mass.: Duxbury Press, 1974), p. ix.

10. William Thompson, "Regime Vulnerability and the Military Coup," *Comparative Politics* 7:4 (July 1975), pp. 459–487.

11. Morris Janowitz, *The Military in the Political Development of the New Nations* (Chicago: University of Chicago Press, 1964), p. 11.

12. See Amos Perlmutter, *The Military and Politics in Modern Times* (New Haven: Yale University Press, 1977).

13. See S. E. Finer, *The Man on Horseback: The Role of the Military in Politics* (Baltimore: Penguin Books, 1976).

14. For example, Suchit Boonbongkarn, "Military Intervention of Thai Armed Force," in Sukpanich, *The Military and Politics,* and David Morell, "Thailand: Military Checkmate," *Asian Survey* 12:2 (February 1972), pp. 156–167.

15. Chai-anan Samudavanija, *Election, Political Parties, Legislature, and the Military* (Bangkok: Bankit, 1981), pp. 303–356.

16. Donald E. Nuechterlein, *Thailand and the Struggle for Southeast Asia* (Ithaca, N.Y.: Cornell University Press, 1965), p. 108.

17. Chulacheeb Chinwanno, "Conflicts in Indochina," *Journal of Social Sciences and Humanities* 3:2 (September-December 1979), pp. 70–86.

18. David Morell and Chai-anan Samudavanija, *Political Conflict in Thailand: Reform, Reaction, Revolution* (Cambridge, Mass.: Oelgeschlager, Gunn & Hain, 1981), pp. 82–83.

19. See Chulacheeb Chinwanno, "Crisis, Choice, and Change in Thai Politics: October 14, 1973, Incident" (Paper presented at the Association of Asian Studies Convention, San Francisco, March 1975).

20. Morell and Samudavanija, *Political Conflict,* pp. 273–276.

6
Militarization and Political Institutions in Chile

Carlos Portales

The presence of the military in Latin American domestic politics has undergone a process of institutionalization in recent years. Internationally, the result has been an increase in the chances of interstate conflict within the region. For people who are concerned with the authoritarian trends that that militarization implies on the level of internal politics, as well as the increase in international conflicts that may occur, the study of this phenomenon acquires special relevance. Understanding the causes of militarization, as well as its relationships with and its effects upon politics, is indispensable if one is to establish objectives of demilitarization that will contribute to the desired processes of internal democratization and to a lessening of the chances for international conflict.

The purpose of this chapter is to analyze the responses of Chilean political institutions to the processes of militarization that have occurred in different periods of the country's history and to analyze the consequences that these institutional solutions have had for civil-military relationships. In this endeavor, militarization will be understood as the "process whereby military values, ideology, and patterns of behavior achieve a dominating influence on the political, social, economic and external affairs of the State."[1] This process may differ in nature depending upon the interrelationships among the sociopolitical, economic, and organizational factors that bring it about.

In contrast to this process is civilian control of the military. According to Huntington,[2] civilian control may be "subjective"—if it is based on the maximization of power of certain government institutions, particular social classes, or constitutional forms that prevent the existence of an "independent military sphere"—or "objective"—if the professionalization of the armed forces is emphasized, stressing a functional distribution of power between civilians and the military. The Chilean cases that I have chosen for analysis illustrate this interrelation in different historical periods: that of the formation of the nation-state, the crisis of the "outward-oriented" development model, and the crisis of the "inward-oriented" development model. The Constitutions of 1833, 1925, and 1980 have all been different responses to the problem of militarization. The first two represent cases of military subordination to civilian power, and the last is an attempt to institutionalize the presence of the military as an independent actor in political life and to reinforce the militarization of civil society. References to the functioning of the constitutional systems of 1833 and 1925 and to the policies followed regarding the armed forces will make it clear that the objective pursued was one of demilitarization, in contrast to the policies of the present Chilean regime. In conclusion, I analyze the factors that tend to prolong the militarization of the present period.

The Armed Forces During the Nation-building Period

The long Chilean tradition of military subordination to civilian power cannot be understood without reference to the conservative oligarchic regime established after the civil war of 1830, which ended with the defeat of the liberal groups and the establishment of a civilian-controlled republic with strong authoritarian features. In contrast to other Latin American republics, the period of insurgent struggle and of political intervention by military chieftains who emerged from the struggle for independence did not last long in Chile. Conservative party control was institutionalized in the Constitution of 1833, which established a strict subordination of the military to a strong presidency.

The constitutional text prescribed the nonparticipation of the armed forces in national politics: "The Armed Forces and Police are essentially obedient. No armed body may deliberate" (art. 157). "Any resolution taken by the President, the Senate, or the Chamber of Deputies in the presence or on the demand of an army, a general at the head of his troops, or any popular assembly, with or without arms, in disobedience of the authorities, shall be null and void" (art. 158).

The president was granted extensive powers over the armed forces: to make all military appointments; to confer, with the approval of the Senate, the highest military ranks beginning with colonel in the army and captain in the navy (art. 82, no. 9); to organize and dispose of land and sea forces as he saw fit, with the approval of the Senate (art. 82, no. 16); personally to command these forces, with the approval of the Senate (art. 82, no. 17); and to declare war with the prior approval of the Congress (art. 82, no. 18). With regard to problems of public order, the president was granted extensive powers that permitted him to decree special states of emergency.[3]

Congress, on the other hand, was given the power to approve or reject a declaration of war (art. 36, no. 2); to fix annually, by law, the land and sea forces to be maintained in times of peace and war (art. 36, no. 3); to permit the entry of foreign troops onto Chilean territory, fixing the duration of their stay (art. 36, no. 7); to authorize the departure of national troops from Chilean territory, fixing the time for their return (art. 36, no. 9); and to allow the quartering of permanent army forces at the place where congressional sessions were held, or within ten leagues thereof (art. 36, no. 7). The only direct participation of a high-ranking armed forces officer in the bodies created by the Constitution was that an army or a navy general could be appointed by the president to serve on the State Council, a presidential advisory body.

It was intended that this normative system would put an end to the constant intervention of the military in the struggles of the different groups fighting for dominance within the emergent state. The problem had not been one of action by a professional army but rather of the use that political leaders and army officers had made of their power in a period when the question of hegemony within the country had not clearly been settled and political institutions had not yet been consolidated. Similar situations in other nations on the continent were to continue throughout the nineteenth century and, in some cases, into the twentieth.

After 1830, the landed oligarchy in Chile, led by a group of politicians headed by Diego Portales, the leading Chilean governmental figure of the period, became the hegemonic power within the state. The establishment of a political system with a very strong presidency and a military subordinated to civilian power did not just express itself in the constitutional text but was a political reality. Presidential power was strengthened by the control the government exercised over congressional elections, in which, for many years, a majority supporting the president was always chosen. With regard to the military, Portales forced veteran officers who had sympathized with liberal groups and simultaneously reorganized the militia, which was the true armed force of the landholding sector, to resign from the war for independence. "Upper class youth was to serve as the militia's officers, the people as its soldiers."[4] This armed counterpower was instrumental in neutralizing the military's political influence. Power, centralized in the presidency, was exercised for a period of twenty years by two former generals, Joaquín Prieto (1831–1841) and Manuel Bulnes (1841–1851), but as representatives of civilian power, not as a result of military intervention.

A system of subjective civilian control of the military, based upon the social hegemony of the landowning class and strong presidential power, was thus established. As a result of the low level of organization of the armed forces, it was possible to achieve military subordination in spite of the relative weakness of the new political system.

This system of civil-military relations was maintained for almost a century, despite internal social and political changes and the country's active foreign policy, which had an effect on the size and organization of the armed forces. Although this authoritarian order was not completely free from public disturbances and even armed uprisings (in 1851 and 1859), the liberalization of the system after the middle of the century assured the continuity of civilian power.

The active foreign policy pursued by the country during this same period[5] involved Chile in several wars, with the consequent growth and improved organization of its armed forces. But neither the war against the Peruvian-Bolivian Confederacy (1836–1839) nor the War of the Pacific against Peru and Bolivia (1879–1883) resulted in a drastic alteration of civil-military relationships. General Manuel Bulnes, commander of the army that defeated the Confederacy, was elected to the presidency in 1841 as the constitutional successor to General Prieto, and in 1881, General Manuel Baquedano, chief of the forces that had just conquered Lima, refused the presidential candidacy of the Conservative party at a moment when the war was still going on.

The tradition of military subordination was maintained as well during and after the civil war of 1891 when the armed forces split, the army taking sides with the president, and the navy, with the congressional majority. The political and economic issues on both sides were defined by civilian leaders. Admiral Jorge Montt was elected president after the victory of the congressional faction, and he governed in accordance with an interpretation of the Constitution that limited presidential powers. Tensions caused by the emergence of new social groups that expressed themselves in the political arena did not for the moment result in the breakdown of military subordination to civilian power.

However, the establishment in 1891 of a sui generis parliamentary regime, justified by an interpretation of the Constitution that allowed Congress to approve and to censure cabinets but refused the president the power to dissolve Congress, undermined one of the bases of civilian control: the power of the presidency. The civil war of 1891 was also the turning point in the professionalization of the armed forces. Military preparation had been weak during the nineteenth century, and throughout the War of the Pacific, the strategy and the conduct of the war had been controlled by the two civilian ministers of war who held office during the period. The defeat of the army in the civil war opened the way for a reform of that institution under the Prussian military mission of Colonel Emil Köerner.[6] At the same time, an English mission improved the organization of the navy. These professional transformations during the last decade of the nineteenth century and the first years of the twentieth were to influence heavily the intervention of the armed forces into polities during the 1920s and 1930s.

Military Subordination Under the Constitution of 1925

The military takeover in September 1924 put an end to the constitutional system of 1833. The military movement opposed the policies followed by the parliamentary majority, pressed for the approval of social legislation, and finally supported an alteration in the system of government itself, modifying constitutional norms in order to strengthen the power of the presidency. This breakdown of Chile's political institutions was the result of a profound crisis of oligarchic control and of the "outward-oriented" development model underlying it. The export economy, which had been based on nitrates, had collapsed after the discovery of artificial substitutes, and the traditional forms of sociopolitical control could no longer cope with the growing demands of those sectors of the middle and working classes that had achieved some degree of organization and power in Chilean society. On this occasion, however, the military did not simply support certain civilian groups in the struggle but developed a movement of its own, which continued to be active for almost a decade. The mere approval of the new Constitution of 1925 did not put an end to the militarization of Chilean politics, and civilian control was not really reestablished until 1932.

The principal political reform contained in the new Constitution restored the separation of powers between the president and Congress and strengthened the president's control of the executive by granting him the power to appoint ministers of state without congressional approval. The articles concerning the relationships between the military and the government reproduced almost word for word the provisions that had been contained in the Constitution of 1833. Articles 22 and 23 of the Constitution of 1925 corresponded to articles 157 and 158 of the text of 1833. They established the absolute subordination of the armed forces and police to the civilian authorities, the nondeliberative character of those institutions, and the nullity of all government resolutions adopted under threat of force. The new Constitution also established that no armed body could requisition property or exact aid of any kind unless authorized to do so by civilian authority (art. 10, no. 4—art. 150 in the Constitution of 1833).

The president was empowered to "maintain public order and the external security of the Republic, in accordance with the Constitution and the laws" (art. 71). He was given extensive authority with regard to the armed forces: "to organize and dispose of land and sea forces, as he sees fit" (art. 72, no. 13); "to make all military appointments, in accordance with relevant legal provisions, and to confer, with the approval of the Senate, the highest military ranks beginning with colonel in the Army and captain in the Navy" (art. 72, no. 7); "personally to command land and sea forces, with the approval of the Senate" (art. 72, no. 14); to declare war with prior congressional authorization (art. 72, no. 15); and "to declare the state of assembly in one or more provinces invaded or threatened with invasion in case of foreign war, and the state of siege in one or several points of the Republic in case of foreign attack" (art. 72, no. 17). He could furthermore declare a state of siege in cases of internal disturbance with the approval of Congress or, if Congress was not in session, without it but only for a predetermined period (art. 72, no. 1). Finally, the president was authorized to decree additional expenditures, not exceeding annually 2 percent of the total amount authorized in the General Budget Law, in the case of foreign aggression (art. 72, no. 10).

It fell to Congress to fix the complement of standing land and sea forces in times of peace and war (art. 44, no. 9), thereby eliminating the periodicity of such laws established by the Constitution of 1833; "to permit the entry of foreign troops onto the territory of the Republic, while at the same time determining the period they may remain" (art. 44, no. 10); "to authorize the departure of national troops from the territory of the Republic, determining the time of their return" (art. 44, no. 11); and to approve or reject any declaration of war proposed by the president (art. 44, no. 12).

The Constitution also established the public obligation of military service, to be regulated by law (art. 10, no. 9, para. 5 and para. 6). Finally, it exposed generals and admirals of the armed forces to political trial for seriously jeopardizing the security and honor of the nation (art. 39, no. 1d).

The constitutional text, voted less than a year after the military burst into political life, was not enough to resist the process of militarization. The movement that had been unfolding within the armed forces since the beginning of the century combined criticism of parliamentarianism with an industrializing ideology. Its postulates included institutional demands for professional independence from congressional interference in military promotions and other internal armed forces matters. The movement also stressed the inadequacy of the industrial base, an essential source of supply for the armed forces in a period when foreign resources were totally lacking.

The Constitution might have formally strengthened the executive branch, but it could not increase the relative weight of the emerging but weak industrial sector facing a declining but still strong oligarchy. The possibilities for civilian promotion of an industrial development program were also limited by military distrust of the emergent lower-class movement.[7]

Against this background, General Carlos Ibáñez del Campo seized power in 1927 and began to enact industrializing policies: the introduction of protective tariffs; provision of tax incentives; and the expansion of the internal market as a result of the reorganization of the state apparatus (which implied the growth of the bureaucracy), of public works expenditures, and of the income redistribution generated by the application of new social legislation.[8] These measures did not have the hoped-for activating effect on the economy, because of the severity of the 1929 world economic crisis. Moreover, the government's dictatorial character alienated very diverse sectors of the population, which finally united in a broad civilian movement that encompassed practically the entire political spectrum.

Military subordination to civilian power, as established formally in the Constitution of 1925, did not really begin to take hold until toward the end of 1932, a year after Ibáñez's fall. The election to the presidency of Arturo Alessandri, who had been a populist leader in the 1920s, meant the reestablishment of "civilianism" under the hegemony of the right, representing the landholding oligarchy. The founding of a civilian oligarchic Republican Militia of a clearly extraconstitutional character was a reaction against the military interventions of 1932, which at one point had given rise to a short-lived Socialist Republic.[9]

The stability of the new civil-military relationship was only assured when the Popular Front came to power in 1938. This center-left political coalition favored an industrializing policy that led to the development of an industrial bourgeoisie that was extremely dependent upon the state apparatus. This same government was the instrument for shaping a compromise between the middle and working classes, which, at the same time, constituted a source of stability for the system.

Against this sociopolitical background, the armed forces founded their institutional identity on autonomous professional development under the supervision of the constitutional authorities,[10] a system of objective civilian control.

If we compare the process of militarization of Chilean political life at the beginning of the country's independent existence with that which unfolded during the years 1920–1930, we find that both occurred in the context of crises of the political system, which, in turn, were the result of a deeper social hegemonic crisis. During the independence era the movement had been led by the leaders of an army that was still weak in terms of professional development, but in the 1920s it emerged from a professionalized institution with strong corporate features. In the first case, the military had no governmental model of its own to offer while in the second it did, and only its failure, together with the reorganization of the dominant sectors, permitted a return to a military subordinate to civilian power.

Subordination and Professional Development

If the post-1932 application of the constitutional norms of 1925 is analyzed, we find that the armed forces remained subordinated to the president but that their activities tended to remain outside democratic control, particularly the control that should have been exercised by Congress. One might say that a space was created for them to pursue their institutional development unmolested, within a formal framework of subordination to the constitutional authorities.

On several occasions, Congress surrendered to the president its powers to alter regulations concerning military professional advancement and staff and retirement rules (e.g., in 1944, 1948, 1961, and 1971); in other instances, it acceded to a restrictive interpretation of these powers. A landmark case occurred in 1966 when the Senate Defense Committee undertook to examine the conduct of several high-ranking officers during a past state of emergency, prior to granting the essential Senate approval of their promotions. The executive, however, argued that an inquiry into the officers' professional behavior fell within the jurisdiction of the military courts and that Senate interference in such questions would be detrimental to the principle of absolute obedience of the armed forces.[11] The Senate backed down and accepted the executive's position.

Generally speaking, the broad outlines of defense policy were excluded from national debate, with the consequent introduction of doctrines in the armed forces that would prove disruptive to the system later on. In 1942, law no. 7, 144, created the Superior Council of National Defense to "advise the government in the study and solution of problems referring to national defense concerning the external security of the country." This body was composed of the ministers of national defense, treasury, and foreign affairs, as well as the commanders-in-chief and chiefs-of-staff of the armed forces. In 1960, making use of powers granted him by Congress, the president replaced this council with another called the Superior Council of National Security (D.F.L. no. 181, March 23, 1960). This new body was granted broad jurisdiction over all matters concerning the "security of the nation" and the maintenance of its territorial integrity. Here, the concept of national *security* is added to that of national defense, a concept that, as we shall see later on, had been incorporated into the military's ideological outlook. The president himself presided over this council, which was composed of the ministers of the interior, national defense, foreign affairs, economy, and treasury, as well as the commanders-in-chief and the chiefs-of-staff of the army, navy, and air force.

The progressive blurring of differences between external and internal security is another important phenomenon to be considered in the analysis of civil-military relationships during this period. It must be recalled that in 1927, during the administration of General Ibáñez, the different police forces were unified into the Cuerpo de Carabineros de Chile. This militarized police force was thereafter to be responsible for the maintenance of internal public order. Although under presidential command, like the armed forces, it was placed within the Ministry of the Interior, not the Ministry of Defense. Some authors believe this was done to create a counterweight to the armed forces.[12] The existence of this singular police force was nonetheless no obstacle to the use of the armed forces by various administrations to curb problems of domestic order, although the legal procedure employed involved violating the Constitution itself.

The constitutional text provided that the norms restricting constitutional rights in cases of internal disturbance could only be applied after the declaration of a state of siege by Congress or, in exceptional cases when it was not in session, by the president. Congress also had the authority to pass a special law empowering the president to restrict personal liberty and freedom of the press and to suspend or restrict the right of assembly. In order to circumvent the congressional approval required in such cases (e.g., to declare a state of siege), different administrations made use of the declaration of zones of emergency. This extraconstitutional juridical form was originally devised during the Second World War to permit the placing under military jurisdiction of those parts of the national territory designated by the president in case of foreign attack, invasion, or sabotage directed against national security. These provisions were gradually extended to cover situations of internal disturbance.

In 1947 and 1948 such zones of emergency were established by special laws passed by Congress (laws 8837, 8942, 8960). However, between 1948 and 1958, in a gradual process culminating in the Internal State Security Law of 1958 (no. 12927), Congress abdicated its constitutional powers in this area. In technical violation of the constitutional text, the president thereby acquired powers to decree zones of emergency without prior congressional approval. In 1960 a statute was enacted that authorized the declaration of zones of emergency in cases of public calamity, such as earthquakes (no. 13959). The executive branch was thus conceded broad powers to declare such special zones without congressional control. In this context, the armed forces were repeatedly called upon to perform police functions when internal order was threatened.[13]

Furthermore, the armed forces were progressively authorized to participate in different aspects of national life: in the production of arms and military equipment; cartography; aerial photogrammetry; the control of fluvial, ocean, and air traffic; sporting activities; labor education; telecommunications; meteorology; etc.[14] The military institutions, which were not subject to democratic control, thus increasingly permeated state activities.

In 1971 a constitutional reform was enacted to reinforce the institutional segregation of the armed forces in order to avoid the democratizing influence of the recently elected Popular Unity government. The Christian Democratic party, as a precondition to voting for Allende in a decisive joint session of Congress,[15] insisted on the passage of a specific constitutional amendment tightening the norms regarding the autonomy of the armed forces. The text approved stated that

> the Public Force is solely and exclusively constituted by the Armed Forces and the *Cuerpo de Carabineros,* institutions which are essentially professional, hierarchical, disciplined, obedient, and non-deliberative. The complement of these institutions must be fixed by statute. Recruitment into the Armed Forces and *Carabineros* may only occur through their own specialized, institutional schools, except in the case of personnel to perform exclusively civilian functions. [art. 22]

The purpose of guaranteeing the corporate segregation of the military in 1971 cannot be analyzed in a vacuum. One must take into account the fact that the armed forces had established international ties that had generated a high degree of organization and professionalization, and furthermore that Chilean society was entering a period of deep polarization, the consequence of the exhaustion of the import-substitution model of economic development and of the attempt to apply a socialist model to replace it.

The Chilean armed forces, like their counterparts in the rest of Latin America, had developed a special relationship with the U.S. armed forces. In 1936 the countries in the region had subscribed to a U.S. hemispheric security policy, and following the Second World War, the Interamerican Mutual Assistance Pact and the U.S. Military Aid Program had institutionalized military-political relationships among the hemisphere's military organizations. Between 1946 and 1977, the Chilean armed forces received U.S. military aid totaling $172.7 million,[16] and between 1950 and 1977, 6,833 Chilean military personnel were trained under the auspices of the U.S. International Military Educational and Training Program.[17] The consequences were an increased professionalization of the Chilean armed forces as well as the transmission of anti-Soviet ideological positions. As Chile's national security doctrine developed, these elements were combined with geopolitical ideas that had deep roots in Chilean military thought.[18] The political role that such conceptions suggested was to have important implications at a moment when the society was again suffering a crisis of hegemony.

The government's attempts to apply a socialist model of development resulted in severe social polarization and were met with a resistance that led to confrontation. The rebellion of the political right—and that of the center, which had fallen into a position of strategic subordination to the right—led to the coup d'etat on September 11, 1973. The collapse of the system of objective civilian control of the armed forces was the end result of Chilean social dynamics as well as of a peculiar process of military development segregated from the civilian sphere.

Militarization and the Government of the Armed Forces

Since 1973, military supremacy within the political system has supplanted civilian control of the armed forces. The first decree of the governing junta (law no. 1, September 11, 1973) assigned the armed forces a supraconstitutional role, proclaiming that "the Public Force represents the organization that the State has given itself to protect and defend its physical and moral integrity and its cultural and historical identity" and undertaking the commitment to restore "Chileanness" (*chilenidad*), justice, and the ruptured institutional order. The junta, which was composed of the commanders-in-chief of the army, the navy, and the air force and the general director of the Carabineros, later explicitly assumed constituent, legislative, and executive powers (art. 1 of law no. 257, June 17, 1974). Only the judiciary remained formally untouched, but government policies and judicial self-effacement have combined, in practice, to restrict severely the judiciary's constitutional powers.

This transformation of the role of the military in the Chilean political system has become somewhat permanent as a result of the militarization process related to the new internal socioeconomic project, which was imposed under the aegis of the armed forces, and of the professional development of Chile's military organization. The international political and military situations in Latin America have also had a part in these developments.

As I have already noted, the breakdown of the constitutional regime and of the subordination of the armed forces to civilian power occurred in the context of a hegemonic crisis and a crisis in the economic development model. However, in 1973, in contrast to 1925, the armed forces had not developed an alternative model; they simply reacted against a movement and a government that they perceived to be acting contrary to their concept of national security.

The rooting out of the socialist model and of the forces that supported it required the destruction of democratic political forms and the dismembering of the social bases of the preexisting state. In this context, the military adopted the development model subscribed to by sectors that were related to international finance capital and that, based on a monetarist liberal ideology, sought to make the Chilean economy a part of the transnational world. The new model's dynamism was supposed to result from its relations with the international market.[19] This new model implied a deep transformation not only of the state and the economy but of Chilean society, and consequently it required a permanent and systematic use of force.[20] The merging of the military concept of national security with the project of transnationalization in this reshaping of society has been a prime factor in reinforcing the process of militarization.[21]

The postwar process of military professionalization, which resulted from contact with the U.S. armed forces, not only produced changes in the organizational forms of the Latin American and Chilean armed forces but also engendered a qualitative change in the demand for arms. During the 1950s, such demands were mainly satisfied through a transfer of Second World War and Korean War surplus materials, and in the early 1960s, U.S. emphasis on internal security led to a transfer of antisubversive war materials. In the mid-1960s, however, a split began to appear between U.S. objectives and the demands of Latin American armed forces, whose interest in acquiring sophisticated arms was contrary to U.S. arms transfer policies. Despite U.S. emphasis on internal security, Latin American armed forces had not abandoned their concern about external defense since their concept of national security encompassed both dimensions. The degree of professionalization attained spurred the demand for more sophisticated arms, as well as for the resources needed to obtain them. These demands, a consequence of institutional development, have been a second factor favoring the process of militarization in Latin America.

Finally, the change in the character of U.S. arms transfers to Latin America was only possible because of a modification of the international political and military context, in which the détente between the United States and the Soviet Union permitted a diversification of arms suppliers as well as a weakening of inter-American ties. Under these international conditions, and on a continent where the military establishments have grown in power and in numerous cases control the government, old interstate conflicts have sprung up again.[22] The resulting arms race, posited as a necessary response to potential conflicts, has been a third factor reinforcing the militarization process.[23]

The reasons for the increased militarization that I have indicated are destined to have longer-range effects than those that existed in previous periods. The transnationalization of the Chilean economy is founded upon a deep change in internal social relations, and its guarantor is the armed forces. The demise of the democratic system of 1925 has led to a dismembering of social arrangements that for forty years had permitted increasing popular participation. The role of the state in the management of the economy has been drastically reduced, and the initial purge of the labor unions and subsequent changes in the labor laws have resulted in a deep decline in wages. The social security system has been transformed into a profitable business for the private sector, which has resulted in the elimination of employers' contributions and a reduction of benefits for pensioners. All cultural activities are subject to censorship, and the entire educational system, public and private, is strictly controlled by the state.

All these measures have been carried out in a country that has been ruled for almost ten years under conditions of a state of siege and state-of-emergency decrees. Military officers have been in direct and permanent charge of the government and of public order in every administrative region of the country. At the same time, the high levels of profession-alization of the armed forces in neighboring countries and the arms race within the region have reinforced military intervention in state affairs. All of these factors contributed to the creation of a new constitutional framework that awards military values, ideology, and positions dominant influence in state social, economic, political, and international policies.

"The Constitution of National Security"

Although the Constitution of 1980, by its own terms, will not come fully into effect until 1989, a study of it illuminates the new type of civil-military relations being sought by the current Chilean regime: the establishment of a tutelary "national security" power to safeguard the values embodied in the Constitution and the political system it creates. This national security power is conceived of as being an essential instrument in assuring the subordination of civilian to military values and patterns of behavior in the country's political organization and processes.

National Security as a Key Concept

Article 1 of the Constitution proclaims that the state must preserve national security (para. 5). The very position of this concept in the text reveals its importance in the new political system that is being established.

The provisions governing constitutional amendments indirectly reaffirm the weight attributed to that concept: The chapters on the "Basis of the Institutions" (I), on the "Constitutional Court" (VII), on the "Armed and Police Forces" (X), and on the "National Security Council" (XI) may only be altered if the modifications in question are approved by a two-thirds majority of all members of both houses in two consecutive Congresses (art. 188). For all practical purposes, then, these chapters simply cannot be amended.

It is every citizen's duty to preserve national security as well as "to honor the Fatherland, to defend its sovereignty, and to contribute to the preservation of national security and the essential values of Chilean tradition" (art. 22, para. 2). The obligation of military service derives directly from this duty (art. 22, para. 3).

National security is held to justify numerous limitations on the rights established elsewhere in the Constitution: on academic freedom (art. 19, no. 11, para. 2), on freedom of association (art. 19, no. 15, para. 4), on the freedom to work (art. 19, no. 16, para. 3), on the right to strike (art. 19, no. 16, final paragraph), on free enterprise (art. 19, no. 21, para. 1), on the right of property (art. 19, no. 24, para. 2), and most notably in the cases of mining property (art. 19, no. 24, para. 10), copyrights, royalties, and industrial property (art. 19, no. 25, para. 4).

Further, the existence of a specific threat to national security may lead to the establishment of one of the constitutionally authorized states of emergency—in theory, temporary states—during which most civil and political rights are effectively abolished. In case of foreign war, a state of assembly may be declared (art. 40, no. 1); internal war or uprisings justify the declaration of a state of siege (art. 40, no. 2); and severe disturbances of domestic public order, or any other threat to national security of domestic or foreign origin, permit the declaration of a state of emergency (art. 40, no. 3).

The National Security Power

The constitutional text nowhere explicitly defines the concept of national security. In practice, the armed forces themselves are to give it operational content through a series of complex constitutional mechanisms. The Constitution gives the armed forces a high degree of autonomy and makes them the true trustees of the new constitutional system.

The cornerstone of the mechanism is the concept of sovereignty. Article 5 states that sovereignty "resides essentially in the Nation" and "is exercised by the People by plebiscite and also through the authorities that this Constitution establishes." However, some of the most important authorities in whom the actual exercise of sovereignty is thus vested are not subject to electoral control, either direct or indirect. The most important example is the armed forces and the Carabineros, who are empowered to guarantee "the institutional order of the Republic." In its role of guarantor, the military has almost complete autonomy with regard to the other authorities established in the Constitution.

The Status of the Armed Forces

Article 90 states that "the Armed Forces are composed solely of the Army, the Navy, and the Air Force; their purpose is to defend the Fatherland; they are essential for national security and they guarantee the institutional order of the Republic" (para. 2). The same article adds that "the Carabineros shall also have, together with the Armed Forces, the mission to guarantee the institutional order of the Republic" (para. 3). In contrast with the function of ensuring national defense, which is basically a professional one, the function of preserving national security, as it has been defined by Chilean military doctrine, goes beyond professional parameters to encompass the social and economic organization of the country as well as its internal politics. The obligation to guarantee the institutional order of the republic has a clear political character: to supervise the functioning of the new constitutional system.

The Constitution establishes that "the Armed Forces and Carabineros, as armed bodies, are essentially obedient and non-deliberative. Forces depending upon the ministry in charge of National Defense shall be furthermore professional, hierarchical, and disciplined" (art. 90, para. 4). Professionalism is to be guaranteed by the standards regarding admission into the armed forces and the Carabineros (art. 91) and those related to appointments, promotions, and the retirement of officers (art. 94). Military hierarchy and discipline limit armed and police force members' rights to legal defense, which are "governed in administrative and disciplinary matters by their respective internal statutes" (art. 19, no. 3). In this manner, the values of hierarchy, obedience, and nondeliberation, which are rooted in the Chilean military tradition of professionalism, become the instrument of the armed forces high command or, more precisely, of the commanders-in-chief, permitting them to exercise the trusteeship granted by the Constitution and avoiding politicization and the eventual fragmentation of the military institutions.

Corporative semi-autarchy, the source of the military's political power, is secured by severe limitations on the president's power to select the commanders-in-chief of the army, navy, and air force and the general director of the Carabineros. The relevant provision indicates that they "shall be appointed by the President of the Republic from among the five senior generals eligible under their respective institutional statutes; they shall hold office for four years, may not twice serve, and may not be removed during their term of office" (art. 93, para. 1). The constitutional text does state that "in certain cases the President of the Republic, in accordance with the National Security Council, may retire from active service the Commanders-in-Chief of the Army, the Navy, and the Air Force, and the General Director of Carabineros" (art. 93, para. 2). However, since the commanders-in-chief and the general director make up the majority of the National Security Council, this provision could only be applied very exceptionally, and in no case in which the three commanders-in-chief and the general director were united in opposition.

Thus, a distorted professionalism becomes apparent. The professional tradition developed under the Constitution of 1925, which supported military subordination to civilian power, is transformed into societal and institutional subordination to military patterns defined by the commanders-in-chief.

The National Security Council

The National Security Council is the channel established by the Constitution to express the will of the commanders-in-chief and the general director of the Carabineros (chap. XI). The other members of this body are the president, who is its chairman, and the presidents of the Senate and the Supreme Court (art. 95, para. 1). The council may not meet unless at least a majority of its membership is present. At least one commander-in-chief or the general director of the Carabineros must therefore attend for the council simply to enter into session (art. 95, para. 3).

The principal prerogative of the National Security Council is "to express to any authority established by the Constitution its opinion with respect to any fact, act, or matter which in its judgment seriously threatens the institutional order or may compromise national security" (art. 96b). These resolutions or opinions may be made public or not as the council decides in each case (art. 96, para. 2).

Besides this broad trusteeship granted the council, it may, at the president's request, advise him in any matter linked to national security (art. 96a); on its own responsibility, give its advice with respect to matters that under the Constitution must be treated by statutes proposed by the president (art. 96c and art. 60, no. 14); and request from all political and administrative authorities any and all information related to internal or external state security (art. 96d). The council's further powers (art. 96a) include consenting to a presidential decree of a state of assembly, state of siege (pending congressional approval), state of emergency, or state of catastrophe. The application of the constitutional states of exception thus requires the agreement of the armed forces, with the exception of a state of siege, which must eventually be approved by Congress (art. 40). The National Security Council also has the power to declare the existence of a threat of war, thereby authorizing the Central Bank (an autonomous institution under the Constitution) to acquire, grant, or finance special credits to the state and public or private entities (art. 98, para. 3).

The National Security Council also chooses "a former Commander-in-Chief of the Army, of the Navy, and of the Air Force, as well as a former General Director of Carabineros, all of whom must have served for at least two years, as senators for an eight-year term" (art. 45, para. 3d). The council appoints two of the seven members, all attorneys, of the Constitutional Court (art. 81c), a special judicial body created to determine the constitutionality of statutes, decrees, etc.

With these extensive powers, the National Security Council, which is controlled by the commanders-in-chief and the general director of the Carabineros, may effectively intervene in any political or governmental matter.

The Armed Forces and Other State Authorities

Further constitutional provisions govern the relationships between the armed forces and other public authorities and also strengthen the autonomy and power of the armed forces in comparison with the norms set forth in previous Chilean constitutions.

Although the president is vested with authority with regard to all matters "concerning the conservation of internal public order and the external security of the Republic" (art. 24, para. 2), and under the new Constitution his powers in these matters have in fact been strengthened with respect to the Congress, his exercise of these powers is nonetheless subject in practice to the agreement of the commanders-in-chief of the armed forces and the general director of the Carabineros.

I have already noted that the National Security Council must consent to the decreeing of almost all the constitutional states of exception; that it may previously express its opinion on matters of statute law that are reserved for presidential initiative; and that it may, in addition, express its opinion to the president or to any other constitutional authority with regard to any fact, act, or matter that it feels seriously threatens the bases of institutional order or compromises national security. Moreover, the president's powers regarding appointments and removals in the armed forces and the Carabineros are restricted (art. 32, no. 18). His authority to dispose of land, sea, and air forces, and to organize and distribute those forces, must respect the requirements of national security (art. 32, no. 19). In case of a declaration of war, in addition to the traditional requirement of congressional authorization, the president also must first hear the opinion of the National Security Council (art. 32, no. 21).

Congress retains its power to impeach "generals or admirals of the Forces of National Defense for seriously compromising the honor or the security of the Nation" (art. 48, no. 2d, and art. 49, no. 1) and has the power to determine "the land, sea, and air forces to be maintained in times of peace and war" as well as the norms permitting the entry of foreign troops into the country and those concerning the departure of national troops outside the borders (art. 60, no. 13). Congress also retains the power to authorize a declaration of war, at the request of the president (art. 60, no. 15). Nevertheless, besides the limitations resulting from the powers of the National Security Council, the Senate has lost its prerogative to approve promotions to the higher ranks of the armed forces. Furthermore, members of Congress may be stripped of their office if, orally or in writing, they instigate the alteration of public order, propose changes in the constitutional scheme by any means other than those established in the Constitution itself, or seriously compromise the security or honor of the nation (art. 57, para. 5).

Finally, the powers of the Supreme Court to review decisions of military courts in time of war has been eliminated (art. 79, para. 1). And it must be recalled that the National Security Council is empowered to express its opinion to all other constitutional authorities, including the judiciary.

The armed forces and the Carabineros also have a direct hand in regional government through their representatives on the regional councils of development (art. 101). These councils appoint the mayors who are in charge of municipal administration (art. 108), a key office in the new administrative system.

When the new constitutional system comes completely into force, presumably in 1989, the armed forces and the Carabineros will thus be its tutor and principal buttress, completely reversing the pre-1973 tradition of military subordination to civilian control.

Professionalism, Corporatism, and Civil-Military Relations

Study of the Constitutions of 1833, 1925, and 1980 reveals three different responses to crises in the system of power relations in Chile and to the subsequent irruption of the armed forces into the political realm. The structures created in the 1830s were in answer to the problems of building a political system for the newly born nation-state. The structures established in the 1920s and 1930s were in response to the crises of the outward-oriented model of economic development and of the parliamentary system of government. And the current regime and its Constitution are an attempt to resolve the crisis of the inward-oriented model of economic development and a reaction against the socialist project of the Popular Unity coalition.

The applications of the constitutional systems of 1833 and 1925 were not immediate, and those systems only came into full practical effect once stable hegemonic alliances of political domination were established, led by the landowners at the beginning of the nineteenth century and by the middle classes in the 1930s. The continuity of both systems was assured by their ability to progressively incorporate new emergent social groups. By contrast, the Constitution of 1980 is designed to exclude permanently important groups from socioeconomic development and political life. The system thus requires a military trustee to guarantee its stability.

The level of professionalization of the armed forces at these three points in Chilean history has been very different. In the early nineteenth century, members of the armed forces had almost no professional training, so the remolding of the military by the forgers of the 1833 Constitution was relatively easy. By the beginning of the twentieth century, professionalization and corporative identity had attained high levels; the armed forces' return to the barracks in 1932 only occurred after the practical failure of the military intervention had begun to endanger corporate unity. In the 1970s, not only had professionalization increased, but the armed forces' very concept of their corporate role impelled them to invade almost every important realm of national life.

In each historical case, different levels of socioeconomic and political development, as well as of professionalization of the armed forces, gave rise to distinct systems of civil-military relationships. In 1833, "subjective" civilian control was based upon the social force of the landowners and the political supremacy of the presidency; in 1925, "objective" civilian control was based upon a progressively expanding democratic system and the separation of the political and military spheres; and at present, there is civilian subordination to the military's definition of national security.

The earlier systems of civil-military relations permitted the development of a tradition of military subordination to civilian power. This tradition, created at the beginning of the nineteenth century, was maintained until 1924 and permitted military professional development at the end of the nineteenth and the beginning of the twentieth centuries without risking the political intervention of the armed forces. The crisis of 1924 began an eight-year incursion of the military into politics.

In 1932 the tradition was renewed, and the armed forces were awarded an independent sphere within which they might pursue their corporate development. This independence, however, led to the segregation of the military and thereby facilitated the subsequent development of antidemocratic doctrines and values, which only became visible after 1973.

Under the present military regime, professionalism and hierarchical discipline have been utilized by the commanders-in-chief to avoid the politicization and fragmentation of the military. At the same time, their control of their respective institutions has permitted the political authorities to subordinate civil society to the purposes of the military. This distorted professionalism is institutionalized in the Constitution of 1980.

The rebuilding of a system of civil-military relations that again subordinates the armed forces to civilian power will require not only the establishment of a new democratic regime but a transformation of the military. Objective civilian control will not suffice to alter the military's peculiar concept of its role in society. It will be necessary to establish a new system of subjective civilian control that is based upon the armed forces' strict adherence to democratic principles and upon control of the military by authorities who are directly or indirectly accountable to the people.

Notes

1. This is the definition of militarization given by the World Council of Churches' Working Group on Militarism—see Ulrich Albrecht, "Militarism and Underdevelopment" (Paper presented to the Conference Workshop on Militarism and Disarmament in the Third World, Institute of Development Studies at the University of Sussex, April 1959), p. 4.

2. Samuel P. Huntington, *The Soldier and the State* (New York: Vintage Books, 1957), pp. 80–97.

3. Traditionally, constitutions in civil law countries have contained provisions permitting the executive to suspend certain constitutional guarantees and to

exercise special powers in rigorously defined emergency situations (e.g., a state of siege, a state of emergency).

4. Alberto Edwards, *La organización política de Chile* (Santiago: Editorial del Pacífico, 1955), p. 111.

5. Robert N. Burr, *By Reason or Force: Chile and the Balancing of Power in South America, 1830–1905* (Berkeley: University of California Press, 1974).

6. Frederic Nunn, "Emil Körner and the Prussianization of the Chilean Army: Origins, Process, and Consequences, 1885–1920," *Hispanic American Historical Review* 50:2 (May 1970), pp. 300–322.

7. Genaro Arriagada, *El pensamiento político de los militares* (Santiago: Centro de Investigaciones Socioeconómicas, 1981), pp. 71–107.

8. Augusto Varas, Felipe Agüero, and Fernando Bustamante, *Chile, democracia, fuerzas armadas* (Santiago: Facultad Latinoamericana de Ciencias Sociales, 1980), pp. 66–67.

9. Alejandro Silva Bascuñán, *Tratado de derecho constitucional tomo III* (Santiago: Editorial Jurídica de Chile, 1963), pp. 351–352.

10. Varas, Agüero, and Bustamante, *Chile,* pp. 71–84.

11. Carmen Undurraga and Arturo Frei B., *Bases constitucionales de la fuerza pública* (Santiago: Editorial Jurídica de Chile, 1967), pp. 70–84.

12. For example, Alain Joxé, *Las fuerzas armadas en el sistema político chileno* (Santiago: Editorial Universitaria, 1970).

13. Undurraga and Frei B., *Bases constitucionales,* pp. 167–185.

14. Augusto Varas, "La intervención civil de las fuerzas armadas," in Hugo Frühling, Carlos Portales, and Augusto Varas, *Estado y fuerzas armadas* (Santiago: Stichting Rechtshulp Chili and Facultad Latinoamericana de Ciencias Sociales, 1982), pp. 59–81.

15. Under the Constitution of 1925, the president was chosen by popular election. However, if no candidate had obtained an absolute majority, a joint session of Congress chose between the two candidates who had obtained the highest number of votes.

16. United States Agency for International Development, *Overseas Loans and Grants and Assistance from International Organizations,* Obligations and Loan Authorizations July 1945–September 1977 (Washington, D.C.: USAID, 1978), p. 43.

17. United States Department of Defense, Security Assistance Agency, *Foreign Military Sales and Military Assistance Facts* (Washington, D.C.: Data Management Division, Comptroller, 1977), p. 32.

18. Augusto Varas and Felipe Agüero, "El desarrollo doctrinario de las fuerzas armadas chilenas," FLACSO Working Paper (Santiago, 1979).

19. Alejandro Foxley, "Hacia una economía de libre mercado: Chile, 1970–1978," *Colección estudios cieplan* 4 (November 1980), pp. 5–37.

20. On the effects of the military government's policies on Chilean society, see the papers published by the Latin American Program of the Woodrow Wilson International Center for Scholars, Smithsonian Institution, Washington, D.C., Working Papers nos. 66–72 and 74–76.

21. Guillermo O'Donnell, "Las fuerzas armadas y el estado autoritario del cono sur de América Latina," in Norbert Lechner, ed., *Estado y política en América Latina* (Mexico City: Siglo XXI Editores, 1981), pp. 199–235.

22. Alexandre S.C. Barros, "The Diplomacy of National Security: South American International Relations in a Defrosting World," in Ronald G. Hellman and H. Jon Rosenbaum, eds., *Latin America: The Search for a New International Role* (Beverly Hills, Calif.: Sage Publications, 1975), pp. 131–150.

23. Augusto Varas, Carlos Portales, and Felipe Agüero, "The National and International Dynamics of South American Armamentism," *Current Research on Peace and Violence* 1 (1980), pp. 1–23.

7

The Ghanaian Experiments with Military Rule

Björn Hettne

This chapter summarizes the Ghanaian experience with military rule with the purpose of illuminating the relationship between military power and the civilian order. I shall rely on the intensive case study approach, which in the present instance also implies a comparative approach as Ghana has been ruled by four military governments since 1966: the National Liberation Council (NLC, 1966–1969), the National Redemption Council/Supreme Military Council (NRC/SMC, 1972–1979), the Armed Forces Revolutionary Council (AFRC, 1979), and the Provisional National Defence Council (PNDC, 1982–   ). The frequency of military interventions in Ghana makes that country a particularly interesting case for analyzing the different circumstances under which transitions from civilian to military rule, from military to civilian rule, and from one type of military government to another in a single country take place.

A major issue concerns the development role of the military. Development theory takes the civilian nature of societies for granted, but this assumption obviously contradicts empirical reality in the Third World. Questions to be dealt with in this context range from the efficiency of military regimes in promoting economic development to the whole process of militarization of societies.[1]

Background: The Ghanaian Cleavage Pattern

The origin of the Ghanaian army can be traced back to the late nineteenth century, when the war between the British and the powerful Ashanti empire was coming to a close. In 1897 the Royal West African Frontier Force (RWAFF) was formed by drawing together forces from the Gold Coast, Nigeria, Sierra Leone, and the Gambia. Internally, the RWAFF was used to subjugate the rebellious Ashantis and clear the ground for colonial rule; externally, to defend the British Empire inside and outside Africa. During the First World War, the strength of the RWAFF rose to 30,000, and during the Second World War, when African troops were used outside the continent for the first time, to 146,000.[2] After the Second World War, the rehabilitation of the Gold Coast troops presented certain problems. From that time to independence in 1957 the Ghanaian army was used for maintaining internal security, and thus it constituted a problematic element in Ghana's postindependence politics. It is obvious, even from reading military sources, that the general opinion of the army was low.[3]

At independence, there were almost no African officers in the Ghanaian army, but after the establishment of the Military Academy at Teshie in 1960, the process of Africanization gained momentum. Nkrumah was anxious to achieve a complete Africanization within the shortest possible time,[4] an ambition that should obviously be seen in the context of his Pan-African program. Regarding the other armed forces, there was very little to start from in the early sixties, but for prestige reasons, the military expansion program had to include the air force and the navy.[5]

Ghana, like most other African states, is a multiethnic society. The major ethnic groupings are the Akan (44.1 percent), the Mole-Dagbani (15.9 percent), the Ewe (13 percent), and the Ga-Adangbe (8.3 percent). The largest Akan groups are the Fanti (11.3 percent) in the western region and the Ashanti (13.3 percent) in the Ashanti region in central Ghana. The Mole-Dagbani group consists of a large number of tribes in the North, many of them Muslim. The Ewes live in the East (a large number of them in Togo), and the Ga-Adangbe live along the coast, particularly in the Greater Accra area.[6]

The ethnic character of the Ghanaian army at independence had four major features:[7]

1. The infantry, to a very large degree (60 percent), consisted of uneducated and poor Mole-Dagbani groups from the North.
2. The indigenous officers were mainly (73 percent) recruited from the southern groups (Ga, Ewe, and Fanti).
3. The Ashanti—the "martial race" *par préférence* in Ghanaian history—were underrepresented among officers (7 percent) as well as in the ranks (5 percent), obviously for security reasons.
4. Most command positions were filled by British officers.

Several implications result from this ethnic composition. Most indigenous officers had an obvious interest in Africanization, and the speed of this process was to be a major determinant of career possibilities in the various phases. For example, a forced process of Africanization would create many possibilities in the initial phase but lead to a blockage in a later phase.

As the indigenous officers could be seen as members of a national elite with ethnic-regional subdivisions, they tended to act as spokesmen for their subdivisions. There are several ethnic-regional cleavages in Ghana. One is between the Ashanti and the traditionally subjugated North, where there are a large number of small tribes that all seem to have a "northern consciousness," which, of course, is related to the fact that the North is predominantly Muslim. Then there is a conflict between the Ashanti and southern Akan areas, which is a holdover from the precolonial days when the Ashanti empire controlled all Akan peoples. There is also a conflict between the Akan areas and the Ewe-dominated Volta region. The Ewe live both in Ghana and in Togo, and they have from time to time expressed separatist tendencies. Other sets of cleavages are those between underrepresented groups (Ashantis) and others and those along the North-South dimension, which must be considered potentially explosive. The low degree of political consciousness among the poor northerners did not make the last cleavage immediately relevant. Later a change took place in this regard.

To this traditional cleavage pattern should be added a modern one. In 1947, Kwame Nkrumah, after many years in the United States and the United Kingdom, arrived in Accra to work as general secretary of the United Gold Coast Convention (UGCC). The well-educated, but somewhat alienated, old gentlemen of the UGCC urgently needed someone who could give their organization a more popular backing. However, they soon "found themselves outmanoeuvred, overtaken, left behind. They never forgave Nkrumah."[8] Thus began the political institutionalization and manifestation of another basic cleavage in Ghanaian society, to be symbolized in the leadership of Kwame Nkrumah versus that of Kofi Busia.

Even a superficial acquaintance with Ghanaian politics would convince anyone that the Nkrumah-Busia cleavage does exist, but it is much more difficult to say what it consists of. Of course this conflict should not be thought of as mainly a personal one. The complexity of the Ghanaian cleavage patterns defies simplistic analyses, be they in terms of powerful personalities or, for that matter, in terms of "classes" or "tribes." The Nkrumah-Busia cleavage should be conceived of as a multidimensional one, and the simplest way to account for these dimensions is through a chronological approach.

The 1948 riots are usually considered a watershed in Ghanaian politics. Before 1948 politics had been altogether an elite affair, the most important cleavage being between a modern elite (consisting of the intelligentsia and a few prosperous merchants) and the tribal chiefs.[9] The British had usually favored the chiefs, and paradoxically, they had been more inclined toward an "indigenous" form of constitution than were the educated gentlemen from the coast, who were eagerly waiting for parliamentarism to be established. With the events of 1948 a third force appeared on the political stage, led by the dynamic Kwame Nkrumah. His support structure was the petit bourgeois: teachers, clerks, petty traders, small businessmen, unemployed students, and urban workers—those who wanted to become rich rather than those who were poor. This was the class dimension of the cleavage, but there was also a generation conflict, which was particularly acute in areas where the authority of the tribal elders had remained strong. Nkrumah's supporters became generally known as "the verandah boys."

The natural outcome of this transformation of the political landscape was the coming together of the intelligentsia and the tribal chiefs against Nkrumah's formidable Convention People's party (CPP), which demonstrated its strength in the 1951 election. Busia then emerged as Nkrumah's greatest opponent. By then, the cleavage pattern had grown more complicated. Besides class and age, ethnicity and region had become definitely politicized, as the 1954 election clearly showed. The years after 1954 saw an acute conflict between the centralist CPP, which held government power, and the regional, ethnic, and religious opposition parties: the Ashanti-based National Liberation party (NLP), the Northern People's party (NPP), the Togoland Congress, and the Muslim Association party (MAP). A common demand from these organizations was that a federation be established, consisting of "the colony" (the South), Ashanti, the Northern Territories, and Togoland. The challenge to the CPP was strong enough to make the British hold a third election, in 1956, in which centralism versus federalism was the main issue. Again Nkrumah won, and in 1957 he became the prime minister of a free but still restive Ghana. Busia formed the United party out of the various sectional organizations opposing Nkrumah and became leader of the opposition, an opposition that was ultimately crushed by authoritarian methods.

The political style of the two leaders to a certain extent derived from their different support structures but was possibly also related to more personal factors. Busia believed in his right to rule because of his education and class, and he was status quo oriented. Nkrumah was a mobilizer of a commitment to change, and his right to rule was based on what he conceived of as a higher mission.

These different orientations can be identified in the economic policy during their respective regimes (Nkrumah, 1957–1966; Busia, 1969–1972). In the early 1960s Nkrumah changed strategy and began to apply what was then called "African socialism." This strategy, which was outlined in the Seven-Year Plan for National Reconstruction and Development, basically meant a policy of forced industrialization through import substitution, government controls, and public enterprises. The amount of capital accumulation necessary to carry out this visionary program of industrialization and modernization impoverished the country and undermined Nkrumah's political backing. The policy would have made sense if the suffering it caused had created the base for long-term economic growth, but it did not. The basic weakness of Nkrumah's strategy was its imitative approach, the belief that a reproduction of those economic and social structures that are associated with Western modernity automatically lead to a "takeoff" into self-sustained growth.[10] This result did not occur, and the sacrifices of the Ghanaian people were, on balance, in vain. Busia tried to reverse this strategy when he came to power and initiated a policy that was more based upon market forces, private enterprise, and a liberalization of controls.

It is usual to consider Busia's economic policy as being the opposite of that of Nkrumah: reliance on market forces, willingness to accept foreign investment, export orientation, etc. Tony Killick has argued that this interpretation is misleading and that "continuity rather than change was the outstanding characteristic of policies from 1966 onwards."[11] Although I feel that this is an overstatement, it is clear that the "new" policies were never systematically implemented. Thus, Busia's economic policy was a failure, but it was not necessarily a failure of liberalism as the alternative to Nkrumah's African socialism. In fact, the economic crisis of 1971 was in many ways similar to the one that precipitated the 1966 coup.

Perhaps the contrast between the two dominant leaders was most striking in the field of foreign policy. Before his arrival in Ghana, Nkrumah had been deeply involved in the Pan-African movement, and, as several authors have observed, he used Ghana more or less as a national base for his struggle against colonialism and neocolonialism in Africa.[12] Until 1966, Ghana's foreign policy was completely dominated by Nkrumah, and a significant dualism emerged in the administration of Ghana's foreign relations. On the one hand, there was "the Whitehall system," inherited from Britain and characterized by a "neutral" body of civil servants, and on the other, there was a quasi-revolutionary system centered on the Bureau of African Affairs and the African Affairs Secretariat.[13] What Nkrumah had in mind was a continental government for Africa,[14] but "the 'inheritance elites' had not become their countries' first ministers in order to preside over the liquidation of their new domestic empires."[15] To most national leaders in Africa, Nkrumah's great vision was unacceptable.

Busia was a national rather than an African leader, and it may even be argued that he was less than national, considering the importance of his Ashanti base. In his foreign policy, Busia was cautious and conservative and relied completely on the Whitehall system. Thus, with respect to foreign policy, "Busiaism" implied that Ghana should solve its own problems and not tell other countries what to do. Of course, this isolationism was acceptable both to Western powers and to most other African regimes.

NLC and the Politics of Consultation (1966–1969)

On February 24, 1966, Ghana experienced its first military coup, still a rare phenomenon in Africa at the time. It is not possible to account for the fall of Nkrumah without making an assessment of his regime, but that is not an easy task, since there are few political leaders who have been so differently judged.[16]

I have already compared Nkrumah's internal and external policies, as derived from some "higher mission," to Busia's essentially pragmatic approach. As has been the case with other visionary modernizers, Nkrumah's downfall was built into his development strategy as his visions were shared by so few and the potential beneficiaries belonged to the future. To his contemporaries, the situation looked bad indeed.

At the time of independence, Ghana had foreign exchange resources that were equal to one year's import bill, but by 1966, this comfortable position had turned into a staggering foreign debt. The economic situation was marked by a general condition of scarcity, which has since become a familiar experience in Ghana but at that time was a novelty, and the economic policies of Nkrumah were responsible. As indicated above, the massive program of infrastructural investment failed to generate any economic growth, and the trade agreements with the socialist countries turned out to be unfavorable. African unity, which Nkrumah tended to see as a remedy for all problems, had instead alienated most other African states, particularly those in West Africa. It is therefore true what was said in a commentary after the coup: Nkrumah was a man who lived by theory.[17]

The military was certainly influenced by the growing hostility toward the CPP regime (both inside and outside Ghana), but it also had its own grievances as the higher officers were in general conservative, elitist, and Western-oriented (the Sandhurst syndrome). Evidently the 1960 intervention of the United Nations into the Congo, in which troops from Ghana were involved, was the point at which sharp differences in outlook between the CPP radical wing and the Ghanaian officer corps were brought into the open. At that time Nkrumah decided to send cadets to the Soviet Union for military training in order to break the anglophiliac tradition, and it was then that plotting against the CPP regime began in the armed forces.[18] The army was gradually deprived of its autonomy, and according to one of the 1966 plotters, there was a widespread feeling that Nkrumah was planning to "strangle the Regular Army to death" by setting up the President's Own Guard Regiment.[19]

If one considers the fact that Nkrumah had lost his mass following and was rather isolated during the last years of his regime, his complete lack of confidence in his own army is rather striking. He himself explained that because of his Pan-African program, he preferred an African force of doubtful loyalty to a loyal but partially British force.[20] The hastened Africanization process disturbed the recruitment pattern within the army, which in itself was an important factor behind the coup.

The staging of the coup was an army affair. The commanders of the air force and the navy (which in terms of military power were insignificant) were kept in the dark about what was going on.[21] The main instigators were Colonel E. K. Kotoka, commander of the Second Army Brigade at Kumasi, and I.W.K. Harlley, the police chief. They were both Ewe, but Kotoka also secured the assistance of Major A. A. Afrifa, a young Ashanti officer who was to play an important part in Ghanaian politics until his execution in 1979. The basis of loyalty among the small conspiratorial group was mainly primordial, and the politics of ethnicity was also to dominate subsequent events.[22]

The Western powers (the United States, Britain, and West Germany in particular) were certainly happy to get rid of Nkrumah, but how active were they in bringing about his downfall? According to Nkrumah himself, Ghana had been "captured by traitors among the army and the police who were inspired and helped by neo-colonialists and certain reactionary elements of our own population."[23] However, the part played by this neocolonial factor is not easy to sort out. Leftist authors at once took it for granted that the U.S. Central Intelligence Agency (CIA) had had a finger in the coup,[24] and Basil Davidson has alleged that the United States knew of the coup in advance.[25] A recent Marxist analysis only refers to "the quiet pressures through destabilization measures."[26] Such measures are well documented,[27] but of course they could be interpreted as being the normal procedure of institutions such as the World Bank and the International Monetary Fund (IMF), considering the economic philosophy underlying their activities. The fundamental point here is of course the harmony of interests between neocolonialism and the Ghanaian opposition, not only members of the Busia faction (many of whom were in exile), but also members of the military elite with their British world view. To Ocran, the overthrow of Nkrumah was necessary if Ghana was not to "become a base for communists;"[28] to Afrifa, it was necessary if Ghana was not to become "a satellite of the Soviet Union in Africa."[29]

Ghana's first military government, the National Liberation Council (NLC), was in fact a carefully balanced coalition between the army and the police. The involvement of police forces, which were less concentrated and isolated than the military, made it easier to destroy the CPP. A tribal breakdown of the NLC reveals a clear overrepresentation of the Ewes. According to a widespread view, the NLC was a Ewe government.

The NLC was, however, anxious to widen its support and therefore based its policies on consultations with all relevant groups. As pointed out by Robert Dowse, there was a basic similarity between the NLC approach and the system of indirect colonial rule: "Neither was a 'mobilising regime' in the sense of being concerned to involve the 'masses' in politics. On the contrary a major concern of both was to govern through consultation with various selected groups."[30] The most important of these selected groups were the civil servants, the chiefs, and the professional intelligentsia. Various committees were organized on lines similar to the colonial legislative and executive councils, but of course the civilian influence was restricted to the old opposition against the Nkrumah regime. The NLC turned out to be an obedient tool of the various interests, earlier referred to as Busiaism. As a matter of fact, Busia himself was frantically active as chairman of bodies such as the Political Committee (later replaced by the National Advisory Committee) and the Electoral Committee. In these bodies, the opposition against Nkrumah finally got the political role it had failed to capture in the elections during the fifties. The main complaint of these people now was that they had to share power with the civil service.

The NLC was also accommodating to international interests, and its economic policies consequently complied with the advice of the IMF, the World Bank, and other agencies. The economist G. F. Papanek, heading a team of Harvard experts, found that the military rulers were "remarkably receptive to foreign advisers."[31] The aim of the NLC leaders was to restore some order to a chaotic economic situation, and they believed that the best way to do so was to leave the management of the economy to the economic experts. Nkrumah's Seven-Year Plan was abandoned, all "prestige projects" were to be halted, and the private sector was again to predominate.

Repeatedly, the NLC stressed its transitory character. Originally the name National Revolutionary Council had been proposed, but General Kotoka had made it clear that the aim of the regime was not to change the structure of the society.[32] The NLC rule was a "politics of consultation."

The general pragmatism of the NLC did not prevent it from getting into factional disputes. In April 1967, the key figure in the coup, E. K. Kotoka, was killed by army insurrectionists, and the NLC made the remarkable announcement that the abortive coup had *not* been planned by the Ashanti and Fanti against the Ga and Ewe,[33] obviously what everyone believed. The ethnic composition of the NLC now changed in disfavor of the Ewes, and since the most influential Ewe after Kotoka was Harlley, the police chief, a cleavage emerged between the army and the police. Two years later, in April 1969, General Ankrah (a Ga) had to resign from the NLC after it was disclosed that he had collected funds from foreign firms for political purposes. Later John Nunoo, another Ga, was also dismissed because of his political ambitions.[34] The increasingly tense ethnic conflicts undermined the authority and prestige of the NLC and hastened the transition to civilian rule,[35] which probably came earlier than planned by the military.[36] Because of the internal problems of the NLC, there was also a constant urging for civil rule from the politicians (above all Busia and the Political Committee), who argued that tasks such as "cleaning up the mess" and "wiping out corruption" could be fulfilled by a civilian government.[37]

Obviously, the NLC had certain opportunities to influence the transition process, and its association with the Busia faction became even more evident after the changes in NLC. Its new leader, Afrifa, was a close ally of Busia, whereas both Harlley and Deku supported the Ewe candidate, Komla Gbedemah. The Political Parties Decree made it impossible for active CPP people to take part in the election in 1969. As many as sixteen other parties emerged, but it soon became clear that the only serious contenders for power were the Progress party (PP), led by Busia, and the National Alliance of Liberals (NAL), led by Gbedemah, a former minister of Nkrumah's cabinet who had broken with Nkrumah at an early stage.

Not only was the PP the favored party of the NLC, it was also actively supported by groups alienated from the CPP because of Nkrumah's repressive policies during his last year in power, including organized labor and the cocoa farmers. The skewed ethnic-regional support structure was, one analyst says, a "cliché before there was any evidence to support it,"[38] but the evidence looks like this:

Votes for	Ashanti	Volta (Ewe)
PP	78%	18%
NAL	17%	77%

Another factor that influenced the outcome was the excessive centralism of Nkrumah's regime and the consequent anti-Nkrumaism of local bodies and associations that gave important support to the PP. However, the fundamental cause behind Busia's victory should be looked for in the logic of the Nkrumah-Busia cleavage. With Nkrumah gone, it was natural that his greatest opponent should take over.[39]

NRC/SMC and the Politics of Militarization (1972–1979)

On January 13, 1972, the army intervened for a second time under the leadership of Colonel Ignatius Kutu Acheampong. The resistance against the coup was again minimal. General Afrifa was arrested, accused of plotting a countercoup, and later on leading PP members were taken into custody just as CPP members had been in 1966.[40] Workers' demonstrations were organized in the regional capitals in support of the new regime, and the market women of Accra also expressed their approval. Why did the military intervene again? As in the first coup, a general economic discontent and more specific military grievances reinforced each other.

If the first military government (1966–1969) had drifted toward a market economy, the Busia regime stuck to this course in a somewhat more consistent way, although no explicit economic strategy was formulated. There was, of course, no longer any commitment to African socialism, but on the other hand, there was neither time nor the capacity to develop a viable alternative. In the end, the ultimate factor that determined whether the economic policy of the government would be popular or unpopular was still the world market price of cocoa. In December 1971 a massive devaluation of the cedi was undertaken, which had the effect of reducing real income, particularly for the middle classes who bought foreign goods. Therefore, the decision to devaluate was political suicide. It is quite obvious that the measure was meant to please the World Bank and the International Monetary Fund in order to secure international assistance.[41]

The military grievances can be summarized under four headings: financial problems, career problems, ethnic problems, and the function of the armed forces. The financial problems were generally related to the economic crisis and more specifically to the austerity budget of 1971-72, in which it was explicitly stated that the level of defense expenditure was clearly onerous for such a small country. The consequent cuts affected the general level of maintenance of materials and training, but more personal losses were at least as important (the abolition of a car-maintenance allowance seems to have been particularly resented).

The financial stringency also made the career problems of the younger officers more acute. The Ghana Military Academy took as many as 120 men a year in the early 1960s, but by the end of the decade, the intake had decreased to 25 cadets per annum.[42] In the higher ranks, the normal routine of promotion had been disturbed by the first coup, as officers in favor had been quickly promoted whereas those whose loyalty was in doubt had been held back. Acheampong—the strong man of the second coup—had not been affiliated with the 1966 rebels, and, as he himself complained, Afrifa who then had been a company commander under him was now a retired lieutenant general.

As for the ethnic factor, the Ewe officers had suffered toward the end of NLC rule, and this discriminatory trend was never broken under the Busia government—quite the contrary. The PP victory was a blow to the Ewes, and in an attempt to forestall Ewe action, Busia continued to replace Ewe officers with Akans in the more important positions.[43] By 1972 there was only one Ewe in a senior army rank position.

The last important military grievance was that the Busia government had sought new ways of making use of the army, apart from its traditional function of protecting the country. Thus, the military was deployed against smugglers, in an anticholera drive, for flood relief work, and for reconstruction work. Obviously, this new type of work had been regarded as degrading by the officers.

Thus, the general constellation of factors behind the second coup was rather similar to that of the 1966 coup: a general economic crisis in combination with acute grievances within the military. There are reasons to believe that the latter factor was the more important in both instances. The general economic situation provided the opportunity for the coup, and the factional character of Ghanaian politics always guaranteed some support from one civilian faction or another. Military coups may therefore be said to constitute *the* mechanism whereby one civilian faction takes over power from another.

It has been argued[44] that friendships based on career patterns were more important than ethnic considerations in setting up the National Redemption Council (NRC).[45] However, the Ewe were well represented on the council, and their support was crucial. The new military leaders were young officers with career problems, and in contrast to the previous military rulers, they had not been educated abroad, nor were they great admirers of British institutions.

In a statement explaining his actions in January 1972, Acheampong said: "This coup is not inspired and executed for any particular tribe or political party or section or group of people. . . . no persons should take advantage from the coup; no person will be given unwarranted advantage."[46] However, it soon became evident that the breaking up of Busia's power, in accordance with the logic of Ghanaian politics, implied an orientation toward Nkrumaism, even if this fact was played down by Acheampong, whose real ambition seems to have been to transcend the old Nkrumah-Busia cleavage.[47]

In terms of power structure, and to some extent in terms of ideology, the NRC was Nkrumaist. A return to the extravagance of Nkrumah's socialism was no longer financially feasible, but it was nevertheless clear that the new government did not intend to rely on market forces, as this quotation from the revised budget (February 1972) shows: "The political frame of reference which has guided . . . actions and . . . advice in the past two years must be cast into the rubbish heap of history. This means a departure from the laissez-faire so-called free market economy and the *institution* of effective planning in the allocation and utilization of resources."[48] The very precarious state of the Ghanaian economy, however, called for very specific methods of allocation and utilization of resources. These methods were summarized by the principles of self-reliance, which formed part of the "charter" of the new government.

The first three years of NRC rule were, in economic terms, not unsuccessful, although in view of what was to come, this situation could have been more due to luck than to ability. In 1972 growth was nil, mainly because of a lack of imported inputs, but in 1973 and 1974 the economy recovered, in spite of the rise in the price of oil, to some extent because of increasing cocoa prices. However, from 1975 onward, international inflation raised Ghana's import bill at the same time as several years of severe drought were causing a decline in food production. The government relied on the dubious method of printing money to cover the deficit, which set the inflationary spiral in motion. In 1977 inflation had reached 116 percent.[49]

In the field of foreign policy there were some signs of Nkrumaism. Accra again became a meeting place for African conferences, and the Pan-African orientation of the Acheampong regime was expressed through the less expensive policy of renaming streets after heroes in the African liberation struggle. The idea of a "dialogue" with South Africa, which had been entertained by Busia, was now dropped. Diplomatic relations were resumed with China and, what is more remarkable, with Guinea.

These Nkrumaist measures did not in any way indicate any intention to hand over political power to the CPP people. In contrast to the NLC, which had defined itself as a transitory government and had relied on the civil service, the NRC initiated a process of militarization of the society, for instance, by appointing military officers to the top positions of all major departments, regional bodies, state corporations, and public boards. Furthermore, Acheampong wanted a fundamental constitutional change, which once and for all was to put an end to party politics: a union government, in which all the elements of society—the civilians, the armed forces, and the police—would be included (one nation, one people, one destiny). Such a system, he claimed, could create national unity, end tribalism, and guarantee economic development. In short, the old factionalism between Nkrumaism and Busiaism was to be overcome. In European terms, this might be called a "fascist solution"; at any rate, it failed.

The beginning of Acheampong's downfall can be traced back to 1975 when the NRC became the Supreme Military Council (SMC). The reason for creating the SMC was to restore the military hierarchy that had been disturbed by the 1972 coup. Growing economic problems and an ensuing general discontent had by then weakened Acheampong's position and, in consequence, his ability to resist various kinds of pressures. The next two years saw a number of clashes between the SMC and the general public, culminating in violent disturbances in connection with the 1978 referendum on union government.

The downfall of Acheampong was primarily the result of civilian resistance, mainly from the intellectuals—professionals, university teachers, and students. The professional politicians (who had been out of business for years) joined the resistance, but organized labor kept aloof from the struggle, possibly because of a long-established suspicion of the intellectuals. Without this support Acheampong's fall might have come sooner, but he could also rely on tribal chiefs, particularly in the North.

It is clear that the intellectuals and professionals had reason to be dissatisfied with Acheampong's regime. Not only had the military taken over civilian jobs, its general attitude toward the intellectuals had been one of contempt. Furthermore, the breakdown of the distribution system had become a threat to the whole modern elite, since its most important class distinction was its westernized consumption pattern.

As the time for the 1978 referendum approached, there was a strong mobilization against union government, particularly in the urban areas. The most important organization was the People's Movement for Freedom and Justice (PMF), led by prominent politicians such as Gbedemah (former CPP leader), William Ofori-Atta (a former PP leader), and Afrifa (of the former NLC), who came together "despite political differences."[50] When the results of the referendum were announced, it was generally believed that the election had been rigged, which contributed to renewed mobilization efforts on the part of the movement's organizers. Ultimately the country became ungovernable, and Acheampong had to be sacrificed. On July 5, 1978, junior officers on the Military Advisory Committee succeeded in persuading their seniors, led by F.W.K. Akuffo, to remove Acheampong from power in a peaceful coup.[51]

The creation of SMC II failed to calm the opponents, since Akuffo refused to abandon the idea of a union government without party politics (the name had merely been changed to "national government"). The restraint shown by the workers as long as Acheampong had remained in power was now broken, and in a four-month period there were as many as eighty strikes.[52] For obvious reasons the military wanted to quit the game, and in November 1978, Akuffo announced that the ban on political parties would be lifted on January 1, 1979. The rule of Akuffo had been one of continuous concessions to all kinds of lobbying, and the prestige of the military had suffered accordingly.

AFRC and Politics of Retaliation (1979)

The third coup, in June 1979, differed radically from the previous ones (and most other military coups) in that there was no cunning plot by a handful of officers. On May 15, 1979, as electioneering began to gain momentum, an unsuccessful attempt at a coup d'etat was made in Accra by a number of air force officers led by Flight-Lieutenant Jerry Rawlings. There was talk about Ghana's going "the Ethiopian way," and panic broke out in Accra's Makola Market (the market women were generally held responsible for the food scarcity and the high prices), but the insurrection was quickly put down. It was obvious that this attempted coup was different in terms of planning, organization, and personnel involved. Official statements, anxiously denying any conflict between the air force and the rest of the armed forces, or between the senior officers and the lower ranks, raised quite new questions about the political role of the military in Ghana.

When seven persons (junior officers and corporals—all from the air force) were brought before a court-martial in late May, the motives of the insurrectionists became more widely known because by that time, the government's hold on the press had become loosened as part of the democratization process. When Rawlings boldly stated his motives, such as "corruption in high places," the "tarnished image of the armed forces," and the "activities of Syrians and Lebanese that have deeply eaten into the economy of the country," there was spontaneous applause from the public gallery. This response was extensively reported in the press.[53] Jerry Rawlings directly attacked the government when he said that he had thought things were going to be improved after the removal of Acheampong, a statement that must have expressed a widespread opinion in Ghana at the time. On the last day but one of the proceedings (which certainly would have ended with death sentences), Rawlings was freed as part of a more or less spontaneous mutiny. A broadcast spelled out the aims of the new Revolutionary Council. The new leaders had no intention of clinging to power, their aim was merely to undertake a "housecleaning exercise."[54]

Ghana's third military government, the Armed Forces Revolutionary Council (AFRC), must be unique in the history of military politics. It took power from a military regime and handed it over to a civilian one, after having executed a number of high military officers and put many more in jail. How can these unprecedented acts on the part of a military regime be explained? Rather than interpreting the new government as "revolutionary," it actually makes more sense to speak of containment of revolution. Let us first consider the so-called housecleaning exercise in some detail.

The housecleaning was directed against various social groups that had become associated over the years with corruption or *kalabule,* which was the word Ghanaians used for illegitimate profits made possible by the general conditions of scarcity. Such groups included, for instance, former (and many present) officeholders, capital owners (mainly Lebanese), and the market women.

The first object of the housecleaning exercise was the army itself— or rather the top leadership of the army. Eight senior officers were executed (among whom were three former heads of state: Afrifa, Acheampong, and Akuffo),[55] numerous officers had their heads shaved (and their wives humiliated), and many police officers were locked up by their own men. Apart from such retaliations, which had no or little legal basis, hundreds of military officers were sentenced to very long terms of imprisonment. The official reason for these measures was alleged corruption. In view of the character of this coup, however, the antihierarchy aspect of the whole operation must be emphasized.

Although the military officers were the main targets of the housecleaning, civilian power holders were not spared from retaliations. Many civil servants were dismissed by the AFRC, which yielded to a widespread feeling that civil servants should not escape all blame when governments fall. A large number of people were called to hearings through the daily newspapers, and obviously many of them had their property forfeited. The same fate, of course, befell those people who had left the country after the coup.

As far as the Lebanese were concerned, it was obvious from the start that they would face rough times in Jerry Rawling's Ghana. One of the popular measures undertaken by Busia in 1969 had been to expel Indians and Lebanese in order to stimulate African entrepreneurship. The African capitalists, however, had not emerged, and gradually the Lebanese had returned to revive their businesses. The bombarding of Lebanese enterprises had been stated as being one of the purposes of the unsuccessful coup and in fact had contributed to the general enthusiasm that had helped free Rawlings from prison. The AFRC ordered the deportation of many foreign nationals.

Activities against *kalabule* in the marketplace took rather drastic forms, namely the destruction of Accra's Makola Market in August 1979.[56]

This measure was undoubtedly a popular one, but, as *West Africa* points out, it was a "symbolic destruction of commercial malpractices" and of course did not come close to touching the deeper structural reasons for Ghana's economic maladies. A dark aspect of the operation was its antifeminist trend.[57] The destruction of the Makola Market is perhaps the best illustration of the kind of politics the AFRC stood for: radical populism in what must be considered a revolutionary situation. Jerry Rawlings pointed out in an interview that this was a moral revolution, an effort to clean up with the blood of those people who in a concrete (but not necessarily very fundamental) way exemplified the degeneration of Ghanaian society.

The crucial conflict behind the coup was not the typical horizontal one among various ethnic military elites, but a vertical conflict between the officers and the ranks. The leaders of the AFRC were junior officers who had not lost contact with the soldiers and still had a rather clean record. They did what they could to avoid total destruction of the military hierarchy, so the revolutionary actions of the AFRC were on the whole symbolic and their main purpose seems to have been to cool down a situation that was potentially revolutionary.

PNDC and the Politics of National Salvation (1982–)

After the four-month housecleaning operation, Rawlings, as planned, surrendered power to the civilian politicians. Who were they? After the ban on political parties had been lifted on January 1, 1979, about twenty parties had emerged, eager to shoulder the responsibility for Ghana's civilian future. A couple of weeks before the election in June 1979 their number had been reduced to a handful, and it was not difficult to discern the old Nkrumah-Busia cleavage behind their unfamiliar names.

The United National Convention (UNC) had grown out of the People's Movement for Freedom and Justice, an organization that had rather successfully opposed Acheampong's union government concept. The UNC was led by William Ofori-Atta, a former minister in the Busia regime who was now eager to demonstrate an independent stand. Closer to Busia's humanism and liberalism was the Popular Front party (PFP), which was led by old Busiaists like J. H. Mensah and Victor Owusu.

On the Nkrumaist side the major party was the People's National party (PNP) led by the moderate or right-wing pre-1966 politicians of the CPP. The Social Democratic Front (SDF) was partly sponsored by the Trade Union Congress (TUC), and it carried on the socialist policies of the left wing of the CPP. Thus, the election was mainly a fight between Nkrumaism and Busiaism, and this time the moderate Nkrumaism of the PNP and Hilla Limann won. The political development in Ghana had come full circle.[58]

On September 24, 1979, the rather unique ceremony of transfer of power took place in Accra. As most observers then noted, Rawlings "stole the show." Soon after the installation of the civilian government there were, as could be expected, complaints that the gasoline shortage was more severe, the queues were longer, and the bread loaves smaller than when "Rawlings was there."[59] The implications for the civilian government were obvious: "Behave yourselves or Jerry will come and get you." A new path in the development of civilian-military relations in Ghana had been opened, and in two years Rawlings was back after a new coup that took place on December 31, 1981. This time he intended to stay in power.

In a widely quoted interview after having transferred power to the civilian authorities Rawlings had said that the new government was "on probation,"[60] and as Hansen notes, the political class under the nominal leadership of Limann literally invited Rawlings and his men back. It became clear that "the petty bourgeois which had taken over control of the state apparatus had no historical mission other than self-enrichment."[61] It became clear that Rawlings was backed by the same classes as in the 1979 coup: the lower ranks of the armed forces, the workers, the students, and left-wing academics, but he himself seemed both more disillusioned and more politically conscious.[62] There was no talk of "cleaning operations" anymore. In order to be saved, Ghana had to undergo deep structural changes.

Externally, the country was to be separated from the world market and freed from the dominance of foreign capital. Internally, a completely new democratic political structure was to emerge, with people's defense committees on the grass-roots level and the Provisional National Defence Council as the highest political authority, with Jerry Rawlings as the chairman. At a time when dependency theory was being undermined both by the collapse of radical regimes striving for self-reliance and by the success of countries exploiting their comparative advantages in the market, a small, financially bankrupt West African country stubbornly refused to acknowledge the new consensus of development theorists. Paradoxically, the catastrophic situation of Ghana may be to its advantage. A self-reliant path is now more or less a necessity since international capital has lost interest in Ghana, or so Limann found when he traveled around the world trying to sell Ghana to reluctant speculators. The external links, which are gradually being broken by corruption and incompetence, can no longer be used as instruments for destabilization. Even Nigerian oil has to a large extent been replaced by Libyan oil, which is currently more acceptable ideologically.[63]

What structural changes were planned for the "neocolony," and how much of the work was implemented during the PNDC's first year? In December 1982 the PNDC announced a four-year economic program. The first year (1983) was to be devoted to reconstruction and preparing the necessary conditions for a three-year medium-term plan (1984–1986). In the plan, Ghana's problems were said to emanate from its neocolonial structure, so the overall goal was to develop the foundations of a self-reliant and integrated national economy. The role of the state in banking and insurance was to be strengthened, and there was to be a state monopoly of foreign trade. But this was only a plan. Few improvements on the economic front were reported during 1982, apart from efforts to keep the prices on a level that kept the basic necessities within reach of the common people. In early 1983, Ghana had to face the impossible task of receiving a million returning workers from Nigeria, because of the Nigerian government's decision to expel all aliens working illegally in that country. Thus, improvisations and chaos continued to mark the situation in Ghana in 1983, and the political implications of the situation are most uncertain.

Rawlings's first year in power was mainly devoted to institution building. A new democratic structure, the people's defense committees, was established—not without confusion and mismanagement. As a matter of fact, the governing of the country took place in a permanent atmosphere of crisis, and the new leaders, particularly Rawlings himself, spent a great deal of time explaining the goals of the revolution to local activists who simply acted in a mood of general rebellion. There were also serious conflicts within the PNDC, which lost a majority of its members during this first year. Conflicts revolved around "the judges affair"—the kidnapping and brutal murder of three High Court judges—and since PNDC members were involved, the image of the new leadership suffered badly, in spite of Rawlings's statement that such acts "were against all the principles which this revolutionary process is designed to advance."[64]

In November 1982, Joseph Nunoo-Mensah, chief of the Defense Staff and one of the key persons in the PNDC, resigned because of the anarchist trend in the country, and only one day later, an attempted coup was made against Rawlings. Behind the coup was a PNDC member, Sergeant Alolga Akata-Pore, whose name had been mentioned in connection with the judges affair. Akata-Pore tried to mobilize the northerners in the army against Rawlings, who was accused of favoring the Ewes. Thus, one year after the December 31 coup, the revolution was in danger of being held up by tribalism as a cover for personal ambitions. Rawlings's main problem was to find the cadres and the institutional framework that could transform the coup into a revolution. It is rather obvious that the soldiers cannot, without a substantial amount of training and political education, be used as instruments for political change in Ghana.

Conclusion

Since Ghana became independent in 1957, three civilian republics have been destroyed by military interventions, and over the years, the span of civilian rule has become shorter. This process of militarization is also evident in the constitutional outlook of the successive military regimes. The NLC (1966–1969) retained what military sociologists describe as a "professional" attitude. The NLC did not explicitly question the desirability of civilian government in principle, and it held that its rule was of a temporary and transitory nature. The NRC/SMC (1972–1979), in contrast, had no intention of giving up power. Instead, a new model of military-civilian relations was launched: the union government. The project was stopped because of a broad civilian mobilization against military involvement in government. The PNDC (1982–   ), finally, has gone even a step further and abolished a Western type of democracy altogether. However, the distinction between "civilian" and "military" tells very little about the actual political content of the various regimes.

To start with, the four regimes that have been overthrown by military coups were quite different. The first two interventions (1966 and 1972) concerned civilian regimes that represented two different political factions: Nkrumaism (of a radical kind) and Busiaism. The third (1979) brought down a military regime of a "praetorian" type, to use Amos Perlmutter's terminology. The fourth coup put an end to a rather unsuccessful experiment in moderate Nkrumaism. The changing political objectives and the diverse social backgrounds of the coups explain why the military governments differed so much in their general orientation: the liberalism of the NLC, the state interventionism (turning into large-scale corruption) of the NRC/SMC, and the revolutionary populism of the AFRC/PNDC.

Ethnic cleavages were important factors in the intramilitary conflicts, particularly in the cases of the first two military governments. The 1979 and 1981 coups reflected a vertical cleavage between officers and men. The attempted coup in late 1982 tried to exploit ethnic grievances, but what is perhaps of greatest significance here is that it failed.

Another factor that could be compared is the general outlook of the coup leaders, for example, in terms of a Western type of professionalism. If the first coup at least partially could be explained by the identification of the officers with their Western military tutors, which created a cleavage between the officers and the anti-imperialistic national movement, this factor quickly lost importance in the successive coups. Acheampong denied that British influence had made any impact upon him, and

Rawlings looks upon the West as the source of exploitation and destabilization. Thus, in the present context, radical nationalism is an attribute of the military establishment, whereas members of the civilian elite are accused of being traitors to the national cause.

According to Perlmutter's typology,[65] members of the NLC were "professionals"; the NRC/SMC, "praetorians"; and the AFRC/PNDC, "revolutionaries." Yet it is historically the same military establishment, and its varying political orientations must be understood against the background of a changing political context and internal power structure. The military is not a homogeneous group, and the civilian-military distinction must not be overemphasized. Authoritarian tendencies were, for example, evident in the civilian regimes of both Nkrumah and Busia, and in some respects the rule of the NLC was more "civil" than Nkrumah's rule. In fact, it was bureaucratic rather than military rule. Furthermore, both the civilian Nkrumah and the military Acheampong were thinking of Ghana's future in terms of a semimilitary organization of society, which also seems to be what Rawlings has in mind. Thus, in reality, the civil-military relationship is a matter of various combinations, and there are distinct interests (civilian and military) behind each. Once the military intervenes in politics, it tends to become a politicizing experience, which makes a repetition likely, not necessarily, however, a repetition as regards political content.

If we take the role of the military in development as an example, it is of interest to find out whether the military regimes pursued different policies and carried them out more effectively than their civilian counterparts. The first issue is in a way simpler to tackle as it concerns qualitative differences rather than quantitative measures, but here the problem is differences with respect to what? As far as the problem of dependence is concerned, one civilian (Nkrumah) and two military regimes (Acheampong and Rawlings) entertained, at least on the policy level, explicit ambitions to make Ghana self-reliant. Nkrumah stressed industrial development within a general scheme of socialist transformation, Acheampong put emphasis on agriculture of a large-scale type, and Rawlings's program is best described as a basic needs strategy.

Three regimes, one military (NLC) and two civilian (Busia and Limann), pursued laissez-faire policies and took the basic soundness of IMF advice for granted. As has been noted, the civilian regime of Busia and the military regime of the NLC were quite similar in orientation. The NLC in fact paved the way for Busia, just as the AFRC paved the way for Limann. The Nkrumaist image of the PNP makes the subsequent policies of Limann rather contradictory, but it should be kept in mind that the members of the PNP were very moderate Nkrumaists and that the "softness" of the Third Republic made the regime opt for a "strategy of invitation" rather than for a strategy of internal structural change.

This fact also explains the frustrations that enabled Rawlings to return to power.

As far as the issue of performance is concerned, it is of importance to keep the time perspective in mind, as well as the relationship between ambitions and outcomes. When assessing the development performance of the various regimes, one must consider the objective conditions for development in every single case. Nkrumah was obviously highly ambitious, and he also started out from a rather solid financial situation—of which not much was left in 1966. All governments after his were faced with more difficult economic prospects. In acute economic crises—and there have been many of them in Ghana—the people have suffered irrespective of what economic policy the incumbent government held on to. Most often these crises were caused by a drop in the cocoa price, and such a price drop precipitated Nkrumah's fall. The NLC benefited from a positive trend in the cocoa price, but this situation did not last during Busia's regime. Acheampong's first years were happy in this respect, but then the tide turned against him. Since the mid-1970s, one has to consider the oil bill, the world economic crisis, and lately, the influx of returning workers from Nigeria.

Since there has been an accumulation of problems, Rawlings must compare badly to any previous leader, simply because of the depth of the economic crisis now facing Ghana. Considering these circumstances, it does not make sense to compare regime performance using quantitative indicators of development. There is no *ceteris paribus* in real life. Thus, an analysis of the three military regimes does not give much support to the assumption that the military in the Third World tends to function as a "development agency." Nor can the military regimes be characterized as "modernizers." In its reliance on the politics of consultation, the NLC revived the old colonial style of indirect government, which radically differed from Nkrumah's visionary modernization policies. When Acheampong was removed from power in 1978, the whole infrastructure of modern development was breaking down, and there was an involuntary trend toward subsistence production in agriculture—which was quite different from what Acheampong had meant by self-reliance. In the case of Rawlings, it is of course too early to judge the results of his program for reconstruction, but obviously, Ghana is not on the modernization path. For the next few years the development strategy will have to be a strategy for national survival.

Notes

1. B. Hettne and P. Wallensteen, *Emerging Trends in Development Theory*, SAREC Report R3 (Stockholm: SAREC, 1978), pp. 61–63.

2. S. Baynham, "The Ghanaian Military: A Bibliographic Essay," *West African Journal of Sociology and Political Science* 1:1 (1975), p. 83.

3. A. K. Ocran, *A Myth Is Broken: An Account of the Ghana Coup d'Etat of 24 February 1966* (London: Longman, 1968), p. xvi.

4. Major General H. T. Alexander, who worked for two years as Nkrumah's chief of staff, says:

> Very early in our association Nkrumah made it clear to me what he wanted: an army of divisional size equipped with all the modern weapons of war, an air force which contained two squadrons of jet fighters, and a large navy and a new naval base. That the money did not exist to pay for all this mattered not a jot; that the expansion could not be produced overnight or in any case achieved efficiently without slowing up the africanization of the officer corps were arguments pushed aside. His target date for completion was 1962. [H. T. Alexander, *African Tightrope* (New York: Pall Mall Press, 1965), pp. 98–99]

5. Ibid., p. 16.

6. J.' Bayo Adekson, "Army in a Multi-Ethnic Society: The Case of Nkrumah's Ghana, 1957–66," *Armed Forces and Society,* 2:2 (1976), pp. 251–272.

7. Ibid.

8. B. Davidson, *Black Star: A View of the Life and Times of Kwame Nkrumah* (London: Allen Lane, 1973), p. 87.

9. For the earlier period the basic work is D. Kimble, *A Political History of Ghana, 1850–1928* (London: Oxford University Press, 1963). For the period from 1946 to 1960 the standard work is D. Austin, *Politics in Ghana, 1946–1960* (London: Oxford University Press, 1970).

10. This idea is well expressed by T. Killick, *Development Economies in Action: A Study of Economic Policies in Ghana* (London: Heinemann, 1978), p. 336:

> In effect Nkrumah mistook the appearances of modernization for the reality. Much effort and many resources were devoted to acquiring the symbols of modernity— the institutions, the machinery, the factories, the apparatus of state. The results were modernization without growth, occurring, I submit, because the strategy overlooked that past industrial revolutions have drawn their dynamism from innovation and adaptation. There was little of either in the many changes introduced by Nkrumah. Most "innovations" were copied unchanged from some Western or Eastern models. They worked out differently, but the differences were not to Ghana's advantage.

11. Ibid., p. 300.

12. I. Geiss, *The Pan-African Movement* (London: Methuen, 1974), p. 418, and Ali A. Mazrui, *African International Relations* (London: Heinemann, 1977), p. 43.

13. M. Dei-Anang, *The Administration of Ghana's Foreign Relations, 1957–65: A Personal Memoir* (London: Athlone Press, 1975), p. 4.

14. K. Nkrumah, *Africa Must Unite* (London: Panaf Books, 1963), p. 216.

15. B. Davidson, *Africa in Modern History* (London: Penguin, 1980), p. 289.

16. It is above all Nkrumah's economic policies that have lent themselves to such varying evaluations, in spite of the fact that their failure—in terms of economic development—should not be in doubt. For an entertaining and

malicious account, see T. Jones, *Ghana's First Republic, 1960–1966* (London: Methuen, 1976). A more sympathetic view of Nkrumah's development strategy as "basically sound" may be found in Roger Genoud, *Nationalism and Economic Development in Ghana* (New York: Praeger, 1969). A very solid analysis based on long experience of economic planning in Ghana is given in Killick, *Development Economies in Action.*

Even from a socialist perspective there are different ways of making the assessment. One way is to make comparisons with some ideal model of socialism, another is to make the evaluation in the context of a concrete historical situation with a limited number of possibilities and a large number of constraints. For the first approach, see B. Fitch and M. Oppenheimer, *Ghana; End of an Illusion* (New York and London: Monthly Review Press, 1966); for the second, see Davidson, *Black Star.*

17. *West Africa*, March 5, 1966.

18. Fitch and Oppenheimer, *Ghana*, p. 6.

19. Ocran, *A Myth Is Broken.*

20. In spite of the bias, Nkrumah's assessment of the situation in the armed forces at this time is not without interest:

> Unfortunately, the preparations for independence have not included the training of anything like sufficient officers or even NCO's to make it possible for me to choose on political grounds who should be promoted. There were in fact, insufficient soldiers with the necessary training or qualifications to fill even half the positions left vacant by the departing British. In order to have any army at all, I therefore had to accept what existed even though I knew the danger of this course. In fact, the most efficient of the British trained Ghanaian potential officer class were the most neo-colonialist. In general, if I was to have any army at all, I had to accept the framework bequeathed to me and an officer corps which contained a high proportion of individuals who were either hostile to the C.P.P. and myself and who were anti-socialist in outlook. Worse still, the fact that the bulk of the infantry came from the North, where education had been almost completely neglected in colonial times, made many of the rank and file soldiers easy prey to anyone who wished to mislead them. [K. Nkrumah, *Dark Days in Ghana* (London: Lawrence and Wishart, 1968), pp. 37–38]

21. In fact Ocran did put the commanders in protective custody and had to apologize afterwards: "My apology was readily accepted. The Air Force Commander, I must say was rather furious at my not confiding in him from the onset" (Ocran, *A Myth Is Broken*, p. 84).

22. Baynham, "The Ghanaian Military," p. 87.

23. Nkrumah, *Dark Days in Ghana*, p. 9.

24. R. Murray, "Militarism in Africa," *New Left Review* 38 (July-August 1966), pp. 35–59, and Fitch and Oppenheimer, *Ghana.*

25. Davidson, *Black Star*, p. 202.

26. J. Marshall, "The State of Ambivalence: Right and Left Options in Ghana," *Review of African Political Economy* 5 (January-April 1976), p. 55.

27. Ruth First, *The Barrel of a Gun: Political Power in Africa and the Coup d'Etat* (Harmondsworth, Eng.: Penguin African Library, 1972), pp. 376–386.

28. Ocran, *A Myth Is Broken*, p. 26.

29. A. A. Afrifa, *The Ghana Coup, 24th of February 1966* (London: Frank Cass, 1966), p. 113 (2d ed. published in 1967).

30. R. Dowse, "Military and Police Rule," in D. Austin and R. Luckham, eds., *Politicians and Soldiers in Ghana, 1966-1972* (London: Frank Cass, 1975), p. 23.

31. First, *Barrel of a Gun*, p. 26.

32. R. Pinkney, *Ghana Under Military Rule, 1966-69* (London: Methuen, 1972), p. 7.

33. Dowse, "Military and Police Rule."

34. First, *Barrel of a Gun*, p. 404.

35. Pinkney, *Ghana Under Military Rule*, p. 132.

36. One year after the coup, Colonel Afrifa publicly stated:

> Much as we would like to leave the scene, as soon as possible, we would wish to complete our task. We cannot risk the lives of innocent soldiers in another revolution: we therefore want to be certain that the conditions are satisfactory for a civilian administration before we hand over power. It is for these reasons that military governments become permanent or try to govern in association with civilians. In fact if we do succeed in handing over power to a civilian government in the very near future, which is our desire, ours would have been one of the very rare instances in history. [*Legon Observer*, March 31, 1967]

37. It is also obvious that the military rulers, recalling their British training, experienced a certain role conflict. In a series of interviews in *Legon Observer* (February 17, 1967) they testified about their strange experiences of being politicians. Ocran, for example, said: "Politics belong to politicians. We who are now partly in politics have, whether we like it or not, contaminated ourselves, and after two or three years of this we cannot continue with our military career."

38. Y. Twumasi, "The 1969 Elections," in Austin and Luckham, *Politicians and Soldiers in Ghana*, pp. 140-163.

39. In this context the comment of Max Assimeng (*Legon Observer*, August 1, 1976) is relevant: "The long struggle for power between Nkrumah and Busia is being interpreted in traditional chieftaincy conflicts. Here is the logic, which has apparently been working in the rural areas: if two candidates are fighting for a stool (or a skin) and one drops out—or is dropped—it follows that the other should automatically take over. In the minds of many people, therefore, Busia is still fighting with Nkrumah, and not fighting Gbedemah."

40. However, in December 1973 another plot by old Nkrumaists (Kojo Botsio and John Tettegah) was put down. Acheampong's coup was not "Nkrumaist" simply because it was directed against "Busiaists," but his regime gradually took on a Nkrumaist flavor due to tendencies inherent in Ghanaian politics.

41. R. I. Libby, "External Co-optation of a Less Developed Country's Policy Making: The Case of Ghana, 1969–1972," *World Politics* 29:1 (1976), pp. 67–89.

42. Plave V. Bennett, "The Military Under the Busia Government," *West Africa*, February 25, 1972, pp. 222–223, and Plave V. Bennett, "Epilogue: Malcontents in Uniform," in Austin and Luckham, *Politicians and Soldiers in Ghana*, pp. 301–305.

43. Baynham, "The Ghanaian Military," p. 91.

44. Bennett, "Epilogue," p. 306.

45. Colonel Acheampong was an Ashanti; Major Baah, a Brong; Majors Agbo and Selormey, Ewe.

46. *Legon Observer,* vol. 8, no. 10.

47. *New African,* December 1977. Nkrumah died in April 1972—still in exile—and in July (after complicated negotiations with President Sekou Touré of Guinea), he was at last buried in his home village of Nkroful in the western region of Ghana. Nkrumah's statue, which had been dragged from its pedestal in 1966, was put into a museum.

48. Bennett, "Epilogue," p. 309.

49. *West Africa,* December 24/31, 1979.

50. *New African,* April 1978.

51. I. Kraus, "From Military to Civilian Regimes in Ghana and Nigeria," *Current History* 76 (March 1979), p. 136.

52. Ibid., p. 138.

53. See, for example, the *Ghanaian Times,* May 29, 1979. It was not easy to get a daily newspaper in Accra in those days.

54. The statement reads as follows:

> Countrymen, we the junior officers and the other ranks, are very much disturbed about the sunken reputation of the Armed Forces. We have felt that the SMC would do a house-cleaning exercise and put the reputation of the Armed Forces on an even keel before handing over. All attempts to help the SMC do this have failed. In these circumstances, we have no alternative but to take over the administration of the country. In the period at our disposal therefore we have plans for a house-cleaning exercise and we are going to act on it immediately. In this exercise, if you have been seconded from the Armed Forces to the civil establishment, you would be called upon to give an account of your stewardship. If you have been honest in your assignment you would not have anything to fear. But if your hands are soiled, then the full rigour of the law will be brought to bear on you.
>
> We wish to assure the nation that we do not intend to cling to power. The Armed Forces Revolutionary Council will ensure a smooth transition to constitutional rule as planned. In this way preparations for the elections should therefore go on uninterrupted. [*West Africa,* June 11, 1979]

55. It is not easy to see any compelling logic in the killing of these three men. Of course, Acheampong symbolized the misery of the preceding years, but after all Akuffo did bring about the downfall of Acheampong, and Afrifa had all along been part of the opposition against the SMC. Perhaps the motives should therefore be looked for in the antihierarchy aspect of the coup.

56. *West Africa,* August 27, 1979.

57. A few market women who charged exorbitant prices were shot on the spot, many more were stripped naked and flogged or sentenced to sweep the streets. See the report by Anne Fraker and Barbara Harrell-Bond in *West Africa,* November 26, 1979.

58. According to Hansen there were three factions in the CPP: the economic nationalists, the welfare socialists, and the Marxists. The economic nationalists, who used state power to create capital for the Ghanaian entrepreneurial class,

dominated the party in the period 1957–1960. The welfare socialists, basing themselves on the ideology of African socialism, accumulated capital for the state itself and held power from 1960 to 1965. Limann represented the economic nationalists (E. Hansen, "The Military and Revolution in Ghana," *Journal of African Marxists* 2 [August 1982]).

59. *West Africa,* October 22, 1979.

60. *West Africa,* February 4, 1980.

61. Hansen, "Military and Revolution in Ghana."

62. At a press conference on January 1982 Rawlings said, "I was slightly naive, in the sense that it never struck me that some kind of supportive system, maybe new institutions, would have to be organized to ensure that the people of this country held on to their newly-won freedom, to ensure that they dictate the terms of their survival" (*West Africa,* January 25, 1982, p. 224).

63. Rumors in Ghana indicated that an invasion was planned jointly by the United States, United Kingdom, and Nigeria. There is, however, no concrete proof to show the existence of such plans.

64. *West Africa,* July 12, 1982.

65. A simple and useful distinction between the various types of military with regard to political orientation is suggested by Amos Perlmutter in *The Military and Politics in Modern Times* (New Haven: Yale University Press, 1977). The *professional soldier* regards his military role as a profession with certain skills, in which he takes pride, and with specific duties, which are prescribed for him by the civilian regime whose authority he as a general rule never questions. The *praetorian soldier* does not recognize the civil authority as supreme and thinks that he has the same right as any other interest group to intervene in politics as it serves his purposes. The *revolutionary soldier* does not distinguish between his military and political roles (in contrast to the professional) but defines his political role in terms of a collectively held ideology (in contrast to the praetorian).

These types must obviously be regarded as ideal types, and within a particular army (and probably within a particular soldier), different principles may be struggling at the same time. A praetorian army will probably have a bad professional conscience when intervening in politics, at least the first time it does so (as in Ghana in 1966). The revolutionary soldier, similarly, may feel tempted to define the revolutionary goals in ways that coincide with his very personal praetorian interests. To confuse things even more, these interests could very well be rationalized in terms of professional values. Enough has probably been said to emphasize the purely analytical function of this distinction.

Part 4

The Search for Alternatives

8

Defense Without Threat: Switzerland's Security Policy

Dietrich Fischer

The world is drifting toward the danger of a devastating nuclear war. Even if a world war under present circumstances might still leave many survivors, this result may be unlikely in the near future if the current trends of accumulation and proliferation of nuclear arms persist. The nuclear arms race seems to have no limits.

In this period of utmost danger, there is everywhere a growing interest in solutions that can guarantee a durable peace. This chapter investigates some of the basic principles of Switzerland's security policy from this viewpoint, to see whether that policy may represent one of several possible models to preserve national and international security.[1]

Transarmament Instead of Disarmament

Practically all people wish to have peace. But on the question, how peace is best to be preserved, opinions diverge. Many people in the West, as well as in the East, are honestly convinced that the best guarantee for peace is absolute military superiority (of their own side, of course). But unless the other side accepts military inferiority, this position inevitably leads to an arms race, which has brought the world into the dangerous situation of today. Other people believe that the best approach is peace initiatives in the form of unilateral disarmament measures, which, it is hoped, will then be emulated by the other side. But history shows that nations that are not sufficiently prepared for defense can attract aggression.

The apparent solution to this dilemma is negotiated mutual disarmament. All nations would enjoy greater security and, at the same time, have a lesser burden of defense expenditures if all would take *simultaneous,* balanced steps toward disarmament. But it is difficult to monitor such agreements reliably. Also, there is no higher authority that could enforce such agreements. Therefore, there is mutual distrust. A certain amount of caution and scepticism is, unfortunately, not always completely without justification. For this reason, disarmament negotiations have not been overly successful so far. They should certainly be pursued with all efforts, but even negotiations among allies—for example, about the allocation of military expenditures within NATO—are sometimes difficult. To expect that negotiations between adversaries will lead to success more easily would be self-delusion. Do these points mean that the situation is hopeless, that there is no way out of this dilemma? Fortunately, there are alternatives.

A country that honestly desires peace can make a contribution to peace without jeopardizing its own security. It can do so by taking purely defensive measures, which do not pose a threat to any other countries as long as those countries do not attack the first country. At the same time, the first country can stop the development of offensive arms, which would be perceived as a constant threat by potential opponents and therefore would fuel the arms race. Such "transarmament" measures reduce tension and the danger of war. Yet rather than endangering a country's own security, they strengthen it. Such measures have the advantage that they can be taken unilaterally, without risk. Unlike disarmament measures, they do not depend on the simultaneous cooperation of potential opponents, cooperation that is usually difficult to achieve.

Should an Opponent Be Threatened?

It is often said that the only language potential opponents understand is military strength. Although perhaps true in some cases, there must be a clear distinction as to *when* that strength should be applied. An enemy should feel afraid when attacking another country, but only then. If a potential opponent feels threatened even when not attacking, then there is no incentive for him not to attack. (Whether such a threat objectively exists and is intended, or whether it is only the subjective impression of an opponent, makes no difference.) Unfortunately, this simple truth does not yet seem to be heeded in many places.

The main principle of Swiss defense policy is called "dissuasion." It not only seeks to increase the losses of a potential enemy if he attacks, it also tries to make peaceful cooperation as attractive as possible.

Military strength can mean at least two basically different things.[2] On one hand, it can mean the capability to attack other countries, or to threaten them with attack. On the other hand, it can mean the capability to resist attacks or threats from outside. The greatest contribution to peace is made by a country that can defend itself and therefore

Table 8.1. Menger's categorization of people's character

	Easily Hurt	Not Easily Hurt
Hurting Others	most difficult character	
Not Hurting Others		most pleasant character

does not attract aggression, but which, at the same time, has no intention of attacking other countries. It is still better not even to possess the capability of attacking others in order to make the purely defensive intention credible. The most dangerous position is the one in which a country that is not able to defend itself threatens others. Such a country can easily provoke an attack by others, or may feel pressured to launch a preemptive attack.

The confusion between "strength" as the power to resist, i.e., invulnerability, and "strength" as a source of tension is common also in the daily use of the word, in many languages, and this confusion has caused real difficulties in the thinking about some of the problems. For example, military leaders in certain countries, in the name of "defense," call for the acquisition of offensive weapons systems that threaten the security of other nations. Even some members of the peace movement have become victims of the same confusion by calling for unilateral disarmament as a means to reduce tension in the world. The demand that a country should be weak in order not to pose any threat to others confuses "posing no threat" with "being vulnerable."

To bring clarity into this confusion, a diagram adapted from Menger can help (see Table 8.1).[3] He categorizes people into those who tend to hurt others (*unhöflich*, meaning impolite or inconsiderate) and those who don't hurt others (*höflich*, i.e., polite, considerate). He further distinguishes between people who are easily hurt (*empfindlich*, sensitive, in the meaning of being easily offended, intolerant) and those who are not easily hurt (*unempfindlich*, in the sense of being tolerant). Menger then analyzes which types of people can get along with each other and which cannot stand each other. He finds, among other things, that people who are considerate and tolerant can get along well with everybody. People who are inconsiderate and intolerant cannot even stand others of the same type, they can get along only with people who are both considerate and tolerant.

Table 8.2. A classification of nations

	Vulnerable	Invulnerable
Aggressive	unsafest posture, most likely to become involved in a war	
Nonaggressive		safest posture, greatest contribution to international peace

Table 8.2 is a classification of nations, which is in some sense analogous to Menger's classification of individuals (although I do not in any way imply that there are considerate or inconsiderate nations, these terms can only apply to their leaders).

A nation is invulnerable if it has both the capability and the will to defend itself against any potential threat. Neither of these two ingredients alone is sufficient. Similarly, a nation is aggressive only if it both possesses offensive arms and intends to use them for aggressive purposes. Since intentions can change relatively quickly, and verbal proclamations of peaceful intentions are not always believed by an opponent (sometimes with good reason), the only safe way for a nation to show credibly that it is not aggressive may be not to acquire any offensive arms (more about the distinction between offensive and defensive arms will be discussed later).

What Is General Defense?

"General defense" means the use of all legitimate means against all possible forms of threats. One can distinguish three principal forms of power:[4] military power (more generally punitive power), economic (remunerative) power, and psychological (normative) power. A comprehensive concept of pure defense should protect a country against all three of these forms of power but should not seek to exert power over other countries in any of these three fields.

Resistance against each of these three forms of power consists of an objective component (the capability to defend oneself), a subjective component (the will to defend oneself), and a combination of these two components. Table 8.3 gives an overview of these six forms of resistance to power. *Invulnerability* is a combination of all three forms

Table 8.3. Forms of resistance against power

Form of Power	Resistance		
	Subjective	Objective	Combined
Military (punitive)	fearlessness[a]	defensive capability	indomit- ability
Economic (remunerative)	self-restraint, modesty of wants	economic strength[b]	self-reliance[a]
Psychological (normative)	self-respect,[a] self-conviction	knowledge	autonomy

[a]These terms are described in Johan Galtung, The True Worlds (New York: Free Press, 1980). The division into subjective and objective components of resistance is an extension of Galtung's classification.

[b]By economic strength is meant the ability to provide for oneself without exploiting others or depending on the goodwill of others, through resources and/or knowledge, skill, ingenuity, etc.

of resistance against threats. Following are some examples of these forms of resistance from the Swiss concept of general defense.[5]

The objective potential to offer resistance against military power from outside is provided by a strong, well-equipped, and defensively oriented army. Switzerland has a comparatively strong and well-trained militia army, 600,000 strong in a population of only 6 million. The army includes about 80 percent of the men between the ages of twenty and fifty, all those who are not physically or mentally impaired.

The subjective will of a people to defend their country is present if the national institutions are felt to be worth defending. For this reason, the Swiss defense doctrine stresses the importance of a just social order that the population will consider is worth defending. (A dictatorial regime that carries out a struggle of oppression against its own population makes itself very vulnerable against attacks from outside, and also from inside. For example, Batista's army in Cuba in 1959 dissolved almost by itself.)

The objective potential to resist economic temptations and blackmail from outside is present if a country can provide for its essential needs out of its own efforts whenever necessary. This provision includes the storage of reserves of food and other commodities that are necessary to sustain the functioning of vital sectors of the economy and of the defense effort. It also includes plans for an increase in domestic production during an emergency. An example is Switzerland's plan for potential food self-sufficiency if imports should be interrupted, a plan initially developed by Fritz Wahlen, who later became a federal councillor and stands out as the originator of economic defense planning in Switzerland. In peacetime, Switzerland imports about 40 percent of its food requirements, but it is not necessary to practice *constant* self-sufficiency, as long as imports from abroad are cheaper. It is sufficient to be prepared for an emergency.

The subjective will to resist economic pressures takes the form of voluntary reductions of demand, rationing, and elimination of all nonessential consumption. Switzerland foresees, for example, a calorie intake reduction of about 30 percent, and especially a drastic reduction of meat consumption, if food imports should be interrupted. If oil imports should be cut off, there are plans for reductions in the consumption of heating oil and gasoline. Substantial reserves are also kept.

The combination of a subjective preparedness to make do with less if necessary and of an objective potential to produce more domestically if required, so as not to become dependent economically, is called "self-reliance."[6] This state is not to be confused with autarky, i.e., permanent self-sufficiency.

Self-reliance brings true security, without threatening or exploiting others. On the other hand, plans for intervention abroad to secure imports—for example, the idea of sending a rapid deployment force to the Gulf if the flow of oil should be interrupted—offer a very dubious contribution to national security. Such ventures could draw the intervening power into an unnecessary war, possibly a nuclear war, and therefore they threaten a country's national security rather than strengthening it.

The objective potential to resist psychological warfare in the form of hostile propaganda and the spreading of false rumors is established through public education that develops critical thinking and a comprehensive and truthful informing of the population. The Swiss security doctrine stresses that "manipulated information which tries to keep setbacks and negative developments secret . . . may, after a while, have the opposite effect from that desired" (sec. 533).

To make the structure of leadership as invulnerable as possible, Switzerland's federal system has been structured so as to be an element of strength. The tightly woven net of organizations, overlapping in part, helps ensure that if the head of one organization falls, only a small domain will be without leadership. Other still functioning organs can immediately step into the breach (sec. 64).

The subjective component of resistance against psychological influence is self-respect. For instance, the Swiss tend to be proud of their own institutions (perhaps a little too much so).

An effective defense must serve two purposes.[7] First, it must seek to prevent aggression, and second, if a country should still be attacked the defense must seek to protect as much as possible what it is intended that it should protect, i.e., serve people's survival and prepare the way for liberation from the aggressor.

Nuclear deterrence, which leaves the civilian population unprotected, has so far fulfilled the first criterion, but it would fail catastrophically on the second count. There are many instances that show that deterrence occasionally does break down, in spite of a country's best efforts. Purely nonviolent resistance, which is advocated by some people, may help keep the damage low in case of a war, but in the present world, it does not seem to offer a sufficiently strong deterrent against aggression. General defense, which combines the use of all purely defensive means to prevent aggression without being seen as a threat by other countries as long as they do not attack, seems to be more effective in preventing war. In Switzerland, the policy of dissuading aggression is supplemented by efforts to protect the population to the maximum feasible extent if Switzerland should nevertheless become a victim of aggression.

Up to this point, defense policy has been discussed without any precise specification of what is to be defended. No goal of defense is legitimate if it would lead to a logical contradiction if other countries were to pursue the same goal for themselves. For example, economic interests abroad, foreign raw material supplies, or the promotion of one's own religion, ideology, or political system must not be "defended" with military force, for if others do the same, war will inevitably result. On the other hand, the protection of a country's internationally recognized territory is a legitimate goal, one that does not lead to war if other countries pursue the same goal. Switzerland considers that an even more important goal of defense is its self-determination, i.e., its people's right to shape their own institutions democratically without the imposition of force from outside. This goal, peace in liberty, does not infringe on any other country's pursuit of the same goal.

Offensive and Defensive Arms

Purely offensive arms threaten the security of a potential opponent but do not contribute to a country's own security. Purely defensive arms increase a country's own security without reducing the security of potential opponents. Many types of arms, of course, can be used for offensive as well as for defensive purposes, and they have to be classified somewhere between these two pure categories. It is nevertheless useful to speak of predominantly offensive and predominantly defensive arms.

Table 8.4.   Some examples of offensive and defensive weapons

Offensive	Defensive
tanks	tank barrage, antitank weapons, mine fields
bombers	anti-aircraft weapons, radar warning systems, bomb shelters
landing boats	shore batteries in fixed emplacements, coastal mines

Table 8.4 gives some examples of conventional offensive and defensive weapons.

An example of purely defensive arms are barrages against tanks. Such artillery cannot be used for an attack, because it is immobile; it only serves a purpose if hostile tanks attempt to cross a certain line. An example of a purely offensive weapon may be the proverbial gunboat, which used to be positioned in front of the capital of a foreign nation in order to extract concessions. A modern successor may be the aircraft carrier, but for true defense, domestic airports are just as useful.

Typically, offensive arms are characterized by long-range mobility, whereas defensive arms are either in a fixed position or have a short-range mobility. Offensive arms are better suited for fighting abroad, while defensive arms are better suited for fighting on one's border or inside one's own territory.

There are even weapons systems that not only reduce the security of a potential enemy against whom they are aimed but also one's own security. These systems could be called "superoffensive." An example is an unreliable radar warning system that could trigger an accidental nuclear war. Reliance on such a system not only threatens the security of an opponent but also a country's own security. On the other hand, there are measures that could be called "superdefensive," which strengthen the security of both parties to a conflict. One such measure is the stationing of a neutral force in a buffer zone along a contested border.

A mathematical analysis has shown that under plausible assumptions, the acquisition of offensive arms contributes to mutual fear and therefore to an intense arms race and defensive arms help to slow down or stop an arms race, independent of any agreement among the contending parties.[8] The following example may serve to illustrate this point. If country X acquires a number of tanks (offensive arms), allegedly for pure self-defense, then potential enemy Y may be afraid that these tanks might be used for an attack on its territory. Y will also want to acquire tanks, preferably more than X has, in order to repel any attack. This action causes more fear and suspicion in country X, causing X to acquire even more tanks, etc. The result is a classic arms race. If, on the other hand, X acquires purely defensive antitank weapons, then Y has no reason for fear as long as it does not intend to attack X. Y does not need to acquire more tanks in response, nor does Y need any antitank weapons of its own. Of course, a country with aggressive intentions may still seek to develop countermeasures to make these antitank weapons useless, but such measures are not necessary for defense, only for aggression. If a country succeeds in producing cheap and effective antitank weapons, then its enemies, no matter how aggressive they may be, will soon stop building tanks. If they did not, they would only ruin their own economies without achieving any of their aggressive aims.

There is a widely quoted proverb, Offense is the best defense. The idea behind it is that pure defense is often more difficult than counteroffense, because an aggressor can choose the location and time of attack whereas a defender must be prepared to resist everywhere and at all times. But if one takes into consideration the long-term consequences of offensive armaments, then a pure defense still has a great deal in its favor.

It is clear that offensive arms can also be used in a purely defensive way against an aggressor. But promises of purely defensive intentions are often met with distrust, not always without reason. Obviously, a country that has repeatedly fought wars outside its borders will have less credibility than a country that has strictly respected its borders in the past.

There is a widespread and deeply rooted belief, not only among ordinary citizens, but also in top government circles of certain countries, that the more a country spends for arms, the safer it is. But this belief depends very much on the type of arms that are acquired. It is clear that generally, a unilateral acquisition of arms tends to increase a country's own security and to reduce the security of potential opponents. But certain arms buildups may increase a country's security in the short run but endanger its own security in the longer run. This is the case if the arms are perceived by a potential opponent as being a threat and thus give rise to an arms race that would not have taken place otherwise. Such an arms race ultimately subjects all involved parties to increased danger.

In certain cases, the acquisition of a weapons system may even pose a direct threat to a country's own security. Typical of this sort of superoffensive arms are weapons that represent a great threat to a potential opponent but are themselves very vulnerable. They could provoke a preemptive first strike. This is not merely a theoretical possibility, and an illustration of such an occurrence is the way the Middle East war of 1967 broke out.[9] Israel and Egypt both had offensive bomber fleets on open, unprotected desert airfields. Each side knew that if it let itself be caught by surprise, the opponent could easily destroy its planes on the ground with bombs from the air and in this way acquire a substantial advantage in a war. After Egypt had closed the Bay of Aqaba to Israeli vessels, and war appeared imminent, it is understandable that Israel did not want to wait and see but quickly destroyed most of the Egyptian air force before it could be used against Israel. If, on the other hand, both sides had possessed hard-to-penetrate air defenses, then it is likely that neither side would have wanted to take the initiative in fighting, unnecessarily sacrificing its armed forces to a superior defense.

A similar situation can develop also with nuclear arms. One of the most dangerous recent developments in this field has been the increasing accuracy of missiles and especially the development of multiple independently targeted reentry vehicles (MIRVs). If a single warhead can destroy an enemy's missile with many warheads, then the temptation is strong on each side to strike first in order to limit losses.[10] A nuclear war is by no means inevitable unless *both* sides acquire a first-strike capability but fail to maintain an invulnerable second-strike capability.

Another dangerous and unnecessary development is the reduction of the warning time between the discovery of an incoming missile (through satellites and radar) and its impact. Whereas the flight time for intercontinental missiles is about thirty minutes, the Pershing II missiles that are being stationed in Western Europe would be able to reach the Soviet Union in only about five minutes.[11] This factor will not only reduce the security of the Soviet Union, but the security of the West as well. The North American Air Defense (NORAD) radar warning system has generated a number of false alarms about a potential Soviet missile attack, partly because of computer failure, partly because of human error. Fortunately, all these warnings have been identified in time as mistakes, but if the time available for discovering a mistake becomes ever shorter, and the proposed strategies of "launch on warning" are followed, then there is a growing danger of an accidental nuclear war.

The following argument justifying such developments is sometimes offered: We want to do our best to prevent a war, and we would prefer not to have to develop such destabilizing weapons systems. But if the other side develops a new weapons system, we have no choice but to do the same, for we cannot afford to fall behind. This argument sounds convincing, but it is wrong. If one side takes steps that make war more likely, it does not help at all for another side to also make war more likely. Measures that *reduce* the threat of war must be taken, and often these are entirely different from what an opponent may do.

A purely defensive measure against nuclear weapons is fallout shelters, which Switzerland has built for the bulk of its population, and continues to expand, even though they can offer only limited protection. But such civil defense programs are purely defensive only if a country does not possess any nuclear weapons itself. If a nuclear power begins to construct shelters, its potential enemies have reason to worry that these might be preparations for a first use of nuclear arms, since shelters would reduce that country's civilian losses during a retaliatory second strike. The combination of defensive and offensive arms can be even more threatening than the offensive arms alone. One must assess the entire system of a country's armaments and defense preparations, not only portions of it, in order to judge whether that system is predominantly offensive or defensive.

Switzerland possesses no nuclear arms nor any other means of mass destruction, and all its general defense measures are in accordance with international law, which prohibits the "indiscriminate conduct of war against the population of the opponent" (sec. 512). Unlike the defense doctrine of many countries, Switzerland stresses the importance of preventing an automatic escalation of conflict in the nuclear age through appropriate, but not excessive, reactions to hostilities (sec. 412).

It is often argued that a purely defensive military posture is very expensive. Even if that were true, cost considerations become secondary when survival is at stake. But the fact of the matter is that true defense is less expensive than an outward-oriented military posture. In 1977, Switzerland spent 2.1 percent of its national income for military purposes, compared with a world average of 4.6 percent and 5.3 percent for the United States and 8 percent for the Soviet Union.[12] Even if not all of Switzerland's defense expenditures are included in the military budget (for example, private contributions to civilian shelters, food reserves, and part of the time spent for training in the militia army), its defense expenditures are still comparatively modest.

Nonmilitary Defense[13]

Armed national defense is concentrated exclusively on inflicting as severe damage as possible on a potential aggressor and through this means, to prevent aggression in the first place or, if that should fail, repel an aggressor and liberate occupied territory. But there is a whole range of other, nonviolent means that can also contribute to making aggression unattractive. One can keep as low as possible any gains that an aggressor may hope to win from conquest. In addition, one can make peaceful cooperation more attractive by increasing the gains and reducing the losses of a potential enemy as long as it does not attack.

Table 8.5. Military (1) and nonmilitary defense (2,3,4)

Enemy Attacks	Enemy Does Not Attack
1. <u>increase enemy's losses</u>: armed defense and/or retaliation	3. <u>reduce enemy's losses</u>: no exploitation; no "loss of face"
2. <u>reduce enemy's gains</u>: nonviolent resistance; industrial sabotage in occupied areas of one's own country	4. <u>increase enemy's gains</u>: scientific, cultural, political, and economic cooperation; trade, diplomatic, and humanitarian services

Those three possibilities, which an effective policy of dissuasion should include, but which are still being neglected by many countries, can be subsumed under the notion of "nonmilitary defense." Among the gains and losses to be considered are not only lives and material goods but also prestige or humiliation, loss of time, and anything else that a decision maker may value. These four possibilities, one military and three nonmilitary, are summarized in Table 8.5, and following are some examples of nonmilitary defense measures that are mentioned in the Swiss concept of general defense.[14]

In order to keep the expected gains of an aggressor as low as possible, (case 2 in Table 8.5), the population is being urged not to cooperate with an occupation force and to offer passive resistance. These tactics would mean that an enemy would be confronted with an ungovernable country. Preparations have been taken to blow up bridges, tunnels, and railway lines in occupied areas; warehouses and stocks of goods would be destroyed before they fell into enemy hands; and industrial plants could be rendered useless for an enemy without destroying them if a few essential parts were removed. During the Second World War, the Swiss government permitted the transport of nonmilitary goods through the Alpine tunnels between Gemany and Italy, but made it clear that in case of an attack on Switzerland, those tunnels would be blown up and made useless for many years. This threat helped prevent an attack on Switzerland. If Switzerland had prohibited the use of those tunnels instead, but an enemy could have gained access through the use of military force, that prohibition would have invited an attack.

In order to make peaceful cooperation as attractive as possible (case 4 in Table 8.5), Switzerland seeks mutually beneficial trade relations with other countries as well as scientific, technical, and cultural cooperation; offers assistance in cases of natural disaster; makes its diplomatic services available to other countries; participates in international organizations; and supports international law. Development cooperation is also part of these measures.

In order to keep the losses of a potential enemy as low as possible if it does not attack Switzerland (case 3 in Table 8.5), the main principle is Switzerland's neutrality. Since Switzerland has no obligation through treaties with third parties to get involved in a war outside of its borders, none of the parties in a conflict sees any need to eliminate the Swiss army as a potential source of danger. Since Switzerland is prepared to fight exclusively inside its own territory after being attacked, it does not pose a threat to any other country.

The decision not to fight unless attacked first was taken by Switzerland unilaterally. Through this means, it increased its own security without threatening the security of others. If it had waited for reciprocal measures from neighboring countries, particularly from Germany before the Second World War, it could have waited in vain. In a similar way, nuclear powers could strengthen their own security by adopting a policy of no first use, regardless of whether they trust their opponents to adhere to the same policy or not.

There certainly do exist circumstances under which the security of a weak country can be strengthened if it becomes a member of a defense alliance—Switzerland itself was founded as a defense alliance of three cantons (Uri, Schwyz and Unterwalden in 1291). But if a war breaks out, its scope is automatically extended if military alliances exist. It may even happen that an irresponsible member of an alliance, sensing that its power is increased because of its alliance, may give in to the temptation to engage in unnecessary provocations of an enemy. In that case, the existence of an alliance would make a war not only more devastating but even more likely. It has been Switzerland's experience that it is an advantage for it not to be a member of any military alliance as long as other potential members are not equally well prepared and equally careful to prevent war.

Many people seem to believe that small nations, unless they ally themselves with big powers, can never be as secure militarily as a big power. It is clear that the military forces of a small nonaligned country will be inferior to those of a great power, but what influences a potential aggressor's decision to go to war or not is not only the cost of the war but whether the expected benefits of aggression outweigh the costs. If the benefits are kept low, even a small army can provide a sufficient deterrent against aggression. There is no reason why the ratio of costs to benefits should be lower for a small country than for a large one.

There are also other ways, besides its neutrality, in which Switzerland seeks to prevent that a potential enemy sees any loss in not attacking. "Switzerland has renounced the use of force in backing its demands vis-à-vis other states" (sec. 423), preferring instead to take any such grievances before the International Court of Justice, and the Swiss government refrains from praising or criticizing foreign governments. In general, it seeks to convince any potential enemy that a Switzerland left in peace and independence is more useful than a destroyed Switzerland.

All of these nonmilitary measures can help make an attack on Switzerland less likely without threatening any other country. Security is strengthened through a variety, or an abundance, of defensive measures. Any country that neglects to supplement its military defense with nonmilitary measures substantially weakens its security.[15]

Is cooperation with a potential enemy appeasement, which is dangerous, as the Munich agreement has shown? It is the exact opposite. Appeasement means to give in to an enemy when it is aggressive, and thus to encourage more aggression. But cooperation during peacetime, which would be withdrawn in case of an attack, discourages aggression.

A Number of Problems

Overall, Switzerland's security policy has served it well. Any country that wishes to apply the same basic principles should find them useful in strengthening its own security as well as international peace. Switzerland's defense preparations do not threaten the security of any other country. It is therefore not afraid if other countries follow the same security policy, but welcome that fact.

Naturally, not everything is perfect; there are also a number of problems. The amount of Switzerland's official development assistance (currently 0.25 percent of its national income compared to the UN guideline of 0.7 percent) is one of the relatively lowest among the industrial nations, even though Switzerland enjoys one of the highest per capita incomes. Of course, financial assistance to unpopular or corrupt governments can hinder the process of development rather than promoting it. There is certainly reason to be cautious about the use to which assistance is put, but well-selected projects, which can permanently improve the situation of the people who are most in need, require urgent support. In order to remove injustices in the world voluntarily, as a form of nonmilitary defense (and certainly also for humanitarian reasons), Switzerland should increase its efforts in this area.

The problem of conscientious objectors to military service requires a more satisfactory solution than mandatory jail sentences. The Swiss defense doctrine states that freedom and democracy must not be defended in a way that is incompatible with those principles. Conscientious objectors should have the opportunity to serve in nonmilitary forms of defense, for a somewhat longer period than is required for military training, if they wish to do so.

Despite an extensive discussion of nonviolent civil disobedience and other forms of nonmilitary defense, no maneuvers are being regularly held in Switzerland for such forms of defense as yet. How can people be credibly expected to practice such forms of resistance if they have never been prepared for such behavior?

Even though peace and conflict research is mentioned as being part of Switzerland's effort to contribute to a decrease in international tension and to the peaceful settlement of conflicts and disputes, the resources devoted to this research have been very limited so far and dependent mostly on voluntary private contributions. In what state would military defense be if it had to rely on voluntary donations? At the first UN Special Session on Disarmament in 1978, Secretary General Kurt Waldheim appealed to all nations to make available one-tenth of 1 percent of their military expenditures for research and education in the field of disarmament. That sum would detract very little from military efforts, and the money could possibly make a significant contribution to national and international security by enabling researchers to explore ways of eliminating the causes of war and of solving conflicts without resorting to violence long before hostilities have escalated to a level at which a peaceful settlement is difficult to achieve.

All of these shortcomings can and should be corrected. In spite of them, Switzerland's security policy seems one of the most successful ones, if one considers the long period of peace that the country has enjoyed.

A Brief Glance at History

How did this security policy evolve in Switzerland? During the first 200 years after its founding, from 1291 to 1515, Switzerland participated in many wars, fighting off attempts at subjugation and conquering some territory. A turning point occurred in 1515 when two Swiss armies, one in the service of the French king and one in the service of an Italian baron, met on opposing sides in a battle at Marignano in northern Italy and almost completely annihilated each other. When the few wounded survivors brought news of this event back to Switzerland, there was deep horror, indignation, and a realization of the futility of war.[16] The conviction gradually evolved that the best policy is to keep out of other countries' disputes by taking a neutral stand, by having a strong defense of one's own borders but not participating in any war on foreign soil.

Today, Swiss people who fight in a foreign army face imprisonment upon their return or lose their citizenship.

Since 1515, many wars have raged in Europe, including two world wars in this century, but Switzerland has enjoyed almost 500 years of peace with only two brief interruptions. From 1798–1815 Switzerland, like most of Europe, was occupied by Napoleon's armies, and in 1847, there was a brief civil war between Catholics and Protestants, but it ended the same year. In the 1960s, there was a growing movement for autonomy among a French-speaking Catholic minority in a German-speaking Protestant canton, but that dispute was solved peacefully without the loss of a single life when, in 1978, those communities that elected to do so were allowed to form a new canton, Jura.

Many consider Switzerland's neutrality selfish and immoral. They maintain that when there is great evil in the world, it is necessary to go to war for the right cause. It is clear that those countries that receive help to liberate them from oppression will be grateful, but Switzerland is so small and weak that it could hardly come to the rescue of other countries that are not able to defend themselves. Switzerland may serve the cause of peace best by remaining neutral and helping all conflicting parties communicate with one another.

Conclusions

The main purpose of this chapter has been to show that it is possible for a country to make a contribution toward peace without sacrificing its national security by

1. increasing purely defensive arms and nonmilitary defense efforts;
2. reducing offensive arms that stimulate arms races, so as not to pose any real or imagined threat to other countries that would make them insecure and thus tempted to initiate a preemptive first strike;
3. making the structure of the entire society as invulnerable as possible through decentralized federal forms of organization, economic self-reliance on various levels, and creating an equitable social order that is perceived as being worth defending; and
4. undertaking peace initiatives by offering assistance to other nations when they need it, sharing useful information, strengthening just international law, etc.

The more nations take such a position, the safer the world will be. Measures to strengthen one's defensive capability, while reducing any offensive threat to others, have the advantage that they can be taken unilaterally, without having to wait for reciprocal steps by other nations, and without endangering one's own national security.

To preserve peace and one's own security, it is necessary to make it clear that aggression can never succeed. But it is equally important to make it credible that one does not pose any threat to others as long as they leave one in peace. To threaten others, or even to allow them to wrongly believe they are threatened, can be suicidal in the nuclear age.

Notes

A preliminary version of this chapter was presented as a paper at the Conference on Militarization, Development, and Alternative Strategies for Security, Oslo, May 25–27, 1981. I am grateful to participants at that conference for helpful discussions. In particular I wish to thank Johan Galtung for valuable insights into the concepts and theories underlying this chapter. Of course, I am alone responsible for the content. A related article is my "Invulnerability Without Threat," *Journal of Peace Research* 19:3 (1982), pp. 205–225.

1. The issue of "structural violence," for example, in the form of international economic inequality, is as important as the problem of direct violence in the form of war. But that issue would go beyond the framework of this chapter and is not discussed.

2. See Kenneth Boulding, *Stable Peace* (Austin: University of Texas Press, 1978), p. 33.

3. In Karl Menger, *Moral, Wille, und Weltgestaltung* (Vienna: Springer-Verlag, 1934). Translated as *Morality, Decision, and Social Organization* (Dordrecht, Holland: D. Reidel, 1974).

4. See for example, Johan Galtung, *The True Worlds: A Transnational Perspective* (New York: Free Press, 1980).

5. A comprehensive oficial statement of Switzerland's defense policy is given in the *Report of the Federal Council to the Federal Assembly on the Security Policy of Switzerland (Concept of General Defense) (of June 27, 1973)* (Bern: Zentralstelle für Gesamtverteidigung, 1973). Section numbers in the text refer to quotations from this statement.

6. See for example, Johan Galtung, Peter O'Brien, and Roy Preiswerk, eds., *Self-reliance: A Strategy for Development* (London: Bogle L'Ouverture Publications, 1980).

7. See Gene Sharp, "Making the Abolition of War a Realistic Goal," Wallach Award Essay (New York: Institute for World Order, 1981).

8. See Dietrich Fischer, "Dynamics of an Arms Race with Offensive or Defensive Arms," Discussion paper no. 81-06 (C. V. Starr Center for Applied Economics, New York University, 1981).

9. This problem is discussed further in George H. Quester, *Offense and Defense in the International System* (New York: Wiley and Sons, 1977).

10. Such proposals may be found in an article called "Victory is Possible" by Colin S. Gray and Keith Payne, *Foreign Policy* 39 (1980), pp. 14–27.

11. McGeorge Bundy, "America in the 80's: Reframing Our Relations with Our Friends and Among Our Allies" (Address to the New York University Sesquicentennial Conference, October 16, 1981).

12. Stockholm International Peace Research Institute, *World Armaments and Disarmament: SIPRI Yearbook 1979* (New York: Crane, Russak and Company, 1979).

13. Much of this section is based on Johan Galtung, "On the Strategy of Nonmilitary Defense: Some Proposals and Problems," in Bartels, ed., *Peace and Justice: Unity or Dilemma* (Nijmegen: Institute of Peace Research, Catholic University of Nijmegen, 1968); reprinted in Johan Galtung, *Essays in Peace Research*, vol. 2 (Copenhagen: Christian Ejlers, 1976). See also Galtung, *The True Worlds*, chap. 5.

14. See *Report of the Federal Council to the Federal Assembly.*

15. Suppose that before the Second World War Switzerland would have taken hostage the diplomatic personnel of a superpower, isolating itself internationally and losing support; would have made itself defenseless by letting its army dissolve itself; would have prohibited the use of German in its schools in German-speaking regions, causing internal disunity and making the country look weak; would have called on the German people through daily broadcasts to overthrow the murderous dictatorship of Hitler. These acts would have violated all of the above principles of dissuasion. It is doubtful, to say the least, whether under such circumstances Switzerland would have been spared war. Clearly, the moral blame for an attack on Switzerland would have rested on Hitler's Germany, but that would not have helped much.

16. It is likely that after a nuclear world war, with the slaughter of hundreds of millions of innocent civilians, the world will come to realize the futility of war in general. But it may be too late.

9
Conflict and Restraint: Poland, 1980–1982

Paul Wehr

In July 1980, a movement of social and political protest began in Poland that was to shake the foundations of that nation and the rest of the socialist world. The formation in Gdansk of the independent labor movement, Solidarity, led to a national struggle for power that lasted nearly eighteen months. The government's imposition of martial law in December 1981 forced Solidarity underground, and it was later outlawed by an act of the Polish Parliament. Yet some of its former leaders remain in hiding or in exile to this day, and occasional demonstrations indicate that popular sympathy for Solidarity continues throughout Poland. However, I have chosen to refer to Solidarity in the past tense in this chapter, because as a formal labor organization it no longer exists.

The conflict between the Polish government and Solidarity could be viewed as simply an abortive attempt at reform crushed by a repressive state. A careful analysis of events that occurred over a two-and-a-half-year period, however, reveals much about how conflict evolves and by what means it can be kept within bounds. We get an unusually clear glimpse into sociopolitical conflicts in an authoritarian state. The Solidarity-government conflict—an important phase in the continuing struggle between the workers' movement and the state in Poland—illustrates a basic contradiction in socialist polities. Elitist control in a state in which the ideological orientation is officially egalitarian inevitably generates popular discontent.

The emergence of a "new class" of political, managerial, and military bureaucrats is at the center of the conflict in Poland. "It is the bureaucracy which formally uses, administers, and controls both nationalized and socialized property as well as the entire life of society. The role of the bureaucracy in society, i.e. monopolistic administration and control of national income and national goods, consigns it to a special privileged position . . . a new ruling and exploiting class."[1] Poland's New Class, similar in so many respects to the power elite that Mills[2] describes as being at the pinnacle of U.S. social, political, and economic structures, is determined to monopolize authority in the Polish social system. Such monopoly, as Dahrendorf[3] makes clear, inevitably gives rise to challenging "interest groups," which often coalesce into broad movements. These groups seek to protect their interests by increasing their share of authority. When the position of the New Class is closely linked to a hated foreign power—in the Polish case, the Soviet Union—nationalist emotions further encourage the conflict, and the legitimacy of the New Class is still more doubtful.

The fiction that in a "people's state" there is no divergence of interests, no social conflict, has been clearly revealed in the Polish case. The Solidarity movement brought the conflict into the open, and this chapter focuses on the constraints on that conflict and the restraints on the use of violence by both sides.

The Conflict

Every conflict formation has elements that can be mapped.[4] It has historical, geographical, political, and economic contexts within which it occurs, and parties with different degrees of power conflict over the goals and issues that determine the distribution of that power. A conflict also presents certain dynamics and modes of communication, performs certain functions, and contains a potential for limitation, including restraints on the use of force and violence. We will look at each of these elements in turn.

Contexts

The Solidarity movement was one of a series of post-World War II political upheavals in Eastern Europe—East Germany (1953), Hungary and Poland (1956), Czechoslovakia (1968), and Poland (1970). Solidarity emerged from a quarter century of Polish labor activism, and, unlike earlier movements, was able to develop both breadth and depth. After the establishment of Workers' Councils in 1956, the workers' movement struggled for economic and political reform, protection of workers' rights, and democratization of the work place. The councils provided a link among the working class, the intellectuals, and students.[5] The councils reappeared periodically, though as Kolankiewicz and Taras[6] note, by the mid-1970s they were no longer active bodies.

Bureaucratic resistance to reform initiated after the 1956 uprising was stiff, and by 1958 it had forced the abandonment of Wladyslaw Gomulka's New Economic Model. It also forced the replacement of Workers' Councils by Independent Workers' Conferences—a decided setback for industrial self-management and worker participation. By 1960, work-place demo-cratization had been brought to a dead halt, and during the subsequent decade, Poland's political culture "was characterized by an ever-greater alienation of individuals and groups within society from the institutions and processes of government."[7]

The Polish economy declined steadily as well, from a 10 percent growth rate in 1956 to one of 5 percent in 1970. In the latter year, food shortages, price increases, high unemployment, and economic stagnation led to strikes and demonstrations which were repressed by the police with a substantial loss of worker's lives. When Edward Gierek replaced Gomulka as head of the party and state, worker demands were still primarily for improved wages and working conditions.

Through the 1970s, the Gierek regime unwittingly increased the likelihood of further labor revolt with a number of its policies—policies that, ironically, were intended to do quite the opposite. The government fired and imprisoned labor radicals, and many Solidarity leaders, including Lech Walesa, were victims of this purging. Gierek further pursued the quiescence of key labor sectors by granting higher wages and increasing consultation with leaders in those sectors.

Gierek implemented a massive program of industrial modernization relying heavily on foreign credits. A managerial "revolution" was nec-essary, so modernization and institutional modifications were made on the lower levels of the labor unions, in local government, and in the party bureaucracy. The intent was to spread authority more broadly, but the consequence seems to have been a more resistant, entrenched, and uncontrollable bureaucratic structure. Decentralized decision making does not seem to have increased.

Under Gierek, the role and prestige of the party was enhanced. "In 1973 the Party received for the first time legislative recognition of its directive programmatic role in society."[8] The party was to a certain extent democratized through purging and an increased involvement of manual workers; on the other hand, party members became an even more visible privileged class within Polish society. Within the party and government, these institutional changes brought the inevitable reaction from those people whose interests were thereby threatened.

During the 1970s, Gierek allowed increasing cultural freedom and consequent links with the West, which permitted members of the intelligentsia to give expression to their own and workers' dissatisfaction. The election of a Polish pope in Rome and his subsequent visit to Poland further stimulated nationalist sentiments.

The 1976–1980 period was one of growing intellectual ferment. An explosion of underground literature celebrated Poland's cultural heritage and circumvented authoritarian government control. The NOWA publishing house alone clandestinely produced 200 censored and banned works during the period. In the "free universities," students, faculty, and workers politicized one another, and they joined forces in 1976 to form what would become the Committee for Social Defense (KOR). Through its newsletter, *Robotnik,* KOR circulated a Workers' Rights Charter demanding the right to strike.[9] That charter heavily influenced the Twenty-one Demands presented by Solidarity to the government in the summer of 1980. What developed during that time was the conception of a popular socialism, a proletarian socialism, a "socialism with a human face." That the movement that erupted in July 1980 was reformist, not antisocialist, is clear from opinion polls.

> Socialism as a means of organizing society appears to be acceptable to most Poles. Two-thirds (66.4%) of a May/June 1981 sample of shipyard workers in Gdansk and Gdynia, the home of Solidarity and the site of several uprisings against the regime, agreed with the statement: "The present political system in Poland is basically good. That which is bad was caused by unfit people in inappropriate places."[10]

Despite some well-intentioned policies, Gierek's economic legacy was dismal. He left behind him an indebted, inflated economy supporting a corrupt and incompetent regime. The government's Popkiewicz Report (May 1981) estimated that $10 billion of "air money" was chasing nonexistent goods around the economy. Food shortages were common. Private agricultural production (84 percent of the total) was especially poor, made worse by deficient transportation and marketing systems. Gierek's attempts to graft entire imported industrial plants onto an infrastructure that was incapable of supporting them were made still less successful by bureaucratic bungling. A licensing agreement with the Massey-Ferguson Company illustrates the point. An entire tractor factory was built, ready to produce, before it was realized that neither plant nor product—both based on the English measure system—would be of any use in a Poland that was on the metric system. By 1980, borrowing for such unsuccessful grafts had helped increase Poland's indebtedness to the West to $25 billion.

By July 1980, then, the political and economic situations were producing the conditions for a revolution of rising expectations: (1) an indebted and disintegrated economy in which a well-paid but unproductive labor force had little to buy; (2) a self-conscious working class that was increasingly hostile toward the ruling class of arrogant, corrupt, and incompetent officials with undeserved privileges; and (3) an intellectual ferment giving voice to popular dissatisfaction. The soil of discontent was ready for the seed of rebellion, which soon broke the surface. The strikes and the formation of Solidarity signaled the failure of Gierek's policies. He was soon to be replaced by Stanislaw Kania.

In July, strikes broke out in several regions in response to sharp meat price increases. Organizer Anna Walentanowicz was dismissed from the Lenin Shipyard in Gdansk, and her fellow workers responded with a sit-in strike, out of which emerged Solidarity and its Twenty-one Demands. The Lenin Shipyard strike was notable for the political as well as economic demands that were made on the government—an important benchmark in the worker-state struggle. The shipyard strike was rapidly linked with strikes in other industrial cities through an Interfactory Strike Committee. By August 31, Solidarity negotiators had reached sufficient agreement with their government counterparts to end the strike. Ahead lay months of working out in practice what had been agreed to on paper—a process that had been only partially completed when martial law was imposed fifteen months later.

The July–August strikes revealed the economic and political power of Polish labor. That power was rapidly augmented as the strikes caused other discontented elements—intellectuals, decentralists, academics—to coalesce into a broad movement. By early September, Solidarity had become not just a labor revolt but a movement of mass discontent challenging the control of a ruling class of bureaucratic, industrial, military, and party elites. Simply put, it was Solidarity against the state. The Twenty-one Demands aimed at no less than full socialist democracy, and the events of July and August 1980 gave the movement a genuine sense of power and autonomy. As a participant in those events observed:

> The first act of the social contract is an agreement among the people on the idea of social reconstruction. The agreement is concluded in the moment when from a large crowd of people somebody climbs up on an excavator and speaks to them on behalf of them; that moment the mobs transform into [a] social movement. This marks the end of [the] . . . "power of [the] powerless" and opens the time of the power of [the] powerful," conscious of themselves.[11]

The Social Contract agreed to by Solidarity and the government suggested what democratic socialism might look like but not how it was to be achieved. It was this quandary—power with no clear design for exercising it—that kept Solidarity in check for many months. From September 1981 to November 1982, Solidarity struggled against an intransigent government to build the institutions of democratic socialism.

Finally, the geopolitical context of the Polish conflict is essential for our understanding of it. Poland is "a land between"—a nation, as Milosz[12] put it, trampled by the "elephant of History." Culturally Western,

Poland is militarily, economically, and politically oriented toward the East. An historical invasion corridor to the Soviet Union, Poland must be made militarily secure and politically stable for the USSR. The Warsaw Pact alliance, with Poland at its strategic center, guarantees that security and stability. As a major coal producer, Poland is also central to the Council of Mutual Economic Assistance (COMECON) and the other East European economies. These immutable geopolitical and economic realities shaped and restrained the Polish conflict at every turn. Solidarity leaders consistently acknowledged Soviet security interests and, until the escalation in September 1981, avoided directly threatening them.

Parties

The primary parties in the conflict were (1) Solidarity, pressing for shared power; (2) the leaders of the ruling Polish United Workers' party (PUWP), resisting that demand; and (3) the Soviet government, pressing the party to resist. Since party and government coincide in socialist states, I will use those terms more or less interchangeably. The conflict was made more complex by the existence of divisions within the parties. In Solidarity, there was a steady erosion of Walesa's power as radicals progressively turned their impatience with government intransigence into an open challenge of Walesa's moderate leadership. Within the PUWP, hard-liners and reformers debated the appropriate response to Solidarity demands. Although little is known about internal conflict among the Soviet leaders concerning the USSR's policy in regard to Poland, one can safely assume some opposition of hard-line and moderate opinion.

Both Solidarity and the party changed during the conflict. Solidarity grew rapidly to a membership of nearly 10 million, and it built a communication network to reach those members. Solidarity's leaders made decisions and negotiated through its National Commission. Yet, in December 1981, it was still a rather loose organization of local branches and disparate geographical regions and was not yet sufficiently developed to keep members in line, as the autumn 1981 wildcat strikes had revealed.

The PUWP, at the outset of the conflict, was tightly controlled from the top along strict "democratic centralist" lines. The effort to transform this governance began with a conference of 500 party dissidents in April 1981 at Torun. From this meeting flowed a strong current of pressure for democratization of the party—"not a challenge to Communist ideology, but a challenge to the gap between theory and practice," as one would-be reformer expressed it.[13] The presence of a million Solidarity members within the PUWP served to encourage party reform. At the July 1981 Party Congress, many hard-liners were swept from the Central Committee, and only four Politburo members were reelected. Secret ballot elections and multiple candidacies for party offices were instituted.

Even the Parliament (Sejm) was showing an independent spirit in rejecting half the legislation proposed by the government. The latter, too, made some attempt to purge its more corrupt members. The imposition of martial law several months later, however, in all likelihood firmly reestablished "democratic centralism."

The Soviet government, although involved less directly in the confrontation, was nevertheless a primary party in the conflict. With its threats of invasion, economic pressure, diplomatic visits, and military presence, it stiffened the Polish government's resistance to sharing power with Solidarity. Although the role of the Soviet forces was proscribed to one of "non-interference in Poland's internal affairs" by the agreement that had followed the 1956 Poznan riots,[14] 30,000 Soviet troops were permanently stationed in Poland. Their presence was irritating to the Poles, and the troops made even more real the constant threat of Soviet military intervention. The Soviet government felt its security interests in Poland would be protected only by orthodox party control, and it would assure that control by force if necessary.

Other states were not idle observers. Czechoslovakia and East Germany were especially active in support of the Polish hard-line leaders. The United States and other Western nations also had important interests at stake. Poland's $27 billion debt to the West reflected the depth of the latter's involvement, and Western governments and banks encouraged what restraint they could with threats of political and economic sanctions.

The majority of the Polish people can be characterized as a secondary party, looking on apprehensively while Solidarity and the government contended. The people were mainly concerned with economic conditions in Poland and desired an accommodation that would improve the economy. That the average Pole was not necessarily a strong supporter of Solidarity and its methods is suggested by opinion surveys in early November 1981, in which only 46 percent of those polled approved a recent one-hour nationwide strike.[15]

The church and the army also played important roles. Although it sympathized with Solidarity's goals, and its clergy gave the union strong moral support, the church's primary concern was for political stability. Church leaders used their long-standing modus vivendi with the government to play the role of mediator—though with their less-than-complete neutrality that was difficult. The Solidarity-government conflict served to enhance the church's position in two ways. As advisers and confessors to a number of important union leaders, the clergy had influence with that group. As a potential mediator and a restraining influence upon Solidarity, the church gained influence with government leaders. To the degree that the church could help keep the lid on a simmering pot, it was valuable to the state. By October 1981, Party

Secretary Kania was calling for a national unity front of state, church, and Solidarity.

Until September 1981, the armed forces remained somewhat above the conflict, ready to intervene if the conflict went too far, too fast. As General Wojciech Jaruzelski assumed first party, then government, leadership, however, the army became a primary party in the conflict.

Leadership turnover further confused the situation. Personalities came and went. Stefan Cardinal Wyszinski, the mediator and counselor of restraint, died and was succeeded by Josef Glemp. Kania ceded party and government control to Jaruzelski, and even the U.S. presidency changed hands during the conflict period. One can only speculate about the impact of such impermanence on negotiations and other important dimensions of the conflict.

The ultimate concern throughout the period was how to keep the three primary parties from becoming violent. Each had substantial power; the stakes in the power game were high, as was the level of emotion; and yet there were effective restraints on both the conflict and the use of force.

Issues

The central issue in the conflict was defined by Solidarity's demands for independent status and for greater participation in national decisions. In socialist polities, authority is concentrated exclusively in a unitary state. That monopoly was challenged by Solidarity. With its large membership—a quarter of the population at its zenith—Solidarity posed a serious challenge indeed.

Precisely how and to what degree power should be shared was the basic theme running through the fifteen months of Solidarity-government negotiations. Solidarity leaders envisioned the emergence of a state-Solidarity partnership in social and economic planning, with the Twenty-one Demands agreed to in the Social Contract as the basis. In that contract, the government had conceded Solidarity's right to exist and had agreed to certain safeguards for the group's independent status. In subsequent negotiations about legislation to implement the agreement, the government resisted on each of the twenty-one points. The law limiting state censorship took thirteen months to enact, and negotiations on legislation to protect independent trade unions, the right to strike, and union access to government radio and television facilities had achieved no real progress by late 1981.

Many other issues were connnected to the central one of Solidarity's participation in national decision making independent of state control. Solidarity would act as a monitor of government economic performance, and socialist democracy, in which basic civil rights would be protected, should replace the existing technocracy of a privileged ruling class. Performance, not party membership, should determine tenure in government posts. Poland's national identity, history, and culture should be celebrated, not repressed, by the government. The government should be accountable to the people for the inefficiency, corruption, and arrogance of its officials. Such goals, clearly stated as they were by Solidarity, threatened the government's power monopoly directly and indirectly, the political structures elsewhere in the socialist bloc.

How deeply Polish workers felt shut out of policymaking is indicated by opinion surveys of the period. Nearly three-quarters of the shipyard workers polled in 1979 felt that the worker had no influence "over what happens in the work place."[16] Feelings of helplessness and nonparticipation were at the heart of the Solidarity movement and its demands for change.

The inability of Solidarity to force guaranteed protection from the government led directly to its defeat. Solidarity's size and the character of its governance made it especially vulnerable to infiltration and attack. Its strengths were also its weaknesses. Its large, loose membership gave it power but exposed it to subversion, spying, and manipulation. Its democratic and open governance drew popular support in part because it contrasted so sharply with the government's style. Its nonsecretive methods were perceived as less threatening, perhaps, by the Polish and Soviet governments. Precisely because of these attributes, however, Solidarity was relatively easy to suppress. The government knew exactly what the group was doing and planned to do, and leaders were easy to locate for arrest. When Solidarity was forced underground, it was almost impossible for it to shift to a clandestine mode of operation.

Dynamics of the Conflict

The conflict was marked by dynamics that Coleman[17] suggests characterize a great deal of social conflict. A precipitating event, the Walentanowicz dismissal, made latent conflict manifest. The subsequent strikes and negotiations clarified the issues and identified the parties. Polarization occurred throughout the autumn of 1980 as people opted for change or reaction, and it occurred not only around the Solidarity and government polar extremes but within those organizations as well.

Thus, we are facing a period—let's hope that it does not last too long—of coexistence on the basis of a division into "we" and "they." This division has in fact existed since long, but was carefully camouflaged. Today, at least, we are ready to admit publicly that the tie between the party and the masses has been severed and is not easy to restore immediately.[18]

Escalation was punctuated by confrontations—among them, the government's refusal to register Solidarity in October 1980 and the police attack on Solidarity in Bydgoszcz in March 1981. Frustration within Solidarity at the slow pace of negotiations to implement the Social Contract fueled the escalation. The government's resistance and maneuvering strengthened the position of the radicals within the union, which, in turn, encouraged the intransigents among government leaders.

The question of termination of the Solidarity-government conflict remains a confusing one. In one sense the conflict was terminated by the formal elimination of one party by the other—first by physical repression as martial law was imposed, then by an act of Parliament abolishing the union. Yet Solidarity continued in an altered form through the period of martial law, and there is still the possibility of its resurgence or reformulation.

One of the most striking dynamics was the explosive growth of Solidarity. That growth depended heavily on the union's ability to communicate with its members, with the Polish people, with its government opponent, and with the world beyond. Solidarity communicated in three important modes: by the mass media, through cultural and political symbols, and by face-to-face and written interpersonal communications.

Solidarity never gained the direct access to state television and radio it sought, though the negotiations of August 1980 were televised nationally. The union had to create its own communications system using the churches, strike bulletins, flyers, and its own national and local newspapers.

Cultural symbols were important communicators for Solidarity. Polish history, Polish Christianity, Polish independence documents and events, the different workers' revolts since 1956—such were heavily used. Great symbolic power also emanated from certain persons and their offices in Poland's present and past—Pope John Paul II, Cardinal Wyszinski, General Wladyslaw Sikorski, Lech Walesa. Monuments to workers killed in Gdansk and other centers of labor revolt, Warsaw's Victory Square, the resurrected Constitution of 1791, the Solidarity logo with its national flag and colors—all communicated ideas, emotions, and states of mind.

Holidays assumed new significance. Rural Solidarity, the agricultural counterpart of labor Solidarity, was established in 1981 on Good Friday. Constitution Day was revived and coincided with the Feast of the Virgin Mary. The May Day parade became more Polish when its route was altered to pass through Victory Square. National, religious, and Solidarity symbols melded in a rich symbolic mixture. In authoritarian systems, in which a lack of free speech sharpens people's skill with implicit and nonverbal expression, such symbolism is especially powerful.

Face-to-face and interpersonal communications within Solidarity occurred through formal and mass meetings and by telephone, telegraph, and letter. Solidarity leaders traveled constantly throughout Poland to build the union's structure and its communication network. This very personal, face-to-face contact was essential for building trust as well. Solidarity's communication with government officials occurred mainly through the joint negotiating teams that were established to produce legislation. There were also occasional meetings between head negotiators such as Walesa and Mieczyslaw Rakowski.

Escalation of the conflict appeared to stimulate another dynamic cited by Coleman. Formal information sources, such as newspapers, cannot meet the increased demand for information, and people come to rely increasingly on word of mouth, which encourages rumor, exaggeration, and other forms of information distortion.

One other dynamic was evident—the operation of what Coleman calls Gresham's Law of Conflict.[19] As the conflict escalated, the more extreme leaders tended to push aside the more moderate. Within the party, the more flexible and conciliatory Kania was replaced by the more rigid Jaruzelski; in Solidarity, Walesa was challenged with increasing success by more radical leaders, such as Andrzej Wiajda.

Functions of the Conflict

A final important element in social conflict is the functions it performs. The Solidarity-government conflict appears to have been in some respects functional for one or more of the parties, and may have even been so for the polity as a whole. Only time will reveal its long-range consequences.

Coser[20] views social conflict as integrative and functional given certain conditions and limitations. We must take care to clarify the term "function" as Coser uses it—to describe a process that creates or strengthens, a process devoid of any normative connotations. We must also remember that a conflict that is functional for a part of the system may at any point in time be dysfunctional for other parts or for the system as a whole.

The Polish conflict validated certain of Coser's propositions about the functions of conflict. That conflict "*serves to establish and maintain the identity and boundary lines of societies and groups . . .* [and] contributes to the establishment and reaffirmation of the identity of the group"[21] was illustrated by the resurgence of Polish nationalism and the growth of worker self-consciousness through Solidarity. Conflict with the government, and indirectly with the Soviet government, thereby strengthened both the Polish nation and its working class.

Coser's proposition that *"conflict with another group leads to the mobilization of the energies of group members and hence to increased cohesion of the group"*[22] also appears to have been validated. Government resistance and threats created cohesion within Solidarity among the diverse political, occupational, and class elements that were seeking change. But for cohesion to continue, as Coser notes, the group must have an underlying value consensus. Among Solidarity leaders, such consensus did not exist, and protracted conflict with the government ultimately produced dissension and a weakening of the leadership group.

Another proposition concerns structural preferences. *"If a relative balance of forces exists between the two parties, a unified party prefers a unified opponent."*[23] This point was evident in the government's ambivalent attitude toward Solidarity's efforts to terminate wildcat strikes and unauthorized demonstrations and to otherwise control its branches. On the one hand, the government wished to limit the union's power; on the other, it wanted a stronger union that could control its members and factions, and with which the government could fashion, if necessary, a stable and cooperative relationship.

"Conflict acts as a stimulus for establishing new rules, norms and institutions, thus serving as an agent of socialization for both contending parties."[24] Leaders in Solidarity and the government learned how to negotiate and through such accommodation produced an independent organization within an authoritarian state. That organization was later suspended, then eliminated, but the skills of negotiation and the precedent of an independent organization persist to influence the future of Poland. Other skills and methods of open, nonviolent conflict—the strike, third-party mediation, threat control—have probably become more deeply rooted in the political culture of Poland. To the extent that that is true, the conflict has strengthened Poland as a nation.

Finally, Coser contends that conflict is functional as *"a test of power between antagonistic parties.* Accommodation between them is possible only if each is aware of the relative strength of both . . . [and] may indeed be a means of balancing and hence maintaining a society as a going concern."*[25] The Solidarity-government conflict was such a test of power. By September 1981, there appeared to be a rough power equivalence that was tolerable to the government. As Solidarity's challenge became less restrained in October and November, the government, anticipating an intolerable flood of change and loss of power, declared a state of internal war. Another explanation might be that the test of power revealed to the government how powerful Solidarity actually was—

Table 9.1. Factors restraining political violence (slashed
entries indicate the presence of restraint before martial law was
imposed and its absence thereafter)

| | Conflict Party Restrained | | |
Restraining Factor	Solidarity	Polish Government	Soviet Government
Adherence to nonviolent means	yes	yes/no	yes
Lack of capacity for violence	yes	no	no
Crosscutting affiliations and bonds	yes	yes	no
Polish nationalism	yes	yes	no
Conflict timing/pace	yes	yes	yes
Threat control	yes	yes	no
Negotiation and mediation	yes	yes	yes
World opinion	yes	yes	yes
Absence of secrecy	yes/no	yes	yes

the government then had no alternative but to crush the movement as
best it could.

Restraints on Political Violence

How did the three primary parties limit the conflict to nonviolent
means for as long as they did? Why was violence not used earlier? Which
factors worked to restrain it in the Polish conflict? Table 9.1 and the
following discussion indicate some of these factors.

Adherence to Nonviolent Means

A major restraint upon the conflict was Solidarity's adherence to
nonviolent methods. When violence did occasionally occur, union leaders
acted as mediators and mitigators, not as instigators of the violence. In
Katowice in October 1981, for example, when a worker-police confrontation turned violent, Solidarity leaders quickly intervened to mediate
a settlement.

Withdrawal of cooperation by striking was the union's most powerful
weapon. Strikes in factories, offices, universities, and agricultural enter-

prises demonstrated Solidarity's power to disrupt. The mere threat of a strike often sufficed to bring the government to the bargaining table. The nationwide warning strike in March 1981 brought government concessions that were enough to avert a general strike.

Noncooperation also took the form of physical obstruction, such as the bus and taxi blockade of central Warsaw in August 1981 to protest food shortages and price increases. Hunger strikes were used by political prisoners to gain release. In some instances, Solidarity branches used nonviolent direct action in defiance of both the government and the union's National Commission. Ten thousand women in Zyrardow, in October 1981, dramatized demands for more food and lower prices with a sit-in occupation of the factory they worked in. A moratorium on strikes agreed to that very month by Solidarity and the government was increasingly ignored by union locals. In direct defiance of it, 180,000 workers in the western province of Zielona Gora carried out a one-hour warning strike. The National Commission finally called a one-hour nationwide warning strike not only to press demands for more union participation in national policymaking but also to end the wildcat strikes. In such cases, the strike was used by Solidarity as much to retain control of its members as to force government concessions. To minimize such internal conflict, Solidarity's research organization conducted opinion surveys to help the union's leaders keep in touch with grass-roots concerns and provide an information base for policy.

Lack of Capacity for Violence

The methods of nonviolent action used by Solidarity served not only to demonstrate the union's widespread support and numerical strength but its peaceful intentions as well. It should be noted, however, that the group's adherence to nonviolent means of effecting change was pragmatic as well as ideological. True, the church urged reliance on nonviolent initiatives and responses, but not all Solidarity leaders accepted nonviolence as a moral position. All did, however, support nonviolent means for practical reasons. First, nonviolent direct action had been substantially successful. It seemed to be working for Solidarity. Second, the alternative approach promised less, not more, success. Even if arms had been available to the union, the consequences of anticipated brutal repression by the government were not attractive. Nor would the organizational structure of Solidarity have lent itself to the carrying out of organized violence. With its exceedingly democratic and open governing process, the movement could not have effectively carried out paramilitary or guerrilla actions. Its only access to violence would have been to encourage its members to engage in violence independently.

Neither the Polish nor the Soviet government had an ideological commitment to eschewing the use of violence. Both refrained, nevertheless, from using it until December 1981, simply for pragmatic reasons. There was neither the need for a violent response to the Solidarity challenge nor a credible justification for doing so that the governments could present to the world and their own peoples. When martial law was imposed, Solidarity's continued adherence to nonviolent means rendered the Polish government's justification for the use of armed force transparent indeed. The imposition of martial law signaled the government's shift from nonviolent to violent response. Even then, violence was carefully and cautiously applied, and one could argue that restraint continued to operate, though somewhat less effectively.

Crosscutting Affiliations and Bonds

The structure of the conflict encouraged restraint as crosscutting affiliations worked against unbridled conflict. For example, the memberships of the PUWP and Solidarity coincided to a degree and both overlapped with the church's membership. Such multiple affiliations seemed to moderate behavior on all sides.

Dahl[26] and Lipset[27] see this process as being peculiar to pluralistic political systems and more specifically, as the primary way conflict is kept within bounds in the United States. Coser, too, links the conflict-regulating function of multiple affiliations closely with pluralistic, open societies.

> We come to see that the multiple group affiliations of individuals make for a multiplicity of conflicts crisscrossing society. Such segmental participation, then, can result in a kind of balancing mechanism, preventing deep cleavages along one axis. The interdependence of conflicting groups and the multiplicity of noncumulative conflicts provide one, though not, of course, the only check against basic consensual breakdown in an open society.[28]

The Polish experience suggests that this dynamic operates in nonpluralistic societies as well. One could argue that Poland was on its way to becoming a hybrid political system—a polity somewhere between the pluralistic and monolithic poles—and that cross pressures and affiliations operate in different degrees in systems along the political continuum.

The number of oppositional pairs within a conflict situation is important. The proposition that the larger the number of conflicts in any particular context, the less likely that any one will become all-inclusive with respect to persons, groups, energies, and resources[29] was well illustrated by the plethora of conflicts that were subsidiary to the Solidarity-government antagonism. These included the intra-Solidarity and intra-government struggles for control, each played out on several levels. Certain binding institutions restrained and stabilized the conflict, as did certain leaders within them. Cardinal Wyszinski linked the church with Polish nationalism as he reminded Catholics on both sides that they were united in their Polishness and their Christianity.

Polish Nationalism

Until the December 1981 imposition of martial law, the army helped bind the nation together. Fiercely nationalistic and truly a people's army in its composition, it remained in the background as a peacekeeper should the conflict get out of hand. The army was reluctant to intervene in the government-labor conflict, because when it had done so in 1970, many workers were killed and injured, and the intervention had caused division within the army itself. At that time, General Jaruzelski stated, "Polish soldiers will never again fire on Polish workers."[30] Since the government, whenever possible, used police and militia rather than the regular army to repress resistance to martial law, the army remained, technically speaking, in compliance with the Jaruzelski dictum. It is unlikely, however, that it still performs the binding function it did prior to the declaration of martial law.

Strong nationalism and a cultural and an economic homogeneity combined to further restrain violence in Poland. Nazi genocide, postwar boundary and population shifts, and the economic structure of the socialist state have given modern Poland an unusual ethnic, religious, and social integrity. This homogeneity permitted dissimilar groups to develop strong affiliations with one another. A case in point was the collaboration of academics and intellectuals with workers in Solidarity research groups and on negotiating teams.

Conflict Timing and Pace

The timing and pace of the conflict was influential. Unlike the Prague Spring of 1968, whose suddenness provoked an invasion, the Gdansk Summer of 1980 had historical antecedents that made it somewhat less threatening. It was only the latest, most serious eruption in a long-evolving conflict between the state and labor—a stepwise escalation with intervening periods of calm. Even the intense Solidarity-government phase was interrupted by periods of negotiation and reflection.

Threat Control

Among the three primary parties, Solidarity and the Polish government exercised caution in the threat images they presented to their opponents. Although occasional verbal extremism occurred, the conflict was marked by relative verbal restraint until late 1981. Solidarity leaders interviewed by me recognized the "limits of the possible," and understood that the pace and scope of change in Poland and Eastern Europe are limited by certain geopolitical realities that constrain both Polish and Soviet leaders. Poland must continue for the forseeable future to be a middle ground— culturally a member of the Western community but politically oriented toward the East. Verbal assurances from Solidarity that it was not threatening the Soviet security community and its communication lines to central Europe were a conscious part of this war of nerves. With some exceptions, until its provocative September 1981 call for independent workers' movements elsewhere in the socialist bloc, Solidarity was also careful to disclaim any pretension of being a model for labor reform throughout the Eastern European countries.

Most Solidarity leaders recognized certain "avoidance taboos" in the conflict—"'things which are just not said or done' regardless of provocation,"[31] and "taboo" was the precise word used by the union's national secretary to describe Solidarity's self-imposed limits on challenges to government authority and Soviet influence.[32] Such verbal restraint was, however, difficult to maintain as the conflict escalated. After decades of government mismanagement and censorship, everyone had ideas they wished to express openly, and union democracy encouraged them to do so. At the Solidarity congress in September-October 1981, verbal restraint failed, and the war of words escalated rapidly. In fact, the Jaruzelski government used incautious statements by Walesa and others made at a Radom union conference in November to justify the government's declaration of martial law.

Negotiation and Mediation

Although restraint on all sides kept armed force and violence at bay for a year, resolution of specific disputes within the conflict was also important. Negotiation, the key process, required both intermediaries, such as the church, and the development of negotiating skills by the disputants. Although the church had opposed the government in the past, its primary goal in the Solidarity-government conflict was political stabilization and the avoidance of bloodshed. It consistently urged moderation and negotiation. Archbishop Glemp was working toward a trilateral partnership of government, Solidarity, and the church when martial law was imposed.

Solidarity and the government negotiated both internally and with one another. Internal negotiation took place in meetings and congresses. Negotiation between the primary parties occurred usually in closed session, sometimes in public, and was occasionally televised. It was carried out by negotiating teams and from time to time by individual leaders. The latter approach, however, caused friction within Solidarity as union democracy encouraged collegial decisions and maximum participation. Nevertheless, Walesa put the indelible stamp of his cautious, pragmatic negotiating style on the bargaining process. As he told the crowds at the Lenin Shipyard after signing the Social Contract, "There are no losers, no winners, no vanquished—we have communicated with one another, the country is watching."[33]

The conflict styles of leaders on both sides fell along a conciliation-confrontation continuum. Within Solidarity, Walesa was very much the conciliator and had a pragmatic sense of what would work. From the government side, Rakowski negotiated effectively. Sometimes negotiators agreed but could not sell the agreement to the people they represented. The first labor law agreement produced by the negotiators was rejected by some Solidarity leaders. Later, in 1981, the government's plan for worker self-management, which had been agreed to by Walesa and his supporters on the National Commission, was only reluctantly approved after long and stormy debate.

The conciliators on both sides were constantly at odds with confrontationists on their own sides. Solidarity had to strike a balance between the confrontation necessary for its own growth and the compromise necessary to avoid government collapse, government repression, or Soviet intervention. The government, on the other hand, had to resist sufficiently to preclude a Soviet invasion while conceding enough to avoid crippling strikes and other challenges to its authority. Finding those balances was difficult indeed.

In complex negotiations, such as those reforming Polish labor law, teams of negotiators would work separately on different sections, then jointly construct a settlement. Each team had its expert consultants, with Solidarity relying heavily on university professors.[34] Negotiation is a skill that had to be quickly acquired in Poland. There was some familiarity with negotiation in pre-Solidarity Poland as Social Conciliating Commissions had been established earlier in response to labor unrest. Through them, workers and officials had gained some experience in negotiation and compromise. The commissions, however, were tied to administrative units, which, over time, had increased in size to the point where the former could no longer function. When the 1980 strikes broke out, the commissions existed in name only. Nevertheless, the practice of negotiation, though rusty from neglect in an authoritarian state, showed a surprising vitality.

The structures for decision making and negotiation also had to be created, first during the Gdansk strikes. Says Polet, "the 'Polish Summer' provides a remarkable lesson in democracy and conflict management."[35] Strike committees were elected in each of the 300 striker-occupied

n as well. His authority lay partly in his intuitive understanding
his people wanted and how far he could push the opponent
achieving it. Within Solidarity, he did not force an issue but
rsuasion and compromise to produce support for his position.
eat of resignation was his trump card if all else failed.
sa was skillful in negotiating with the government as well—
ning some momentum without pushing his opponents to acts
eration. It is likely that Walesa's declining popularity with the
evel Solidarity leaders and in the opinion polls, which showed
d public support for increased union militancy, helped to move
rnment toward force and violence.

pinion

nly public and government opinion beyond Poland served to
the behavior of the Polish and Soviet governments both before
ng the martial law period. The image of state violence used
vorkers in a "workers' state" would have been extremely em-
g and subversive, particularly in the socialist and developing
ut more generally as well. It is somewhat less clear how that
might have influenced Solidarity's behavior. World opinion
restrained Solidarity from violence in that the image it wished
t to the world was that of an organization working peacefully
e and a less violent and repressive society.

Secrecy

ence of secrecy in Solidarity's operations and governance before
sition of martial law appears to have restrained the use of
by the group's opponents. Although secrecy may decrease the
ity of an organization in one sense, it requires a good deal
to maintain and encourages one's opponent toward violence,
y torture and other forms of duress, to break the secrecy.
so intensifies the sense of threat generated by a protest or-
, giving the government both a reason and an excuse for the
ned force. After the declaration of martial law, Solidarity's
o had not been arrested went underground, and secrecy became
A restraint was removed, though Solidarity violence did not

raining Factors

ctors worked to restrain both the USSR from intervening
nd Solidarity from pushing too far, too fast. Soviet preoc-
ith the war in Afghanistan made the prospect of similar
t in Poland unattractive, especially since the Soviets expected

210

factories. These were linked through an Inter
to the Solidarity team negotiating with gover
and-file participation in the negotiation proc
Twenty-one Demands and in two-way consul
conflict management process.

Intra-unit conflict regulation was equally
teams were inclined to come to agreement
groups on both sides tended to be more conf
Within Solidarity, Walesa and his fellow neg
conflict with a more radical majority of the N
wanted more change faster. Within the par
stood against a Central Committee that r
both sides, rank-and-file members appeared to
conciliatory negotiators. This situation was
ulation as a whole. In opinion polls, 65 p
November 1980 expected both sides to mal
had risen to over 75 percent by November
grass-roots support and used it against h
National Commission. He gauged the mod
union members and shaped his position to
became more intransigent, however, sup
leader colleagues. By October 1981, Wa
majority against his most radical opponen
the commission chair, although that was
Solidarity convention, not among the ran
less conciliatory, more radical leaders adv;
confidence in and approval of the union (
government-sponsored opinion polls refl
to 58 percent of respondents reporting t
November 1981.[37] The same polls showe
number of people who trusted the gov
percentage points separated those Solidar

Inequalities within the labor force fi
within Solidarity. Certain industries, fact
occupational groups had enjoyed the f
that privilege persisted to some degree
privileged sectors wanted equality and
merely because it emerged from Gdansk
wildcat strikes undermined the National
in October 1981.

The decline of support for Walesa a
Solidarity was a key factor in the escalati
He had been an important force fo

politici
of wha
toward
used p
The thr
Wale
maintai
of desp
second-
decrease
the gov

World (

Certa
moderat
and dur
against
barrassin
worlds b
opinion
probably
to preser
for chang

Absence o

The ab
the impo
violence b
vulnerabil
of energy
particular
Secrecy al
ganization
use of ar
leaders wh
necessary.
occur.

Other Rest

Other f
militarily
cupation
involvemer

strong resistance to military occupation. Although Solidarity had no plan as such for resisting a Soviet invasion, the question was widely discussed, and Soviet leaders were aware of this fact. Preparations to resist an anticipated invasion were improvised at least twice in 1981. When a March invasion seemed imminent that year, major factories were barricaded, and Solidarity leaders were taken there for protection. Plants close to the Soviet border, which were linked by telex to others further west, functioned as early warning posts.[38] Carefully planned resistance could have been very effective, and even without organized preparation, an invader could have expected a general strike, sabotage, guerrilla resistance, and other measures to obstruct the occupation. Walesa is reported to have said, "Someone can make me do something with a pistol to my head, but I can destroy ten other things when they are not looking."[39] It was hardly coincidental that a dramatization of Jaroslav Hasek's *Good Soldier Schweik*,[40] that master of imaginative obstruction, was playing to large Warsaw audiences in 1981. The Soviets were also deterred from invading by warnings from Western European nations with whom trade and good relations were highly valued. The proposed Soviet–Western European gas pipeline alone was sufficiently important to the Soviet economy to encourage restraint.

Soviet pressure moderated Polish behavior as well. The threat of military intervention certainly restrained conflict within Poland as the Poles' transcending goal was to keep Poland intact and as independent as geopolitical realities permitted. This desire encouraged Solidarity-government compromise and mutual restraint in the face of a common threat—Soviet military intervention. Economic pressure, too, was applied by the USSR, which supplied at the time an estimated 95 percent of Poland's crude oil, 45 percent of its natural gas, and 84 percent of its iron ore.

Polish government leaders were skillful at resolving conflicting views with the Soviets. More than once Kania and Jaruzelski negotiated in Moscow for time and forbearance to avoid military intervention. There appeared to be genuine bargaining going on on those occasions rather than the brutal coercion the Czechoslovakian government had been subjected to in 1968.

Counterforces

The restrained political violence during the Solidarity period is striking in light of the tension and conflict-generating processes at work: the resentment accumulated over years of authoritarian rule and censorship, the lapses in verbal restraint, the leaders' occasional loss of control over subordinates engaging in police brutality or unauthorized strikes—any of which could have triggered civil war and a Soviet invasion. The dynamics of escalation seemed consistently to be working against restraint. There were also the members of state instruments of violence—the motorized militia (ZOMO) and the Internal Defense Forces (WOW), for example—whose selection, training, and isolation from the people put them, in a sense, beyond the restraint system.

By September 1981, these counterforces were actively destroying the complex web of restraints. Solidarity's National Congress in September-October clearly showed the moderates' loss of support as the union was demanding an equal share in national policy formation. The government proposed a Front of National Accord, in which Solidarity would have a role that was decidedly subordinate to that of the party and government; the union countered, proposing a Social Commission for the National Economy, with Solidarity having veto power as an equal participant. Negotiation around these disparate plans for sharing power continued intermittently through November. Throughout the autumn, unauthorized strikes, threats of a general strike, the government's refusal to live up to past agreements, and its use of riot police to disperse public protests produced a continual escalation.

Within Solidarity, the conflict escalated as well. In November, fourteen members of the Regional Commission resigned, charging that Walesa and his advisers were too accommodating toward the government, which, increasing the pressure, was seeking a strike ban and emergency powers from Parliament. On December 4, in Radom, Solidarity's National Commission rejected the government's Front of National Accord proposal as a sham and subsequently called for a national referendum on Jaruzelski's leadership. On December 7, the government published excerpts from secret recordings of the Radom meeting and charged Solidarity with conspiring to overthrow the Polish state. At six in the morning, December 13, a "state of war" and the creation of a Military Council for National Salvation were announced. Two-thirds of Solidarity's activists were arrested and interned in isolation camps. Polish society was militarized. The conflict had entered a new phase.

Restraint Under Martial Law

The imposition of martial law signaled a failure of the tight restraints on force and violence that had characterized the Polish conflict to that point. During the first six months of martial law, the Military Council suspended and repressed Solidarity through mass arrests of its leaders, restriction of communication and travel, and the breaking up of industrial sit-in strikes and street demonstrations. Thousands were imprisoned, hundreds were injured, scores were killed.

Yet even in this state of war as the government called it, the restraints upon force and violence continued to a surprising degree. With several exceptions—most notably, the Zawiercie steel plant and Wujek mine repressions—there was little bloodshed in the enforcement of martial law. Given the emotion and the high stakes on both sides, one would have expected much more. The treatment of the 3,000 internees officially listed by the Military Council seems not to have involved more suffering then is naturally inherent in political detention, separation from families, and deprivation of civil rights. By early May 1982, a third of the people who had been detained had been released. One should not give the military government excessive credit for the relatively low level of overt violence however. Had Solidarity abandoned or even more actively pursued its nonviolent resistance, violence against the union would have been greater. The Polish state had long assured its capacity for repression through its police and militia—who were isolated from the people in special camps and trained for quick and brutal intervention—and when blood did flow under martial law, it was from such intervention. It seems, nevertheless, that the violence restraints and the conflict resolution skills that had operated during the preceding year had not disappeared and continued to work, albeit under difficult conditions and in new ways.

Solidarity maintained its adherence to nonviolent means following the declaration of martial law. It created a Union of Resistance through clandestine bulletins, broadcasts, and word of mouth. In April 1982, Radio Solidarity began its resistance instructions with a slogan from the World War II Polish underground. The Polish government, though, had learned from the Czechoslovakian resistance of 1968, which had used mobile transmitters to great advantage, and Radio Solidarity was not on the air for long.

Drawing on the Polish experience with the German occupation, Solidarity suggested "circles of resistance"—cells of five friends or acquaintances, linked into networks. Solidarity's "Basic Principles of Resistance"[41] emphasized the points of special vulnerability in clandestine resistance and how to protect them.

1. *The protection of union leaders and organizers* by *not* establishing strike committees, which can easily be arrested.
2. *The disruption of the system wherever possible by obstructionism* modeled after *The Good Soldier Schweik*—"You Know Nothing" when questioned by authorities, "you are a moron" when directed to do something conflicting with your conscience. "In this way you create a void around [commissars and informers], and by flooding them with the most trivial matters you will cause the military-police apparatus to come apart at the seams," "work at half-pace the way we did under the Germans."

3. *Social quarantine and social solidarity.* Help your friends with "social self-help funds" but "shun the company of informers, conformists and their ilk."
4. *The need for active involvement of all.* "Paint slogans, hang posters on walls, distribute leaflets, pass on independent publications."

Two striking aspects of this resistance to the military government were the continuing commitment to nonviolent action and the prominence of women in it. An account of the strike at Krakow's Lenin Steelworks reads:

The managers also tried to get us to leave the plant because there would be intervention. Many people [left]. . . . Not a single woman ran away. . . .

When the [riot police] and army entered the steelworks grounds, the entire Strike Committee . . . along with the students and women, gathered together in the main hall . . . [our leaders] told us not to resist, to keep together, to protect our friends. Bortnowska especially kept up our spirits: she joked, she gave us courage, she laughed at our fear. . . .

We formed a circle and joined hands, the women and students in the center. The students, dressed in workers' uniforms and hard hats, were determined to face everything. They wanted to fight, but we would not let them. . . .

At nine . . . the [riot police] entered the hall. There were about 500 of them. They were armed with truncheons, shields and face-protectors. We narrowed the circle, hands joined. The women were crying. We prayed for the [police], for their wives and children. One of the ZOMO officers took off his helmet along with us. I saw tears in his eyes. In an instant he was seized by other ZOMO officers and thrown out of the hall. . . . None from our division was beaten . . . none resisted . . . the ZOMO claimed that they had orders to beat us if we offered resistance.[42]

The government continued to apply restrained force throughout the period of martial law, partly because Solidarity resistance was progressively weakening and partly to avoid provoking its resurgence. Government suppression of open political demonstrations in May and August was restrained. By late 1982, curfew and travel restrictions had been lifted, and most political prisoners, including Walesa, had been released. At the end of the year martial law was formally suspended.

Important restraints on the use of violence and force by the primary parties during the conflict period overshadowed the absence of such restraints. In the limited analysis presented in Table 9.1, the former outnumbered the latter more than two to one. More important, those restraints carried over into and through the period of martial law. An important question for conflict researchers, statesmen, and political activists alike would be how to strengthen and increase the number of such restraints in future civil conflicts. An especially difficult problem is how to inhibit those "runaway processes" that Coleman suggests may take a conflict beyond the point at which the restraints no longer operate. The Poles did remarkably well, in this instance—operating by rule of thumb, so to speak. They might do even better in the future, using some solid analytical observations from conflict research.

Conclusion

From this examination of the Polish conflict as well as a number of restraints that kept armed force and violence at bay for a surprisingly long time, several conclusions can be stated with some confidence. First, Solidarity developed some innovative methods for increasing democratic participation within a rigid political system. Through an imaginative use of nonviolent action, Solidarity leaders discovered what Sharp[43] has called the "social roots of political power." Imagination, wisdom, and caution produced a sharp conflict with minimal violence—a good base from which to resume the conflict if and when conditions permit.

Second, the imagination of Solidarity contrasts sharply with the unimaginative response of Jaruzelski and government intransigents. One could argue that pressed from the front by Solidarity and from the rear by the Soviet government, Jaruzelski had no option other than martial law. This analysis suggests otherwise—that a Solidarity-government partnership was possible, one that built on rather than exploited the restraints both sides had exercised to that point. It would seem that a great potential for resolving the Polish contradiction was lost when the decision to repress Solidarity was made. That decision may have become unavoidable once leaders trained in political skills were replaced by those prepared in military ones. Militarization of the conflict, in my view, was a grave error—a particularly unimaginative response.

It is too early to assess the impact of the conflict and the restraints, to judge whether the gains for Poland outweighed the losses. On the positive side of the ledger, the conflict functioned to create an important new institution in Polish political culture, which in turn strengthened national consciousness and encouraged new political skills on both sides. The arts of negotiation, nonviolent direct action, and restraint have been learned and will not be easily forgotten. They and the Solidarity movement have become an important part of Poland's political culture. The violence of foreign invasion and occupation and consequent international instability were avoided, no insignificant value in an increasingly militarized and nuclearized world. The Poles were also reasonably humane with one another throughout the conflict, again no mean achievement.

On the negative side, questions remain. What impact has the military repression of Solidarity had on Poland's political psyche? Will the disillusionment that followed immediately on the heels of elation deepen the despair of the Polish political man and woman? Will this despair, and the realization that nonviolent action and negotiation to bring about change did not work, lead dissidents to armed force? One must also ask, of course, what was the alternative to Solidarity? Would a more conventional movement, clandestine and armed, have been more successful, even possible? How else than with the approach Solidarity took could the runaway processes of conflict have been controlled?

The conflict over Solidarity is not an isolated one. It is another important benchmark in the modification process working within East European political systems. Hungary, Yugoslavia, Romania, Poland, East Germany, Czechoslovakia, each has developed its own response to conflicts over nationalism, class, and power.

There is important research yet to be done on the Solidarity conflict. What can we learn about the general usefulness of the Solidarity "model" in other authoritarian societies under dictatorial regimes? Is secrecy under such conditions necessary and functional? Specialists in social and non-military defense should learn more about Solidarity's plans for resisting a Soviet invasion and their possible deterrent effect. Much more needs to be known about the conflict regulation and violence restraints this chapter has touched upon in only the briefest way. A critical analysis by Polish social scientists who participated in the conflict would suggest how it might have been successfully carried on.

The Polish experience, properly researched, may suggest new ways to achieve purposive change in failing political systems—ways that are less violent and dangerous for the states involved and for the global system. The more skillful a people becomes at transforming and defending national institutions without provoking the use of armed force, the better its chance for survival in a dangerous world. As for the case in question, only with time will we know whether Solidarity was merely a short-lived aberration or, in Walesa's words, was "the weapon of the twenty-first century."

Notes

The author acknowledges the helpful comments of Peter Wallensteen and the support of the Institute of Behavioral Science, University of Colorado, in the preparation of this chapter.

1. Milovan Djilas, *The New Class: An Analysis of the Communist System* (New York: Praeger, 1957), p. 35.

2. C. Wright Mills, *The Power Elite* (New York: Oxford University Press, 1959).

3. Ralf Dahrendorf, *Class and Class Conflict in Industrial Society* (Stanford: Stanford University Press, 1959).

4. Paul Wehr, *Conflict Regulation* (Boulder, Colo.: Westview, 1979), chap. 1.

5. Ingemar Nilsson, *Arbetarråden: Polen och Ungern,* Federativserien 20 (Stockholm: Federativ Forlag, 1976), p. 50.

6. George Kolankiewicz and Ray Taras, "Poland: Socialism for Everyman?" in Archie Brown and Jack Gray, eds., *Political Culture and Political Change in Communist States,* 2d ed. (New York: Holmes and Meier, 1979), p. 107.

7. Ibid., p. 118.

8. Ibid., p. 120.

9. Robert Polet, *L'Été polonais,* Special edition of *Cahiers de la Reconciliation* (Namur, Belgium) 12 (December 1980), p. 8.

10. James P. McGregor, "Polish Public Moods in a Time of Crisis: Findings of Polish Surveys Since August 1980" (U.S. International Communication Agency, Washington, D.C., 1982), p. 7.

11. Jerzy Jedlicki, "Form and Content of the Polish Social Contract," in Jan Danecki, ed., "The Transformation in Poland: Some Points of View" (unpublished collection, Research and Prognostics Committee "Poland 2000," Praesidium of the Polish Academy of Sciences, Warsaw, April 1981), p. 5.

12. Czeslaw Milosz, *The Captive Mind* (New York: Knopf, 1955), p. 213.

13. Professor Lech Witkowski, one of the organizers of the party reform meeting in Torun, quoted in *Svenska Dagbladet* (Stockholm), April 16, 1981 (author's translation).

14. Alexander Mirecki, "Polen: Krigsmakten och de politiska kriserna," *Internationella Studier* 2 (1981), p. 6.

15. McGregor, "Polish Public Moods," p. 14.

16. Ibid., p. 11.

17. James Coleman, *Community Conflict* (New York: Free Press, 1957).

18. Wladyslaw Markiewicz, "On the Origin of the July-August Strikes in Poland," in Danecki, "The Transformation in Poland," p. 18.

19. Coleman, *Community Conflict,* p. 14.

20. Lewis Coser, *The Functions of Social Conflict* (New York: Free Press, 1956).

21. Ibid., p. 38 (emphasis added).

22. Ibid., p. 95 (emphasis added).

23. Ibid., p. 132 (emphasis added).

24. Ibid., p. 128 (emphasis added).

25. Ibid., p. 137 (emphasis added).

26. Robert Dahl, *Pluralist Democracy in the United States: Conflict and Consent* (Chicago: Rand-McNally, 1967).

27. Seymour Martin Lipset, *The First New Nation* (Garden City, N.Y.: Doubleday, 1967).

28. Coser, *Functions of Social Conflict,* pp. 78–79.

29. Raymond Mack and Richard Snyder, "The Analysis of Social Conflict— Toward an Overview and Synthesis," in Fred Jandt (ed.), *Conflict Resolution Through Communication* (New York: Harper and Row, 1973), p. 67.

30. Mirecki, "Polen," p. 7.

31. Mack and Snyder, "Analysis of Social Conflict," p. 83.

32. Author's interview with Andrje Celinski, Gdansk, June 26, 1981.

33. Polish film *Robotnicky '80* (1981).

34. Author's interview with Jacek Kurczewski, member of Solidarity's labor law reform negotiating team, Warsaw, June 25, 1981.

35. Polet, *L'Été polonais*, p. 2.

36. McGregor, "Polish Public Moods," p. 17.

37. Ibid., p. 20.

38. Interview with Celinski, June 26, 1981.

39. *Time,* November 2, 1981, p. 37.

40. Jaroslav Hasek, *The Good Soldier Schweik* (Harmondsworth, Eng.: Penguin, 1951).

41. Committee in Support of Solidarity, Press Advisory, Special Edition, "Basic Principles of Resistance," in *Solidarity Information Bulletin* 8 (New York, January 2, 1982).

42. Committee in Support of Solidarity, Press Advisory, Special Edition, New York, January 1, 1982.

43. Gene Sharp, *The Politics of Nonviolent Action* (Boston: Porter Sargent, 1973).

10
Incompatibility, Militarization, and Conflict Resolution

Peter Wallensteen

Incompatibility and Militarization

Existing or perceived incompatibilities might lead to the formation of actors and to conflict behavior, conflict behavior might become armed, and thus social relations might become militarized. Militarization, in other words, relates to incompatibilities within societies. Obviously, there are many different incompatibilities, and the road from incompatibility to militarization is by no means linear. However, militarization is hardly possible without incompatibility, and we thus face the task of suggesting which incompatibilities are the more likely to give rise to militarization.

Incompatibilities can exist in a society without resulting in conflict, indeed, incompatibilities might not even be thought of as such but rather as a "normal state of affairs" or as "problems" rather than incompatibilities. It might often be the work of prophets, academics, or creative personalities to make certain incompatibilities visible and manifest. Still, even pointing to a given incompatibility might not result in action. Action requires an actor. Thus, the process of conflict formation initially is the process by which an incompatibility becomes manifest (seen as an issue and equipped with an actor pursuing the very issue); at a later stage the process refers to the intensification of conflict behavior.

At any given time there will be a multitude of manifest conflicts in society, from the rivalry between individuals, to the struggle between oppressors and oppressed, to the competition between big powers. Only a certain number of these conflicts will become militarized, i.e., waged by armed means by armed actors. The crucial question concerns, not the process of a manifestation of conflict, but the process of a militarization of conflict. Why do certain conflicts become militarized? The follow-on questions are, of course, What can be done in the case of such armed conflicts? How to demilitarize them? and How to develop a state of affairs in which actors can be satisfied and/or an issue can be pursued without violence? The last is here referred to as conflict resolution or durable settlement. Theoretically, there is also the possibility of transforming incompatibility into compatibility by eliminating actors and issues altogether, a state of affairs that could be either complete integration of the formerly contending parties or the complete extinction of one of the parties by the other. Indeed, integration might be the concept used to post hoc describe a process of extinction, and elimination might be the feared result when parties oppose integration. This "ultimate" termination of conflict is at the same time theoretically as well as normatively questionable and will not be addressed in the present context. However, it should be remembered that a great number of actors actually strive to achieve conflict termination, on their terms, rather than conflict resolution.

Incompatibilities Leading to Militarization

In the study of war between states, it is then assumed that four incompatibilities will sooner or later (inevitably?) result in a military confrontation between states. As these incompatibilities form crucial aspects of entire philosophies of war and peace, they actually are elements of schools of thought. Of course, no attempt at a total explanation would exclude one or the other, but the emphasis of different analyses often gives rise to a different ordering of the variables involved. The four schools have already been labeled and need not be outlined in more detail here: Geopolitik, emphasizing incompatibilities over territory; Realpolitik, emphasizing incompatibilities over military power; Idealpolitik, emphasizing incompatibilities over legitimizing principles; and Kapitalpolitik, emphasizing incompatibilities over economic development.[1] In the study of relations between major powers during the 1816–1976 period, it was found that Idealpolitik explanations might have the greatest saliency.[2] However, we are concerned not only with relations between major states but also with small states and nonstate entities. An attempt to use the same typology for nonstate actors is presented in Table 10.1.

The table suggests some analogy between interstate relations and relations between state and nonstate entities. Nonstate actors that could be involved in armed conflicts are, for instance, separatist groups, criminal gangs, revolutionaries, or economic organizations. As always, armed conflict is a two-way affair: Arms can be used by the state or by the nonstate actor. Furthermore, the perceptions of the conflict might differ, and do so most seriously in the state-nonstate relationships. As states often can draw on mutual recognition as well as on an organized power

Table 10.1. Incompatibilities and forms of militarization

Incompatibility Over	Type of Armed Conflict Between States	Type of Armed Conflict Between State and Nonstate Entity
Territorial extension	Border conflicts, rivalry over strategic points, expansionism	Regionalism, nomadism
Military capability	Wars for/against global or regional order	Maintenance of law and order versus criminal or terrorist activity
Legitimizing principle	Wars for/against certain social order	Maintenance versus replacement of certain social order (revolution)
Economic advancement	Wars for/against economic imperialism	Modernization versus traditionalism, labor versus capital

base outside the immediate reach of other states, there might in fact be greater possibilities of communication on an equal basis in state-state relations. In the state-nonstate relationship, the state is a superior party in most respects: It is in control of territory, armed forces, legitimation, and economic resources. The armed opponent will have severe difficulties in communicating its view. As a matter of fact, since the use of force is itself illegitimate, the state can portray any conflict as an attempt to disrupt law and order. Armed opponents, in other words, will have difficulty avoiding being defined as simple criminals rather than as the political opposition.

This problem points to the difficulty of defining a conflict. For instance, conflict resolution assumes that the parties (as well as outsiders) agree on what the conflict is really about, which, in turn, might be determined by the parties' philosophy as well as ultimate aims. Obviously, a party can choose the conflict description it wants and, thus, select one that is favorable to its ultimate aims. Interestingly, it is not impossible to suggest what these ultimate aims could be. They might not be dramatically different among different parties. As a matter of fact, when dealing with states, many writers find that the preservation of the state is the probable ultimate aim. The preservation of a given state is often termed "security," and "threats" are actions that endanger the security of the state. In order to achieve security, a state might become highly expansionist or provocative (endangering its own security in its very quest for security), as is witnessed by the behavior of Stalinist Russia, Nazi Germany, and the nuclear arms competitors. Given that all states strive for this—however elusive—goal of security, what then would be the ultimate aims of various nonstate groups? The goal might be the same, security—security for a group without a state to protect it. However, behind the struggles of the Kurds is the idea that security can only be attained through the creation of a Kurdish state. Similarly, of course, Jews and Palestinians have been arguing for their own states. In the same way, conflicts between the state and criminal nonstate groups often concern the survival of either organization: The state wants to preserve its (near) monopoly on violence; criminal groups want to defend themselves against outsiders that threaten their (lucrative?) trade. Ideological revolutionaries want to abolish an order they believe to be unfit and to replace it with the "correct" order, so that the influence of other groups, which are not particularly well represented in the present setup, will be increased.

This point suggests that human beings are "organizational humans" above anything else. An individual within a certain organization might identify with it, and ultimately, the preservation of the organization might become the rationale for action. Obviously, organizations are created by humans, and perhaps they are created by individuals who need an organization to work within and who cannot be satisfied with the existing ones. The ultimate goal of organizations is preservation, and for groups without organization, to have an organization of their own. Table 10.1 suggests four incompatibilities over which organizations can be created, ways that have a strong potential for making a conflict an armed one. A stable society would, in other words, be one that is rich in organizations and flexible enough to accommodate new organizations. Indeed, this seems to be a fitting description of the Western industrialized countries, which are rich in internal conflict but not in internal armed conflict. The reverse seems true for many of the poorer countries that have a high degree of centralization and little room for organizational diversity, in spite of a great diversity in cultures and ethnic societies (for example, Ethiopia and Iran).

As of now, however, there is little data on the different types of militarization that could exist. For interstate relations, it is suggested that, at least for the major powers, conflicts over legitimate principles might be the most common. For smaller states, or for relations between small and large ones, no comparative investigation exists, but it might be suggested that territorial and military considerations are more important in the former relations; economic dependencies, in the latter.[3] On a more general level, it should be observed, however, that interstate confrontations and wars are not that frequent, as would be suggested by concepts like "anarchy" in describing these very relations. The *potential* for violence might be higher when the disputing parties are both heavily armed, and once a war breaks out, devastation becomes extensive and indiscriminate. Thus, actual outbreaks of war might be less frequent, partly because of the prior knowledge of the consequences of such an action.

However, conflicts between states and nonstate actors do not have the same obvious obstacles built into them. The state is, in a sense, less constrained in its internal behavior than in its external. A consequence is that internal wars, as well as repression, might in fact result in more deaths than do most external wars.

Two studies have presented some preliminary findings that point in the suggested direction. According to the first, conflicts in drought-stricken African states in the early 1970s were more frequent within states than between them.[4] According to the second, the mapping of all types of armed conflicts for two consecutive years (1979 and 1980) suggested that on a global scale armed conflict was more frequent within states than between them.[5] Neither study has, however, incorporated more refined magnitude measures. The former study suggests, further-more, that issues relating to economic and social incompatibilities rarely give rise to military action, but rather result in a lower-scale conflict behavior. In contrast, territorial demands (from outside actors or from internal groups) have a strong military-escalating potential. These points would suggest that certain incompatibilities have a stronger militarizing effect than others: in particular ideological, territorial, and military incompatibilities.

This does not exclude the possibility that economic scarcities can result in militarized conflicts, but it does suggest that scarcity conflicts have to involve other issues in order to move up the escalation ladder. However, this entire field of linkages between different types of incom-patibilities and escalation remains underresearched. For instance, relations between actors that have only one, specified incompatibility might be as strained as those between actors that have a whole set of diffuse incompatibilities. As a matter of fact, the clear-cut nature of the former situation might make it more "dangerous" whereas the tension of the latter might make the actors more cautious.[6]

Incompatibility and Conflict Resolution

Theoretically, the resolution of an incompatibility is only a matter of imagination as most incompatibilities also include points of compatibility.[7] In practice, incompatibilities are very difficult to transcend, as they become entangled with the behavior and the perceptions of the parties

Table 10.2. Substantial forms of settling incompatibilities

Incompatibility Over	Armed Conflict Between States	Armed Conflict Between State and Nonstate Entity
Territorial extension	Mutual division of territory, mutual exclusion from territory	Autonomy, transparency
Military capability	Balance of power, agreed order, mutual disarmament	Demonopolization, power circulation
Legitimizing principle	Détente, peaceful co-existence	Power circulation, decentralization
Economic advancement	Mutual sharing, growth	Mutual sharing, growth

involved. Thus, to suggest ways in which conflicts could be settled, under the assumption that each party has the right to remain a party, might not be what either of the parties actually wants. Struggle might be preferred, and only reluctantly is the alternative of an equitable settlement accepted as victory becomes more remote and the costs of conflict behavior become greater than the costs of locating compatible interests. This cost-benefit calculation, of course, includes not only military destruction but also shifts in alliance patterns, changes in priorities, and changes in the cohesion of the individual parties involved.

However, for a conflict to move from the battlefield to a negotiated agreement, there must be ideas about the possible final outcomes as well as about the processes by which such outcomes can be reached. The former includes visions of demilitarized settlement; the second, visions of demilitarized behavior.

Table 10.2 illustrates demilitarized forms of conflict resolution, assuming that the aim is to find a solution that lies somewhere between capitulation and continued armed contention. Substantial settlements of conflicts between states assume mutual understanding, in a formal or an informal way. Given the lower concentration of power in the interstate system as compared to the intrastate system, this understanding might be more easily achieved. Normally states, even those at war with one another, extend each other formal or informal recognition (if nothing else, by actually fighting one another). Settlements of internal conflicts, however, involve an existing distribution of power or an existing territorial arrangement, which means that conflicts can easily be of a more fundamental form and that the room for mutually acceptable solutions decreases.

However, these differences should not be exaggerated. The low distribution of power among states has its counterparts inside existing states. There is a considerable wealth of groupings, and individuals can become actors in quite another way than in interstate relations (in which individuals almost automatically are classified by their citizenship rather than by their competence).

Examples of lasting settlements that fall into the eight categories of Figure 10.2 are not difficult to come by. Major powers have always found the division of a contested territory preferable to war, particularly if the territory itself is not of immediate strategic significance. European powers had little difficulty dividing territory on other continents during the nineteenth century, but considerable disagreement arose over areas on their own continent.[8]

Settlements of questions of military power have taken several forms, the most frequently quoted, but not necessarily the most successful, being balance of power (in a multipolar and in a bipolar form). Others are agreement on intergovernmental order (the League of Nations, the United Nations) and reduction of military power (disarmament).[9]

Settling conflicts over legitimate order is more difficult. However, principles of coexistence have been applied, not only for the battle between democracy and communism, but also for relations between Protestants and Catholics, Islam and Christianity, and other similar systems.[10] Finally, economic conflicts that are concerned with equitable shares can be handled (almost daily, e.g., through trade negotiations) and could be given reduced priority through continued economic growth.[11]

It should, however, come as no surprise that most of the forms that are seen frequently in the interstate system have their parallels in the intrastate system. Obviously, territory can be divided within states as well as between them. Thus, much of the impetus for Biafran independence in Nigeria has been reduced, not only by the military defeat (which could stimulate revanche instead), but through the changed and decentralized Nigerian federation that was created during the 1970s (even making a political comeback possible for Odumegwu Ojukwu). Also, the post-Franco Spanish Constitution allows for regional autonomy, even with different solutions for different regions, a most daring example. Most solutions stress equal treatment of each region which reduces the room for handling peculiarities of different situations (witness Ethiopia's intransigence in regard to Eritrea). A third example is the creation of a new canton in Switzerland, Jura, to handle particular grievances experienced within an already existing canton.[12]

However, additional insight might be gained by noting that transparency can be increased, and often has to be increased, if a lasting settlement is to be found. Two Nordic examples, albeit not entirely successful ones, concern the Samic population, which can move freely across the borders but still lacks the authoritative representation it would need to find durable security, and the Åland Islands, which, while part of Finland, retain their Swedish nationality, including a flag and restrictions on land purchases by non-Swedes. (In fact, the people of the Åland Islands might be much better off as a noted minority in Finland rather than as a forgotten periphery of the majority country.)

Questions about the concentration of military power have their forms of internal settlement as well. Seldom, however, would such questions be isomorphic to questions relating to interstate balance of power—for instance, maintaining two armed factions, somehow both accepting the same governmental framework. Rather the questions relate to the balance between military and civilian power that provides the necessary decentralization of society. The presence of an active, well-organized civilian society means that power becomes more equitably distributed, thus restricting the power held by the military leaders. A civilian society can also serve to make military power less attractive, in particular if remunerations are higher in civilian activities. The breakdown of the largely military-based European dynasties shows the strength of civilian societies, at approximately the same time major corporations and major trade unions helped tilt the societal balance of power in a demilitarizing direction.[13] If, in addition, there is agreement on the regular succession of power (through elections or other procedures), the attraction of state control becomes further reduced, to the point at which Western societies today need skillful negotiators more than forceful decision makers in order to manage the delicate balancing between different interests.

However, the Western experience might have limited applicability in Second or Third World countries. The degree of centralization in the Soviet Union, China, most Latin American countries, and elsewhere might be much higher than it ever was in the West. This fact means that rather than reducing the strength of the central power, economic development might in fact augment military-related central authority. Neither in the Soviet Union nor in China is the party willing to loosen its grip over society as a result of modernization. As a matter of fact, the idea of a possible alternative model in Poland scared not only the Polish Communist party but also its sister parties in government.[14] Also, in Thailand, as well as in Chile, the military expands rather than retracts as a consequence of economic growth.[15]

Thus, to expect that economic growth will do the job of democratizing societies might be very naive. If the question of power distribution is not directly faced, it will not be faced at all. The successful demilitarization of Greece and Spain suggests that there are possible roads toward demilitarization. However, in these cases the confrontation directly concerned this question.[16]

A convenient form of settlement has been found in the interstate system for incompatibilities over legitimizing principles. By letting each prince choose the religion for his principality, within a given state only one principle is expected to be followed. To have a federation in which one member state is run by a monarch, another by a president, and a third by the party secretary is, so far, unheard of. However, such a situation does exist, at least on a more local level, as for decades, Communists have controlled major cities in some Western capitalist countries (e.g., Italy). Such coexistence has been possible only under one condition: that the parties—at least for the time being—accept the same procedure of power succession, a certain form of elections, a certain form of representation, etc. Given this basic procedural agreement, there should be little problem in having Boston run by the great-granddaughter of George III or Communist party control in New York. The question of legitimation boils down to the issue of selection and election. If the involved parties can agree on this issue, coexistence should be possible between strong contenders within the same country. If, however, one party claims that it is the "leading" one and does not extend the same rights to other parties, resistance is bound to emerge, and settlements will not be possible. As is the case with international settlement, internal conflict resolution assumes mutuality and equality among the parties. A great deal of conflict actually concerns this very issue: whether one party accepts another as legitimate. If not, Ghana's experience of dramatic power shifts between the main contenders suggests the likely development. Ultimately, a personalist, law and order, populist leadership is probable.[17]

Thus, consensus has to be established within a given unit in order for internal coexistence to become possible. Once this consensus has occurred, many pieces fall into place. In Zimbabwe, Ian Smith based his regime on a contempt for democratic principles in order to retain European control. Gradually, although at a high price, this position was eroded, and ultimately, the diminishing white power could not be maintained even with dictatorial means. By accepting a generous African offer in exchange for a consensus on majority rule, agreement became possible. The basis for consensus was an agreement on the voting rights of and the extension of equal rights to all parties involved.

Obviously, the principle agreed to need not be "one person one vote," as many such settlements could result in overrepresentation. One could also envision other principles for power succession, such as the one attempted in Colombia, which has alternating four-year mandates for each party (Frente Nacional). In a democratically inclined world, such agreements might, however, be hard to "sell," both to the public in the country concerned and to the international audience.[18]

Finally, the settlement of economic conflict should be considered. Among the four types of incompatibility, this one is perhaps the most difficult to disentangle. In one sense, everything is economic, which makes the economic issue trivial; in another sense, economics can be narrowed down to a triviality, such as salary increments. The class perspective strikes a reasonable balance between these two extremes. Obviously, there are, in any society, not only economic stratifications (rich and poor) but also structural dependencies (exploitation). This pattern is more general than the simplistic notion that by abolishing one class (more or less defined in legal terms), the entire problem of class conflict can be done away with. As long as there is stratification and structural dependence there are classes. It is difficult to assume that class conflict will inevitably result in revolution or internal war as such a possibility cannot be more true for this category of conflict than for any other. The Scandinavian experience suggests that when class is almost the only issue around which society is grouped, the situation is less likely to lead to confrontation.[19] Rather, various forms of coexistence have been worked out, with each party having a share of the influence and wealth. Supported by economic growth, these experiences have been comparatively nonviolent. One might even suggest that countries that have had armed class conflict have had the class pattern reinforced or intermingled with other incompatibilities. The Russian Revolution certainly was more the result of military disaster, the inadequacy of the postczarist regime, and general economic chaos than of a particular intensification of class antagonism. Similarly, the Chinese Revolution, which was built on peasant mobilization, also drew strength from national disasters and the inadequacy of the Kuomintang alternative. Bolsheviks and Maoists could draw support from nationalist sentiments, particularly during the Second World War.

Armed conflict between state and nonstate actors can thus have four different roots: nationality, force, ideology, and class. In an ideal homogenous society consisting of one nationality, one armed actor, one ideology, and one class, "peace" would exist. Indeed, totalitarian societies often present themselves this way, but in fact, such societies seem to witness bitter internal conflict, particularly within the leadership. The Soviet Union and China, both presenting themselves according to this picture, have seen very devastating developments. An ideal heterogenous society, with many nationalities, a less centralized armed force, competing ideological frameworks, and open class conflict, would seemingly be in constant change, with collective or individual violence. Indeed, there is some evidence to support this, notably India and the United States, which are both closer to this picture.

Surprisingly little research has gone into the question of durable settlements for either interstate or intrastate relations. Indeed, much effort has been devoted to the procedures and institutions that contribute to or are needed for a given settlement, but what makes such settlements survive for an extended period of time? This is, after all, the most crucial aspect of any settlement. A fair agreement that is not expected to outlive even the signatories would probably not be readily accepted or only accepted as a temporary lull in an ongoing battle. A considerable number of settlements in the post-1945 period are of this temporary nature. The divisions of Vietnam in 1954 and 1973 were temporary measures, and they did not last long, and all the settlements over Chad during the 1970s and 1980s have been extremely short-lived. However, some other agreements have been more lasting, to the point at which they are considered today as being completely "natural," an attitude that of course is the most indicative one as "natural" states of affairs are seldom challenged. In this category, there is the reunification and neutralization of Austria in 1955 and perhaps the settlement over Zimbabwe.

The delicacy of durable settlements is illustrated by the number of short-lived agreements, and the comparative study of unsuccessful as well as successful cases of settlement appears to be a most urgent undertaking.

Certain principles seem important if a settlement is to be durable, and many of them are, in fact, found in the vocabulary of international law and international relations: mutual respect, equality, noninterference, nonaggression—all being equally applicable to state-state relations and state-nonstate relations. A most important aspect is that there must be a similar understanding of the role played by the parties, a mutual role perception. Thus, a prerequisite for the settlement of the white-black conflict in Rhodesia/Zimbabwe was the de facto acceptance by the whites that they were nothing but a minority and the Africans' agreeing to treat the whites as a particular minority. Similarly, Austria, by accepting neutralization in exchange for reunification, agreed to play a more withdrawn role (which, in light of its history, was a striking concession). Furthermore, if the contradiction between civil and military authority is going to be settled, the settlement has to rest on a role perception in which the military accepts civilian control, perhaps in exchange for a certain military autonomy or a certain allocation of resources. This appears to be the Spanish equation.

Basic to the survival of settlements is the distribution of power between the contending parties. Durable settlements are probably enhanced by a fairly wide and equal distribution of power. The dilemma seems to be that the wider the distribution and the more autonomous the different units, the greater the difficulties in finding a settlement that all units agree to as long as they are part of the same system. Thus, a proliferation of opposition groups, for instance, in Lebanon or Northern Ireland, means that there almost always is some group that sees a chance of capitalizing on continued resistance (to improve its own position) and consequently blocks other groups from entering into or keeping a given settlement.

The international system is analogous to such internal situations: The great number of states makes joint decisions on global issues difficult to achieve, and the global system easily becomes unmanageable. The other extreme, however, a reduction in power distribution and an extreme concentration of power, also seems to pose great danger, as is witnessed by the rivalry between the two superpowers or by the rivalry of two polarized forces in an internal war (e.g., Spain in the 1930s). Perhaps there is an optimal distribution of power that is conducive to durable settlements, one that restricts the number of actors to a medium level in a given system. Such a situation can be arrived at, either through an amalgamation of many actors (when the number is too large), a fragmentation of actors (when the number is too small), or through redrawing the borders of the system (to become larger or smaller) by refining the definition of the incompatibility (a step-by-step approach).

The most problematic aspect of a durable settlement then is its sensitivity to changes in distribution of power. In one way, a given settlement means an agreement on a given state of affairs, a freezing of the situation. The parties to the agreement might have a joint interest in preventing the appearance of new actors or new issues, as they could jeopardize the understanding that had been reached. However, new issues and new actors are bound to appear, not simply because there is always a need for renewal, but also because attitudes, resources, and populations change. The most important property of a lasting settlement is its ability to accommodate change or to channel change so that the basic settlement is not endangered. Thus, to have all parties agree to an arrangement becomes an important task (an educational task, politically as well as pedagogically), which means that certain questions cannot be raised. As this situation invites conservatism, settlements might always carry the seeds of their demise. However, durable settlement need not necessarily be eternal settlement.

Conflict Behavior and Conflict Resolution

The settlement of a given incompatibility requires a transition from militarization to resolution. First of all, military conflict behavior must cease, as continued threat or use of military force will obviously impede any transition. Even the weapons themselves will be powerful obstacles to any working out of an agreement. In fact, once a conflict has passed the threshold between nonmilitary and military forms of behavior, a qualitative shift has occurred, and it becomes very difficult to return to nonmilitary behavior. Demilitarization is possible only via the complete victory of one party over the other, or via a settlement that returns the armed forces to the barracks. The threshold of militarization might be a small and easy one, but the threshold of demilitarization is very hard and very difficult to cross. It is often noted that wars are easily initiated but take a long time to terminate. Similarly, it might be easy for armed forces to seize power, but recivilianization is a considerably more complex process. The reason is simple and straightforward: As long as a conflict is waged with nonmilitary means, some psychological damage is caused, but once military means are introduced, physical destruction is added and the human suffering becomes more intense, less easily forgotten or forgiven.

Thus, conflict resolution cannot be brought about as long as fighting goes on. Equally difficult is working out relationships between civilian and military leaders as long as the latter suppress the former. Thus, a state of cease-fire has to be introduced to reduce the acute suffering and allow room for negotiation and contemplation. This is, however, easier said than done. As the negotiations will concern the basic incompatibility, and as conflicting interests do not easily evaporate, each party might want to use the threat of or actually apply force as an instrument of pressure on the other, thereby keeping the tension high. Still, in relations between two armed forces, cease-fire arrangements have a long history, for internal as well as for external wars. Understandings can be worked out, armistice lines can become respected, barriers can be created, withdrawals agreed upon, and demilitarizing zones between the parties introduced. In interstate as well as in intrastate conflicts, third-party forces can be used in order to supervise the cease-fire (e.g., multinational troops in Lebanon, inter-African forces in Chad, UN forces in the Sinai, etc.).

The problem becomes more delicate in confrontations between military and civilian forces, such as in confrontations between a military regime and the civil opposition. The symmetry of the intermilitary situation does not exist, as one party is militarily superior and the other one works with nonmilitary means (strikes, demonstrations, petitions, public criticism, etc.). It becomes particularly important to analyze situations in which military regimes have had to withdraw in spite of their military superiority. This problematique seems to be surprisingly little researched, although it should be of fundamental importance in our age. Obviously, there must, at the same time, be constraints operating on the military side, restricting the use of military suppression, and organizational strength on the civilian side, in order to make attempts at a forceful suppression that is so comprehensive that large segments of society become directly affected. Constraints on the military side can be, for instance, factionalism within the military,[20] external pressure,[21] or public contempt for actions taken by the military (e.g., excessive repression that reduces the esteem of the military). In such situations, the civilian opposition will increase its position in public and international opinion by the very fact that it is facing arms in an unarmed manner.

Modern history has many examples of a gradual or rapid withdrawal of military leadership from goverment power. It could be, as some analysts suggest, that gradual withdrawal results in a more permanent withdrawal (as in the case of Mexico),[22] but also a quick process could be successful (as in the case of the collapse of the Greek junta in 1974). Two observations seem particularly relevant to this process. First, a military regime that returns government control back to civilian hands is seldom the same as the one that originally took control. A significant shift has taken place within the military regime itself.[23] A second observation is that such civilian control is actually relying on a coalition between civilians and the military.[24] These observations have been made with South American and Thai conditions in mind, respectively, but they appear equally pertinent with respect to European situations: Portugal, Spain, and Greece all emerged from military control through a two-phase process, in which the original introducer of military control first lost power and the military leaders also had functions within a civilian-controlled constitution.

The process by which military conflict behavior ceases is a necessary element of any demilitarization attempt. Mostly, the demilitarization of conflict behavior will be part and parcel of a settlement of the basic incompatibility, which means that there is a trade-off between these two aspects of conflict resolution. The ultimate mixture and durable qualities are determined by the negotiation skills and the ingenuity that emerges during the course of the conflict. The initial destruction of a conflict can thus only be stopped through the imaginative means of the humans involved. Consequently, no two settlements are strictly comparable, which means that each situation requires its own effort. Throughout history, humans have shown themselves capable of transcending conflicts, reducing destruction, and terminating war. Although the odds today might be worse than ever, that only means that the task is the more urgent.

Notes

1. For an introduction, see P. Wallensteen, "Incompatibility, Confrontation, and War: Four Models and Three Historical Systems, 1816–1976," *Journal of Peace Research* 18:1 (1981), pp. 59–64.

2. Ibid., pp. 83–86.

3. Ibid., p. 86.

4. P. Wallensteen, *Disaster and Conflict: Conflict Formations in the Sahel and the Horn of Africa, 1971–1976* (Uppsala: Department of Peace and Conflict Research, 1981), p. 29.

5. G. K. Wilson and P. Wallensteen, *Aktuell förteckning: Väpnade konflickter 1979 och 1980* (Uppsala: Department of Peace and Conflict Research, 1982).

6. Wallensteen, "Incompatibility, Confrontation, and War," pp. 85–86.

7. The elaboration of the concept of incompatibility is found in P. Wallensteen, *Transcending Incompatibilities: Fundamentals of Conflict Resolution* (Uppsala: Department of Peace and Conflict Research, in progress.

8. See P. Wallensteen, *Structure and War: On International Relations, 1920–1968* (Uppsala: Rabén and Sjögren, 1973), p. 159.

9. An important point of discussion is whether such systems have to be established on a global or a regional level.

10. Concepts similar to peaceful coexistence are found for most ideological systems. Normally, coexistence is regarded as a transitory form or a step toward the full realization of the system at a later stage. However, as long as no time limitations are considered, periods of coexistence can be durable enough.

11. A related question is, of course, to what extent economics can be used either to buy off opponents or as a means of punishment. Here, however, the issue is a question of basic incompatibility.

12. Next to brutal suppression, federation seems to be the most frequent form of settlement, preferred above actual separation.

13. However, given three powerful actors—state, capital, and labor—alliance patterns might also go in a different direction. For instance, state could combine with capital in crushing labor (fascism), or labor might use the state to contain capital (socialism). Perhaps the liberal-socialist coalition (capital + labor) confronting monarchies in the nineteenth century was more of an exception. Nevertheless, it took place and had profound consequences.

14. For Poland, see P. Wehr, "Conflict and Restraint: Poland, 1980–1982," chap. 9 in this volume. See also the special issue of *Journal of Peace Research* 19:2 (1982), *Poles on Poland,* and J. Galtung, "Poland August–September 1980: Is a Socialist Revolution Under State Capitalism Possible?" *Journal of Peace Research* 17:4 (1980), pp. 281–290.

15. For Thailand, see C. Chinwanno, "Militarization in Thai Society," and for Chile, see C. Portales, "Militarization and Political Institutions in Chile," chaps. 5 and 6 in this volume.

16. Again, these changes took place within a Western framework, perhaps more parallel to nineteenth-century Europe than to the present-day Third World (see note 13). In Spain, the monarchy seems to increasingly play a role similar to the one in northwestern Europe; in Greece, the monarchy met the same fate as in France and Italy.

17. See B. Hettne, "The Ghanaian Experiments with Military Rule," chap. 7 in this volume.

18. There does not seem to be any serious contender to the free election paradigm and the dictatorial syndrome although random selection sometimes has been tried.

19. Politics in these countries largely follow a left-right dimension in the way parties, organizations, mass media, and public opinion orient themselves. That this tendency also holds true for attitudes toward international events has been amply demonstrated, at least for Sweden—see O. Petersson, *Väljarna och världspolitiken* (Stockholm: Norstedts, 1982).

20. Morell points to the many cleavages existing within the military: between branches, between overseas trained and locally trained military men, between active and retired officers, between patrons and clients, etc. (D. Morell, "Alternatives to Military Rule in Thailand," *Armed Forces and Society* 1:3 [1975], pp. 298–299).

21. M. C. Needler, "The Military Withdrawal from Power in South America," *Armed Forces and Society* 6:4 (1980), p. 623, extends such a role to the United States in certain situations. Also, in connection with the fall of the shah in Iran, U.S. pressure to avoid repression of the opposition has been cited. The U.S. record is by no means only a restraining one. On the contrary, U.S. involvement has probably been more frequently cited on the opposite account.

22. This point is argued by Ben-Dor, who cites Egypt as an additional example—see G. Ben-Dor, "Civilianization of Military Regimes in the Arab World," *Armed Forces and Society* 1:3 (1975), pp. 317–327.

23. See Needler, "Military Withdrawal from Power," p. 621.

24. Morell, "Alternatives to Military Rule in Thailand," p. 298.

About the Contributors

CHULACHEEB CHINWANNO is Assistant Professor in political science and also Director of the Center for Asian and Pacific Studies at Thammasat University, Bangkok, Thailand.

DIETRICH FISCHER is Assistant Professor of economics at New York University.

JOHAN GALTUNG is founder and former Director of the International Peace Research Institute, Oslo, Norway. He was the Editor of the *Journal of Peace Research* from 1964 to 1974 and Professor of peace and conflict research at the University of Oslo from 1969 to 1978. He is presently attached to Berghof Stiftung, West Berlin.

BJÖRN HETTNE is Associate Professor and Director of the Department of Peace and Conflict Research, University of Gothenburg.

KEIICHI MATSUSHITA is Professor of political science, Hosei University, Japan. He is also a member of the Board of Directors for the Japan Political Science Association.

CARLOS PORTALES is a researcher at FLACSO in Santiago, Chile, and teaches part time in the M.A. program of the Institute of International Studies of the University of Chile. He is also Secretary General of the Chilean Peace Research Association.

CHARLES TILLY is Distinguished Professor of sociology and history and Director of the Center for Studies of Social Change at the New School for Social Research, New York. Until 1984, he was Professor of history, Theodore M. Newcomb Professor of social science, and Director of the Center for Research on Social Organization at the University of Michigan, Ann Arbor.

PETER WALLENSTEEN is Associate Professor of peace research at Uppsala University, Sweden. He served as a visiting professor in the Department of Political Science at the University of Michigan in 1984 and is the author of *Dilemmas of Economic Coercion: Sanctions in World Politics* (1983).

PAUL WEHR is Associate Professor of sociology, University of Colorado, Boulder, Colorado, where he is also on the professional staff of the Institute of Behavioral Science. He is past Executive Director for the Consortium on Peace Research, Education and Development.

Index

Acheampong, K., 154–160, 163–165
Actio-Reactio model, 3–6, 14, 18(n4), 57
Afghanistan, 19(n14), 37, 54–55, 61, 95, 210
Afrifa, A. A., 151, 153–155, 157, 159
Akata-Pore, A., 162
Akuffo, F.W.K., 157–159
Aland Islands, 226
Alessandri, A., 129
Alexander, H. T., 166(n4)
Allende, S., 132
Angola, 84
Ankrah, T. A., 153
Antiwar movements, 96, 99
Arms race, xi, 56–57, 135, 173–174, 180–181, 188
Arms trade, xi, 16, 76, 84–88
Assimeng, M., 168(n39)
Australia, 30, 59(table)
Austria, 50, 52, 82, 229
Autistic model. See Eigendynamik

Bacteriological weapons, 2
Baquedano, M., 126
Batista, F., 177
Belgium, 50
Berlin, 52
Biafra, 225
Bolivia, 126
Brandt, V., 25
Brazil, 32. See also Newly Industrializing Countries
Bretton-Woods system, 28
Bulnes, M., 125–126
Burma, 76, 112
Busia, K., 147–157, 159–160, 163–165

Canada, 50–51
Carter, J., 58
Castro, F., 27
Chad, 229, 231
Chauvinism, 97
Chemical warfare, 2
Chile xiv, 55, 123–144
  civil wars, 124, 126
  democracy, 130, 134–135, 141–142
  national defense, 130–131, 134, 137, 140
  national security, 131, 133–140, 142
  and the United States, 19(n23), 55, 132–134
China, People's Republic of, 25, 84(table), 156
  civil war in, 39
  economic growth of, 24, 29–38, 43–46
  internal development, 10, 17, 226, 228
  and Japan, 30–38, 45–46, 67(n45)
  and nonalignment, 54
  and Southeast Asia, 30–34
  and the Soviet Union, 8–9, 20(n36), 34, 36–37, 46, 54
  and Taiwan 32, 38–39
  and Thailand, 116–117
  and the Third World, 40, 46
  and the United Kingdom, 46
  and the United States, 32, 34, 60, 67(n45)
  and Vietnam, 34, 46, 95
  and the West, 30–35, 46
Chulalongkorn, King, 112

Civil defense, 183
Clauswitz, K. von, 97
CMEA. See Council of Mutual Economic Assistance
Cold war, 9, 37, 116
Coleman, J., 199, 201, 215
Colombia, 228
Comecon. See Council of Mutual Economic Assistance
Commando units, 17
Conflict behavior, xii–xiii, 58, 219, 231–232
Conflict formation, xii–xiii, 2–3, 7–9, 15–16, 23–24, 33, 62(n1), 71(n95), 192, 219
Conflict resolution, xiv, 8, 16, 53, 57–58, 81, 207–209, 219–221, 223–234
Congo, The, 150 ·
Conventional warfare, 2, 17, 58, 94, 104, 180
Coser, L., 201–202, 205
Cosmopolitanism, 97
Costa Rica, 20(n34)
Council of Mutual Economic Assistance (CMEA, Comecon), 53, 59(table), 196
Counter-insurgency, 8
Cuba, 27, 85, 177
Czechoslovakia, 55, 82, 192, 197, 211, 213, 216

Dahl, R., 205
Dahrendorf, R., 192
Davidson, B., 151
Defense, 10, 11, 17, 106–107, 112
  in Chile, 130–131, 134, 136–137, 140
  in Ghana, 154, 162
  in Switzerland, 173–177, 179, 183, 185
  in Thailand, 115–116
Defensive arms, 176–177, 179–183, 188
  and offensive arms, 183
  and security, 180–182
de Gaulle, Charles, 67(n53), 71(n95), 83
Deku, A. K., 153
Demilitarization, 3, 17, 20(n27), 123, 224, 226–227, 231–232
Democracy, xii, 96–99, 113, 118, 120, 123
  and Chile, 130, 134–135, 141–142
  and economic growth, 226–227
  and Ghana, 158, 162–163
  and Poland, 193, 195–196, 204, 207–208, 215
Denmark, 48, 51–52
Dependency theory, 161
Détente, 20(n32), 71(n95), 135, 224(table)
Deterrence, xii, 1, 58, 107, 179, 185
Development, civilian, economic, social and/or human, xi–xiv, 3, 11–17, 50, 52–55, 57, 96–97, 134, 156
  cooperation, 185–186, 188
  in Ghana, 149, 150, 165
  military role in, 164, 165
  models of, 11, 54
  theory, 145
Disarmament, 3, 14–17, 56, 58, 173–175, 187, 225
Dowse, R., 152

East-West Conflict, 8, 9, 24, 51–59, 116
  development as the issue, 52–55
  resolution of, 53